GALLIPOT EYES

'I didn't choose Oaksey, it chose me', writes Elspeth Huxley in her preface to
this evocative diary of village life. She has lived there for thirty-five years,
makes no special claims for its antiquity or beauty but maintains simply that
Oaksey, like all the other 10,000 villages in England and Wales, is unique.

She kept this diary from April 1974 to March 1975. Interwoven with her
daily preoccupations (christening presents for the twins; which way up to
plant asparagus crowns) she describes the people around her and the ever-
changing patterns of village life. We get glimpses of things that have caught
her fancy: fox-cubs at play under her window, an elderly neighbour put to
flight by an ITV camera team, a church spire against a winter sky. With the
schoolmaster she digs at the foundations of a buried medieval castle built by
the earls of Hereford, and in the local library discovers the first identifiable
lord of the manor to have been a Saxon diplomat whose flirtation with Duke
William's future wife may have cost him his lands and his freedom after the
Conquest. From later history she presents some surprising 'finds', such as the
rector who proclaimed the Old Testament to be a pack of fairy tales and the
lady of the manor who rose at six every morning to make tea for her eight
maids.

Although the old ways and skills are disappearing fast, village life remains
an essential and enduring part of English society. In this delightful cameo,
Elspeth Huxley has captured its charm and changes with all the craft of a
born writer.

Elspeth Huxley was brought up on a coffee farm in East Africa to where her
parents had emigrated before the First World War. After university (reading
agriculture at Reading and Cornell, New York) she married Gervas Huxley
in 1931. She spent a number of years travelling round Africa and Australia
with him, writing crime and travel books before returning to farm in
Wiltshire. As well as being a freelance broadcaster and journalist, Elspeth
Huxley has written numerous books including biographies of Livingstone
and Florence Nightingale and the best-selling autobiographical novels *The
Flame Trees of Thika* and *The Mottled Lizard*.

GALLIPOT EYES

A Wiltshire Diary

Elspeth Huxley

CENTURY

London Melbourne Auckland Johannesburg
in association with The National Trust

First published in 1976

Copyright © Elspeth Huxley 1988

All rights reserved

This edition first published in 1988 by Century, an imprint of
Century Hutchinson Ltd, in association with The National Trust
for Places of Historic Interest or Natural Beauty, 36 Queen
Anne's Gate, London SW1H 9AS

Century Hutchinson Ltd, Brookmount House, 62–65 Chandos Place,
London WC2N 4NW

Century Hutchinson Australia Pty Ltd,
PO Box 496, 16–22 Church Street, Hawthorn, Melbourne,
Victoria 3122, Australia

Century Hutchinson Group New Zealand Limited,
PO Box 40–086, Glenfield, Auckland 10, New Zealand

Century Hutchinson South Africa (Pty) Ltd,
PO Box 337, Bergvlei, 2012 South Africa

Cover landscape painting by Alfred Clendening

British Library Cataloguing in Publication Data

Huxley, Elspeth
    Gallipot eyes: A Wiltshire diary:
    (National Trust classics).
    1. Oaksey (Wiltshire) — Social life and
    customs
    I. Title   II. Series
    942.3'12   DA690.02/

    ISBN 0-7126-2377-9

Printed in Great Britain by
Richard Clay (The Chaucer Press) Ltd,
Bungay, Suffolk.

Published in association with The National Trust, this series
is devoted to reprinting books on the artistic, architectural,
social and cultural heritage of Britain. The imprint
covers buildings and monuments, arts and crafts, gardening and
landscape in a variety of literary forms, including histories,
memoirs, biographies and letters.

The Century Classics also include the Travellers, Seafarers and
Lives and Letters series.

CONTENTS

Contents

Contents

March · *170*

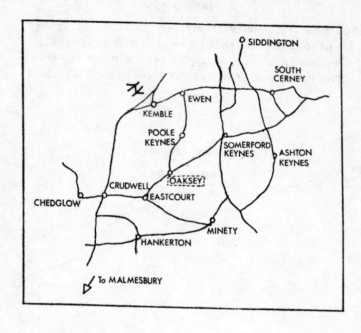

They feed chiefly on milke meates, which cools their braines too much, and hurts their inventions ... their persons are generally plump and feggy; gallipot eyes, and some black; but they are generally handsome enough.

JOHN AUBREY on North Wiltshiremen

PREFACE

There are, I believe, ten thousand villages, or thereabouts, in England and Wales, and at times it seems as if every one of them has had, or is about to have, a book written about it. What, another? you can all but hear people say.

Yes, another; no two villages are quite the same just as no two people are, and writers go on writing about people. The other day I remarked to an acquaintance how difficult it was to find fruitful subjects for biography, because almost everyone of interest has been 'done', often dozens of times. He agreed. 'But then, you might just as well have said the same about the Virgin Mary to a medieval or Renaissance painter.'

This book is not intended as a village history, like several excellent village books that have lately been published. There is more about the present than the past. Nor is it meant to prove anything: that villages are good or bad, their inhabitants happy or miserable, better or worse than they used to be. It's what its title says: a diary. I kept it for a year and then stopped.

For most of us, trivialities make up our daily lives; trivialities therefore make up most of this diary. If it can be said to have anything so ambitious as an object, I think it is to suggest how closely past and present are intertwined, mixed up together like land and water in a delta or marsh. This is no doubt the case in any human community, but in the smaller unit more noticeable and easier to trace than in the larger, more amorphous city or region. You can put under a microscope a cluster of cells, but not the living animal from which they were taken.

Another reason for another book about another village is the accelerating pace of change. There's no need to dwell on this; we all know how quickly former ways of living, thinking and behaving are disappearing, and that what's replacing them won't be the same. That is why I talked mainly to members of the older generation, who can recall a past already as foreign to the young as the plains of Tartary; in a few years, it will be too late.

There are obvious limitations to this method, if you can call it that, of inviting reminiscences from older folk. Memories are fallible, for one thing; for another, while you can tell some of the truth, you cannot tell the whole truth about people who are still living, or whose children are. I've not attempted to disguise the names and identities of my neighbours. Sometimes, therefore, warts must be ignored. It's not only a question of the laws of libel, hurt feelings come into it too. I could, of course, tell the whole truth as I see it, or have heard it, and then emigrate to Australia; but I am too old to do that.

A diary, I suggest, is the literary counterpart of an artist's sketch-book, full of gestures towards a major work which may never get done, of glimpses of little things that take the fancy: a tree-root, a storm-cloud, the turn of a wrist, a child kicking a ball. A finished painting would be a much more satisfactory achievement, but even sketch-books have their niche – some do, that is, and I can only hope that this may be one of them.

Why pick on Oaksey? There's nothing special about this particular village. Almost any of its ten thousand fellows would probably have done as well. It's a pleasant little village, but so are many others. It's always been, I think, a borderline case. On the border between Wiltshire and Gloucestershire, between the Cotswolds and the vale, between the midlands and the south-west; in the Middle Ages on the borders of the Forest of Braden; before that, of the kingdoms of Mercia and Wessex; almost on the borderline between the Thames flowing east and the Avon going west; if matters go on as they are doing, it will soon be on the borders of Swindon, though we haven't reached that pass yet.

I didn't choose Oaksey, it chose me because I live there. It was only when I started on a diary that I realized how little I knew about it, and still do; how many stones remain unturned. The greatest surprise has been to discover how much can be discovered about a small and unimportant place, delving only in fits and starts, with no pre-knowledge or experience of how to go about it, all too little time, and all within a year.

This has been possible, of course, only because a number of historians have done the serious delving and published their results, and because there is a trained, competent and, in my experience, invariably helpful and interested body of librarians, archivists and others, ready and able to tell the seeker where to look and what to look for. I am exceedingly grateful to them all. To make a list of names would be invidious, but I do especially want to thank the staff of the public library in Malmesbury, and also in Devizes, and the County Record Office in Trowbridge; the editor of the *Wilts and Gloucestershire Standard* for letting me browse among the files; and, of course, all the people in the village and its neighbourhood who, so to say, have helped me with my inquiries, lent me documents, and welcomed me into their homes.

April 1974

2 April – TO THE SHOP

'Cold wind.' 'Bitter.' 'Turned nasty.' 'M'm.' 'Rain holding off.' 'Hope so.'
I walk up the lane exchanging brief ritualistic greetings with my neighbours
as the Japanese (one imagines) bow and grin; Baloba tribesmen (one
reads) used to fling themselves to the ground and roll from side to side
stark naked, roaring with laughter; and dogs sniff each other's bottoms.
Thus we establish contact without commitment, or starting up an
argument.

Reg stands, as ever, at the gate, looking up and down the road for
something to stir, watching tractors clattering to and from Park Farm,
smiling and calling out 'nice day', or 'cold wind' or (very occasionally)
'warm day' to any passer-by who looks friendly. What he likes best is some
small useful job, like wheeling a barrow, helping to unload a lorry or
carrying a milk-bottle from the van to his father's house. He spends hours

indoors with jig-saw puzzles and is very good at them, even those with two thousand pieces.

His father Tom is over eighty now, upright, lean, clean-shaven; nearly fifty years in Oaksey hasn't modified the accent of the Scottish Highlands. His garden is always tidy and well-kept, his hedge clipped and grass verge mown.

Ann emerges from her gate, mounts her bike and pedals off down the road to the Park for her morning's stint. At the garage Doug has shut the double doors against the wind and has the radio going inside, as well as a drill; he is always working, Sundays included. When first we came here to live there were two cars in the village, plus a few belonging to surrounding farmers; now there are well over a hundred, mostly parked nose to tail outside the council houses in Bendybow from teatime on, so you can hardly edge your way along. There are a few two-car families.

Old Tom – another Tom – who lives next to the shop is out with his labrador. Over the years I've watched them both getting older, slower, and in the case of the labrador, fatter; but twice a day out they go for their stately progress, down the Eastcourt Road one day, Kemble Road the next. Age and non-mobility keep exactly in step. Which will be the first to decide that it's too cold, too wet, too inclement for the daily plod?

Tom spent nearly all his working life at Street Farm, a hundred yards along The Street, with Stanley Sarah. Mr Sarah, pushing eighty, has retired too, but still provides the village with a talking-point when, every three months or so, he swaps his current motor car for another. Formerly, he had two other major hobbies. Attending farm sales was one. When the auctioneer's bell rang, his lean, bespectacled figure was in the forefront, ready for the first lots to come up: heaps of rusty chicken-wire, bundles of broken rakes and forks and spades, old bathtubs, rusting oil-drums, ancient chests-of-drawers, sometimes a treasure like an old hand mangle, pots for forcing rhubarb or an ancient fiddle (in the agricultural sense, a hand drill).

He used to play a fascinating game of wits with the auctioneer, its aim to bid for each of these lots, in those days in shillings, without getting one knocked down to him. Partly a game of skill and partly a gamble, like Russian roulette. He couldn't always win, and then another game followed, even more enthralling: to pass on the lot to one of the dealers without loss, and if possible with a profit, even sixpence. Perhaps that very evening, the opportunity might arise to indulge his other hobby, that of shooting foxes at night with a torch fixed on to his rifle. He kept free-range hens, so he was no lover of foxes – or of the local Hunt, which in his view was merely a source of amusement and gentle exercise for its quarry. His best bag was forty foxes in a year.

Forsythia is out all along The Street, blazing gold in front gardens; shallots are showing; a thrush is nesting in the unclipped bit of hedge at the bottom of my garden. A huge, wide drill rattles by, swivelled sideways to get through gateways. Machines get bigger and bigger. When we came all the field gates were ten-footers, oak. Then they became twelve-footers, metal. Now, Jim tells me, he has taken down all his gates at Park Farm (those that have survived his highly mechanized system of farming) and put up double ones, fifteen feet wide to allow the mammoth combines to get through. He says that merely to instal these new gates cost him a thousand pounds.

4 April – COURGETTES

Mine is not a large garden but from about March on it begins to seem like Hidcote or Bodnant, and as the year progresses creates more and more gloom and despondency; there are even weeds that grow all through the winter. Obviously, it must be diminished – if not in overall size, then in activity; simplified, one should perhaps say. For a start, no vegetables; everyone agrees that it's more expensive to grow vegetables than to buy them. They are slave-masters in league with the freezer.

Everything comes on at once and I suppose before the days of freezers one simply threw the surplus away, or kept pigs. Nowadays you can't jettison hours of forking, pounds spent on fertilizers, a lifetime it seems of toil and sweat. So for hours and hours you shell and string and slice and blanch and dry and pack and label bags and bags of provender, and stow them in a freezer already full of things you have forgotten about, or that have lost their labels.

Courgettes are the worst. Last year I put a lot of seed into those little pots that arrive as flat discs, and rise up when you soak them. I put three seeds into each pot, and to my amazement all of them germinated. So in due course I had a mass of little courgette plants, far more than I needed. These I transferred, with some difficulty, into two mounds of rotting turf that were getting into everyone's way at the bottom of the future orchard (four apple trees and four plums).

They liked it there. They all took, spread, flowered, and before long little courgettes started to appear. In surprising numbers. But the really surprising thing about courgettes is how, in the wink of an eye, almost literally while your back is turned, a small courgette of the right size for eating becomes a gigantic marrow, almost too heavy to carry and encased in a hide too hard for anything but a dinosaur to eat.

I used to suppose that this sort of thing happened only in the Tropics. Not at all, it happens right here, in North Wilts., on the cold clay, its BBC status hovering uneasily between West Midlands and the South West. There is something indecent about it, and certainly alarming. You feel menaced. Another extraordinary thing is how the baby marrows conceal themselves. At least twice a day, more often half a dozen times, I thoroughly explore every marrow plant on those mounds, lifting the leaves, poking about among those thick, hairy, twisting stems for little objects like fat green cigars, and then twisting these off. When I am absolutely certain that no baby marrow has evaded the search, I stagger back to the house with a couple of full baskets, feeling safe for at least twenty-four hours.

That evening, passing the mound last thing with a sense of modest triumph, something under a leaf catches my eye. I push the leaf aside; and there, lying with obscene complacency amid the twisted stems, faintly striped with yellow, shining with health and fulfilment of its destiny, reposes the most gigantic marrow. It *does* laugh at you. It positively cannot have been there that morning.

Sighing, I fetch a large serrated kitchen knife, practically a saw, to sever its umbilical cord, and totter with it in my arms to the house. I now have an almost insoluble problem. Already I'm exhausted by days and days of cooking little courgettes and getting them into the freezer, which is now crammed with the things. You cannot do this to a marrow. A reasonably small one can be stuffed, but already I have stuffed several, and this one is not reasonable. I could make jam, but one large marrow makes an awful lot of jam. I have already tried, with absolutely no success, to give marrows away. Most people either have a marrow plant or two – never more than two – or they don't like marrows. Nowadays they're not even wanted for the harvest festival.

Someone to whom I poured out my trouble said: 'Feed them to pigs.' An excellent idea, but where are the pigs? The time has long gone by when every villager had his pig in a shed at the bottom of the garden. Oaksey has no pigs. The only man I know who keeps pigs has a unit with about a thousand of them in rows and rows of heated cells, fed automatically from hoppers operated no doubt by computers; even my output of marrows could not be integrated into this system.

To cut a long story short, in the end I found a farmer on a remote hill farm in Wales who had a pig, and was prepared to offer it a marrow or two now and again. Had I costed the delivery of marrows up the valleys and into the hills, completing their journey by Land-rover, they would not have proved at all an economic feed.

5 April – HEDGEHOGS AND GATEPOSTS

Dick Sampson brought his tractor with a kind of scoop to level a little piece of rough ground, all tumpy yellow clay and nettles, running to a point by the hedge at the bottom of my garden. While he manoeuvred his tractor to and fro between the raspberries and a young walnut tree with the precision of a champion rider in the dressage class at Badminton, his helper Noel talked about hedgehogs. They're getting scarce round here and I think cattle grids are partly to blame. I often used to see hedgehog corpses floating in the flooded pits under the grids on the Park Farm road. Now I don't see them any more. Of course, it could be that hedgehogs have learnt to find their way round.

'Ever seen a fox catch a hedgehog?' Noel asked. 'He rolls it over and over like a football till he gets to water, then the hedgehog opens up and he gets his teeth in.'

He was knowledgeable too about the needs of lambs. 'If a lamb's dropped cold and wet,' he said, 'warm milk will curdle in its stomach. Give it a drop of gin, now, no more than a teaspoon, and the milk won't curdle. I used to carry a bottle of gin in my pocket and never lost a lamb.'

Dick is a specialist in fencing and also a musician; he used to play the fiddle but had to give it up because, when he isn't putting up fences, he's too busy with the paperwork that all but submerges the self-employed. His is an artistic family. Two of his sisters sing in the Malmesbury Abbey choir and one of them runs an art gallery in Circencester.

He told me that my gatepost had rotted away in only three years because it's made of English oak. Hearts of Scandinavian pine is what I should have had, not English oak. Disillusioning. In former times, he said, oak was felled only in winter when the sap was down. Now it's felled all the year round; in summer, the wood is too full of sap to take the preservative, so it lasts no time at all.

At the bottom of the garden I've left a tall, straggly and untidy bit of hedge for shelter, and to provide nesting sites for birds, instead of getting a hedge-cutting machine to trim it ruthlessly down. Noel commented on this. The other day, he said, in the Fen country, where nearly all the hedges have been bulldozed out completely, he saw a surviving stretch of hedge, not more than three hundred yards long, so closely packed with nests of blackbirds and thrushes that the nests were almost touching. A sort of high-rise situation among birds, only horizontal instead of vertical. Territorial instincts must be violated, no doubt leading, as with humans, to bad temper, neuroses and aggression; teenage blackbirds going around in gangs bent on destruction will be the next thing. Alarming: that famous Hitch-cock film was perhaps prophetic.

9 April – LORD OF THE MANOR

As Oaksey has its own Lord, John Oaksey, it's natural to think he's the lord of the manor; but he isn't. A manor is an area of land, not a house – only the police seem nowadays to use the word correctly – and the lordship goes with it. Our lord of the manor, if we actually had one, would be Jim Woodhouse.* The residue of the manor, Park Farm, is his, and so was the manor house, but he had it pulled down and now its foundations are underneath Renée's rose garden.

Today I walked along the concrete strips to Park Farm to jog Jim's memory about a load of manure he's promised me. I know this walk so well and yet there's generally something new to see. Buds swelling on the young lime trees, though no sign yet of greenery under this dull grey sky. Seagulls following a tractor at work on the far side of this large, level field. Nettles beginning. Rooks circling over tall bare trees.

I always enjoy a talk with Jim because he's always cheerful, the exact opposite of what farmers are supposed to be. Things don't go wrong for Jim, ever – or, if they do, instead of moaning he tells you about something that's gone right: the best crop of barley he's ever had, a fabulous yield of potatoes, all his ewes dropping twins except those who've had triplets. A shrewd, hard-headed businessman with a reputation for tough bargaining, who's always been a good neighbour to me.

I caught him in today – generally he's out in his Land-rover with two old labradors in the back – and we got talking about the contrasts between farming today and farming when he came to Oaksey thirty-five years ago, as a young man newly married. He's a Herefordshire man, one of four farming brothers, and before coming here was assistant manager at a farm school in Hampshire. He had thirty-six men working under him, he said. Twelve were carters, for everything was done with horses then. Jim remem-

---

*It is now Judge John Byrne of Papua New Guinea, whose wife bought the lordship for £9,000 at an auction in 1986.

bers a procession of twenty wagons, each drawn by a pair of glossy horses, their ears encased in plaited straw caps with dangling tassels to keep out flies, bringing home the hay between big painted ladders in the June dusk, to be ricked in the yards.

His pay was £10 a week, very handsome at a time when the farm wage was thirty-five shillings; and when he decided to strike out on his own, everyone thought him mad. He had no capital at all. However, a friend offered to lend him £1,000, Renée had just enough to pay the valuation, and they came to Park Farm as tenants in October, 1940, with exactly £985, and nothing else.

The previous occupants had been an organization called the Bruderhof, a Christian community expelled from Germany by the Nazis, who shared everything in common – including wives, according to the villagers, for whom they provided a rich mine of rumour, such as the assertion that the women, who wore long blue kirtles girdled at the waist (the men wore knee-breeches and beards), dropped their babies behind hedges, like cows. As the war developed, they became spies. On the day war was declared about half a dozen Bruders appeared on our doorstep at Woodfolds asking if they might listen to our radio, as they had none of their own. In gloomy silence we sat together listening to the gloomy voice of Mr Chamberlain announcing our even gloomier fate. They thanked us politely, to our surprise in English and in the accent of the midlands; it transpired that these particular Bruders hailed from Birmingham.

When invasion threatened and the Home Guard was formed, rumour got busier than ever: Bruders were said to be constantly flashing lights, transmitting radio messages and generally aiding and abetting the enemy from their vantage point deep in rural Wiltshire. Public alarm was only partially allayed by the arrival of truckload after truckload of enormous, heavy concrete cubes which were placed in rows all over Park Field, like great white teeth emerging from the ground, to hamper the landing of enemy aircraft.

Petitions were sent to the Home Office, our MP badgered, letters appeared every week in the local press, and some Bruders who had gone to Swindon were manhandled in the street. At last it got too much for them, and perhaps official pressure was applied. They sold their oxen together with the ox-cart in which they used to rumble past our windows to the village, on feast-days swathed in green boughs; their few possessions were disposed of, and they sadly departed to found a new Bruderhof in Uruguay.

However Christian the lives of the Bruders, their farming experience was nil; and Jim and Renée found everything in a shocking state: the house damp and dilapidated, buildings dirty and needing repair, roofs leaking, doors off their hinges, loose-boxes deep in dung. They arrived at tea-time to be greeted by thirteen freshly calved heifers, deposited there earlier in the day by a dealer, bellowing their heads off in the yard. None had been handled before, all had to be milked and there wasn't even a milking stool or bucket. Jim borrowed both; he and Renée set to work to capture and tie up the wild kicking heifers and got them milked out by eleven o'clock that night. Next day they started to hand-hoe six acres of mangolds, deep in weeds. 'We used to finish up bucket-feeding seventy calves,' Jim said, 'and get to bed, with luck, about midnight.'

They took over from the Bruderhof a horse, the only one to start with: a stupid, disobedient horse they thought him, until it dawned on them that he understood only German. So Jim found a Brother left behind at Ashton Keynes who taught them how to say 'Gee-up' and 'Whoa' in German, and the horse behaved perfectly after that.

Change came rapidly; from being neglected and starved of capital, farming shot to the top of the priority list as war grew grimmer and food shortages worse. Machinery came in with a rush. At Park Farm the first tractor arrived, the last horse went; then came the first combine, a midget by modern standards, and the rows of golden stooks that I remember patterning the fields were seen no more. The binder, the wagons, all the horse-drawn implements went off to fetch a song at agricultural sales. Then the clanking, itinerant threshing drums disappeared. Each one needed a team of eight men to feed it, rick the straw and load the bags of wheat or barley on to wagons. No more piles of chaff in rickyards, or rat-hunts with terriers when the last of the straw was moved. Farm work was hard work then but team-work; machinery has turned everyone into a solitary worker.

The turning-point for Jim and Renée came when a drier was installed to turn young mown grass into pellets which, being high in protein, to some extent replaced imported animal feeds. By then Jim had ploughed up most of the old pastures, embarked on corn and potatoes in a big way, brought in sheep, and was well on the road to success.

When the drier was working round the clock Jim employed eighteen men. Now his permanent labour force has dwindled to two men and his sons Michael and Graham. In theory, Jim has retired, more or less, leaving the management to Michael. Like most theories it works, if at all, patchily. When the reconstruction of the old granary has been completed, and Jim and Renée have handed over the farmhouse to Michael and his bride, perhaps retirement will become a reality. In so far as farmers ever do retire.

Curious how generations change to fit their times. For hundreds of years,

I suppose, Jim's forebears have lived with and for their livestock: gentled their horses, communed with their cows, all but suckled their lambs. Now, in a single generation, animals have become almost strangers, machinery is all. I doubt if cows mean anything to Michael – there's no dairy now at Park Farm – but a sleek new tractor, a brightly painted combine, almost any kind of farm machine, brings him joy. Although they can't be fondled like a favourite heifer, or bottle-fed in the kitchen like a lamb, I think he really loves and understands those machines, not just in general but as individuals, each with its idiosyncrasies.

Even his pastimes seem to be mechanized. Whereas bird-shooting is his father's passion, Mike has a pilot's licence and belongs to a flying club. Another favourite occupation is blowing up the stumps of trees with dynamite. In his younger days he used to wear a ten-gallon Texas kind of hat and drive the combine carrying a revolver with which to pot hares and rabbits in the corn.

Whether Michael will prove to be as shrewd a man as his father remains to be seen, but I've had faith in his capacities ever since an incident which occurred when he was about six or seven, the same age almost exactly as our Charles. They used to 'play together', if that's the right description of some of their activities; like smoking in hen-houses, clambering over the roof to get into the loft at Woodfolds to demolish a large, carefully saved-up (this was in the war) Dundee cake, and being caught in the nick of time with a box of matches about to set fire to a barn full of hay.

For his birthday, Charles received a tricycle which he greatly treasured and which Michael greatly envied; all Mike's entreaties to let him borrow it were in vain. Charles also had a school cap he was rather proud of. Michael snatched it off one day and threw it up into the branches of a tree. When Charles, enraged, went after it, Michael nipped on to the tricycle and pedalled off down the road.

11 April – MIDDLE GAER

I went ahead in the van loaded with cardboard boxes and everything from wellingtons to wine. Whenever I go on a journey it seems to lodge firmly in my head that we're off to the North Pole for a couple of years, thousands of miles away from the availability of even a box of matches. It's surprising what you need, even for a weekend, for a family of seven, even though three of them are tiny and one a cat. Not only food: a torch in case the electricity fails, a sprayer for the fruit trees, spare electric light bulbs, a box of toys, all the sheets and towels and so on. Departure takes a long time.

It's always a great moment when I arrive. From the narrow lane, so overhung with branches it's a green tunnel between stone walls held up (but only just) by inter-twining roots of trees, you emerge on to a flat semi-circle of grass in front of the small white cottage. All around you lies the spread of mountains and the fall of valleys, cloud-patterned, infinite in their variety. Today the evening sun was slanting down the cwm and shining on the mountains; the trees were floodlit, the distant sheep dotted about the hill Bryawr opposite as white as painted boulders. And everything so quiet that you could hear a bee hum, a sparrow chirping.

Wide-ranging views, fresh unpolluted mountain air, cloud-shadows riding over green hillsides, intermittent sunshine – what more can anyone want? The bleat of lambs, white and newborn; the song of birds in spring-time; and no aeroplanes. Or only very seldom and very high, their drone no more intrusive than the hum of a bumblebee among golden cascading broom.

Above the cottage rises the Gaer mountain, ringed by earthworks of an Iron Age fort and open to the four winds. From its rounded summit, close-cropped by sheep, you can see on the one hand up the Vale of Ewas and across it to the high ridge beyond Llantony, and on the other across the valley of the Grwyne Fawr and the forest of Mynydd Ddu away into the Black Mountains and, beyond, the Brecon Beacons stretching towards the sea.

Hard to beat that for a view – when you can see it; one must make that proviso. We are prone to mists and swirling cotton-woolly clouds when everything drips, and visibility is down to about two yards. Middle Gaer's previous owner told me of a year when rain had fallen every day for six months on end (though I suppose not *all* day); three people committed suicide, and he emigrated to Australia.

He and his family were snowed in once for several weeks. One morning, they saw human footprints going down the lane, to vanish in an extra-deep drift. No footprints emerged the other side. My predecessor awaited the thaw with interest, but nothing came to light when the drift disappeared. He didn't think this especially odd. 'This hill is haunted,' he explained. Beyond the cottage is a decaying farmhouse smothered in nettles, abandoned because it was the abode of a man who shot himself on the stairs. Ifor, the owner, believes that underneath the derelict house is an inexhaustible repository of natural gas which will one day make his fortune, ghost or no ghost.

So I started for this Easter visit with hope and apprehension fairly balanced. It turned out fine but cold with an east wind. My Oaksey neighbour Herbert says it's likely to stay in that quarter until 21 June. He has a wind-vane, and his wife watched it like a hawk on 21 March, because whatever the direction of the wind at noon that day, thence it will blow for three months. The wind was firmly settled in the south that morning, but at five to twelve it veered to the east and there it stayed till five past. Only ten minutes, but that was enough. Now we're stuck for three months with that nasty cold east wind. 'Queer, isn't it,' Herbert said.

13 April – HAROLD

I seldom arrive at Middle Gaer without thinking of Harold. Sometimes I can almost hear his cheerful shout emerging from the wood below the cottage: a high-pitched, long-drawn-out hallo-o-o-a, and see his dog bounding ahead.

In some indefinable way, Harold was attached to the place, though he never actually lived here. But long ago his sister kept house for the Reverend Thomas Williams, a retired parson who bought this little hill farm with a tumbledown cottage and eighteen acres in 1915 for £260 from the Representative Body of the Church in Wales. The Reverend Williams put up a lean-to shed known as the Vicar's room, and on its foundations (in so far as it has any) my kitchen/living room now stands.

Harold loved Middle Gaer as if it had been his own. He knew every inch, and which stretch of the boundary fence belongs to whom. The bit from the iron gate to that oak belongs to me, then a stretch along the steep dip to Parry, then a bit at the bottom to me, then Olsens' up to the other gate, then a bit of mine as far as the alder tree, then Ifor Jones along the old wall, then mine along the top and then Charlie Price down to the iron gate again. The fences are a mixture of barbed wire, tree-trunks, rusty wire-netting, limbs of trees, bits of corrugated iron and here and there an old bedstead, and they represent a constant battle of wits between the farmer and his Welsh mountain sheep, which can get through, round or over anything.

Harold used to appear at any hour and without warning, save for his shout and his dog, followed by a shock of white hair emerging from the bracken. His cheerful face was crinkled like an early English apple, his eyes a clear child-like blue, his cheeks ruddy and his chin close-shaven. His clothes were old but not tattered and he always looked clean and tidy. He had no abode, no trade or profession, no regular income, no means of transport but his feet and sometimes a pony, no possessions but the clothes on his back and a suit for best with collar and tie. He lodged with whichever farmer was employing him at the time. He was a monumental liar, a master sponger and about the best raconteur I have ever met. You could listen to him for hours on end. He also knew a lot about sheep and ponies. From his youth he'd ridden about all over the hills, winter and summer, bareback as a rule, as much at home as a grouse in the heather. As a young man he'd cut a dashing figure at local shows and races; he'd ride anything, win a lot of races, spend his winnings on cider and girls, and be penniless next day.

When Harold married, he lived for years at The Rock, the last cottage up a track leading into the hills beyond the Gaer. Here were born their four sons. His wife died when the youngest was a baby. Then he left The Rock to live in many roughish places with his sons and sometimes, sometimes not, a housekeeper. When the last one went – it's unlikely that he ever paid them – he brought up his sons himself, with the intermittent aid of sisters, half-sisters and semi-aunts; everyone in these valleys is related to everyone else and most of them to Harold.

Harold's parents died within a few days of each other, he told me; she first, and from that moment Harold's father didn't open his mouth to eat or drink. Then on the eighth day he called for two pints of ale, drank them, and died. I remembered one of Gervas' favourite couplets: 'She first deceas'd; he for a little tried to live without her, liked it not, and died.'

One thing Harold couldn't teach his sons was how to read and write; he lacked the skill, but managed well without it. If he received a picture postcard he'd produce it with a little grin and an air of triumph to have it read to him, too good not to be shared. Any official communication, or bill, or possibly summons – in the past some episodes concerning sheep had occurred – was much better left unread. His deals in sheep, cattle, ponies and anything that came along were many and complex, and conducted by telephone, preferably when the owner of the telephone was out; if resort had to be made to a call-box, you would hear that high-pitched 'Hallo-o-a, Harold here', and then a less exuberant voice inquiring 'Will you pay for the call?' – impossible to refuse, Harold would always have something interesting to say.

I rashly involved myself with Harold in running a small flock of ewes on Middle Gaer, as he was living then close at hand at Llwyncelyn. 'Involved' is the word; developments got more and more out of hand; sheep vanished, sheep appeared, sheep strayed, sheep went to market, different sheep came back, and finally an inspector called. The sheep were disposed of. They had been fun while they lasted, and I didn't want to go to gaol.

If Harold had few worldly possessions, he had a lot of creditors. However sharp the look-out they kept for him on market day, his was sharper; they'd see that shock of white hair vanishing behind the back of a cattle lorry and find that it had melted into thin air. What with half-sisters, nieces, aunts' half-brothers' daughters, and just friends, he had so many hide-outs in Abergavenny that it was hopeless to try to track him down.

'You've got to say this for Harold,' people remarked, 'he's a good man with sheep.' Many of the farmers round about have commoners' rights to turn their sheep out on to the open mountains above the last boundary fence, and in the summer, after shearing, Harold would ride up with a bunch of ewes and wethers, pick a spot, and sleep there overnight to let them get accustomed to their new surroundings. These sheep would never stray beyond a certain radius from the place where he'd slept, nor mingle with other flocks grazing on the mountain, nor allow a stranger sheep to join their number. When the time came to move them back he had only to go to that particular spot and there they'd be, to be rounded up in a few minutes by his dog.

The sheep had a stronger territorial instinct than Harold; he was always moving on. Not only could he do anything with sheep but he could also milk a cow, kill a pig, truss a fowl, break a pony, lay a hedge, train a dog, build a wall. He was a first-rate shearer. Farmers were glad to give him bed and board; they deducted his keep from his wages and you'd think this was foolproof, but Harold found chinks now and then. He'd take some eggs or a dressed goose to market for the farmer's wife, who'd never see the money, or move on owing for his laundry, or his pony's keep. But there it was, that was Harold, the farmers said, he was a good worker and he'd always bring back a few sweets for the kids on market days, or lend a hand in the kitchen.

He lodged at one time with a farmer who lived in one half of the house while the wife lived in the other, and they never spoke. They took turns in the kitchen but never occupied it together. Harold never felt quite sure which side of the house he belonged to; he slept in a caravan. At another period of his life he'd lived, or camped out, in a strange, crumbling, dark and clearly haunted old manor house, belonging to the last of seven sons, who occupied one room with an ancient gas cooker without gas. The rest of the room was strewn with old bicycles, fertilizer sacks, incubators, empty bottles and indescribable junk. The farmer used to hang a side of bacon from the ceiling and buy a ten-pound cheese, and cut bits off each when he felt hungry. He was never short of cider which he matured in enormous casks in cobwebbed cellars under the old house. There was a tumbledown chapel used for storing fleeces, and in the old baronial hall an extraordinary *trompe l'oeil*: you held up a candle to an interior window, and saw its flame reflected in smaller and smaller pinpoints of light, apparently to infinity, as if you were looking down an endless corridor lit by torches on each side.

The roof of the house had fallen in, and as you wandered from room to room you knocked into bits of Jacobean oak carving lying about among sacks of rotting potatoes and drying onions, sheep medicines and bundles of old sacking. The seven brothers, Harold said, used to be prize-fighters at fairs, and not one of them married.

By contrast, among his former employers was a rich lady and the best horsewoman, Harold said, he'd ever seen. Her husband was away a lot on business and she had an affair with the vet, which resulted in a baby. For a week or so after its birth Harold heard it crying in the normal way upstairs, and then there was silence. He asked about it several times and got the same answer: 'She's asleep.' After a week, the husband returned, went upstairs, came down looking pale and shaken and telephoned the police. They arrived and took away the lady and the baby and Harold saw her only once again, at Cardiff Assizes. She'd thrust a bottle-brush down the infant's throat.

Now Harold won't come riding or striding up the path any more with his ringing 'halloa-there' and his shock of white hair. For several years he talked of going to Australia to visit one of his sons who'd offered to pay the fare. One day I heard that he'd actually gone. How he had managed with all those forms you have to fill in at airports, and getting a passport, and life in a tidy bungalow in a Melbourne suburb with never a sight of a sheep or a pony, goodness knows. But Harold always managed, and now and again a picture postcard arrived, written by his son. He'd intended to stay for six months. A year passed, eighteen months, and some said he'd gone for good; but I always thought he'd return to the hills.

'Is Harold back yet?' I asked on my next visit.

'Harold's dead.'

He had, indeed, come back, though not to our valley; he'd gone first to Yorkshire to stay with his eldest son. When out riding one day with his grand-daughter, a girth broke, the saddle slipped, Harold was thrown and broke his neck; he never moved again.

'Funny, when you think of it, Harold was just about born on a pony,' people said. He did come back to his native land in the end, to be buried at Monmouth beside his wife and youngest son. No one knew his age exactly since he drew no pension, never having bought a stamp. Seventy, or thereabouts.

If the Gaer is haunted, Harold's ghost has joined the company: a cheerful, active, friendly shade, voluble for ever, dealing I am sure in ghostly sheep and borrowing from fellow-shades to back some spectral horse, and always with a dog at his heels. The wind's sudden rattle in the chimney could be his chuckle as he dodges round the back into the ferns to elude some frustrated creditor. I miss his company.

16 April – JUSTICE

Back home, and my turn for the Bench this week. It's twenty-eight years since I was appointed and I still feel a fish if not exactly out of water, then in the wrong pool.

Today I was thinking how old I have become (although not yet hard of hearing I think) and remembering the day in 1946 when Hugh Baker rode over to Woodfolds on his white horse from Chedglow, hitched his horse's bridle to our picket fence, left his grey bowler in the hall and, after a little general conversation, asked me if I'd like to be a JP. I was astounded; such a thought had never entered my mind and, so far as I could see, I had absolutely no qualifications. However, it appeared that I had. I was under forty (just), a woman, lived within fifteen miles of Malmesbury and was able to sit on a Wednesday, when most people employed by others were not.

Hugh Baker was the chairman, one of the old school: upright in both senses, a perfect seat on a horse, courteous and kind, public-spirited, at ease with everyone from peers to poachers. A bachelor, he lived with a sister in a farm-house full of riding crops, sporting prints, silver cups won at agricultural shows, bound copies of the *Badminton Magazine* and dog-baskets. 'I've done everything in the world I wanted to, and I'm a happy man,' he once told me. One of the aims which he achieved was to breed the champion bull at the Royal Show. He read *The Times* from cover to cover every day; anyone who did that, he said, and did it thoroughly, could hold his own on any topic likely to be raised by anyone he was likely to meet.

In due course I was sworn and became a magistrate. To sit in judgment on our fellow men is something very few of us feel cut out to do. There but for the grace of God . . . I suppose every JP starts off with these misgivings and most JPs never quite shrug them off. Lay magistrates are sometimes said to be too lenient and, if so, this is the reason. We all drive cars, most of us have broken the speed limit on occasion, failed to see a halt sign, omitted to pay sufficient care and attention and even, perhaps, driven with too much alcohol in our blood. So far we may have got away with it but next time it might be our turn to be down there among the customers instead of up here on the stage. Literally a stage; when amateur theatricals are in progress at the Town Hall we make our entry through curtains painted to suggest a woodland glade, castle battlements or a pirate's quarter-deck. Our humdrum appearance must be an anticlimax, to say the least.

In practice, dispensing justice at this grass-roots level isn't quite as un-nerving as one expects it to be. Magistrates, for one thing, aren't supposed to know anything about the law, beyond what we are all supposed to know. The Clerk deals with everything else. Apart from routine matters like extensions to licensing hours, approving plans for alterations to pubs, licensing betting shops and so on, there are normally only two things to decide: whether an individual has done what he's accused of doing and, if so, what is the appropriate penalty.

In practice, generally it's only the second question that concerns us, since the great majority plead guilty to the offence. If a radar check shows that you exceeded the speed limit it's no good saying that you didn't, or denying that you'd had too much to drink if the laboratory test showed that your blood contained more than 80 mg of alcohol. Since nothing is infall-ible, mistakes may occasionally be made, but if so, it is quite impossible for the magistrates to detect them.

Nor is the choice of penalties as great as it may seem. There's a semi-official scale of fines for motoring offences, which take up the bulk of our time, and endorsement of licences is automatic; we have no choice in the matter. It's very, very seldom that we send anyone to gaol; serious cases go straight to the Crown Court either for trial if they're defended, or for sentence if there's a guilty plea. So generally it boils down to a choice between probation and a fine.

Probation has got steadily more popular with everyone, except possibly the probation officers, most of whom are overworked. It's based on our current belief in the innate goodness of man, who will love his fellow men and keep the law unless corrupted by misfortune and circumstances beyond his control: a broken home, bad associates, domestic troubles, lack of education and so on. Those who have erred need help, not punishment; instead of sending sheep-stealers to Australia, we send shop-lifters to a psychiatrist. Probation was originally intended for first offenders but nowadays it's often hopefully extended to second, third, fourth and umpteenth offenders, sometimes because it's hard to know what else to do. Tougher characters consider it a very soft option indeed.

Nevertheless there's the parable of the lost sheep, and the success rate of the probation service is a great deal better than one per cent. Any magistrate can draw comfort from examples of its success. I can think, for instance, of a middle-aged woman who pleaded guilty to a whole string of frauds. She'd been travelling all over the south of England staying for one night in a good hotel, leaving without paying the bill and now and then pawning something she had bought with a dud cheque to pay the bus fare to her next stop.

The usual remand for inquiries produced a sad tale. She was a university graduate fluent in several languages, married to a fellow academic. He'd deserted her, taking their two sons and leaving her with two small daughters and no means of support. At some point she'd collapsed, abandoned her teaching job and her daughters and gone off to live from hand to mouth in cheap lodgings in a small industrial town, supporting herself by casual employment in factory canteens. She'd never applied for National Assistance. Finally she'd abandoned the canteens and lodgings, taken off with ten shillings in her purse and gone from place to place until the police caught up with her in Malmesbury.

Clearly she was a case for a psychiatrist. The snag about probation was that she had nowhere to go. People on probation are required to report to the officer any change of address and employment; she could hardly report any change of what she hadn't got. She could be sent to prison, where she might or might not receive psychiatric treatment, but no one wanted that. The probation officer came to the rescue by taking her into her own home and then going to infinite trouble to search for lodgings and a job.

A few weeks later she telephoned to say that she had placed the woman in employment and was ringing round for the loan of a few necessities, until the woman could get on her feet. The period of probation was two years and when the woman was discharged all was well; she'd held down her job, repaid the loans and retrieved one daughter who was sharing her flat.

With fines, the problem is to make them severe enough not to seem laughably trivial, but not so severe that they can never be paid, in which case the offender gets hopelessly into arrears, comes before the court to get the backlog remitted, and nearly always succeeds.

Benches are sometimes accused of lack of uniformity in imposing fines.

In theory, two people guilty of a similar offence should suffer similar penalties. But suppose Offender A is a married man with five children, an invalid mother to support and a job down at the bottom of the wage scale, while Offender B is young and single, paying £5 a week to his parents and drawing a generous wage. To him a fine of, say, £20 would represent two days' pay and might clip him in the betting shop for a day or two; to A, it would be a real smack between the eyes. So it's uniformity, not discrepancy, that would create injustice.

Another difficulty about deciding on fines is how to keep the minds of magistrates, conservative organs as a rule, in tune with the realities of roaring inflation. When Hugh Baker first became a magistrate the farm wage was twenty-five shillings a week, so five shillings (25p) was a sizeable fine, ten shillings (50p) almost vicious. Displaying no bicycle lights was then the commonest offence. By the time Hugh retired, we'd bumped up the fines to five shillings for no front light and ten for no rear one, and thought that quite enough; the two together amounted to about half a week's farm wage.

His successor (another Hugh) was, and is, almost an ideal chairman for a country Bench: possessed of an easy manner, no pomposity, common sense, a sense of humour, a knowledge of the countryside and that indefinable air of authority derived from Eton, service in the Scots Greys and filling the offices of Field-Master to the Beaufort Hunt and Colonel of the Queen's Bodyguard. When he took over as chairman, farm wages had risen to about £3 a week and so a fine of that amount was considerable, and £5 severe.

Time passed; all of us grew older, inflation began to escalate and then took off into the stratosphere. We've all tried to keep pace but it's hard to eradicate one's ingrained set of values and to treat £10 as a bagatelle. But a bagatelle it is if you're a plant operator on a motorway getting £100 a week and more. In such cases we should think of a number and double it to make the fine hurt; but then the discrepancies would be increased between a fine imposed on the plant operator and that on a farm labourer getting, with overtime, perhaps £30 a week.

People sometimes ask me if I enjoy the Bench but that's the wrong word to use; one doesn't, or at any rate shouldn't, enjoy the misfortunes of others, even minor ones as most of these are. And not always as minor as they may seem. A conviction for exceeding the speed limit can dislocate a man's entire life if he's automatically disqualified under the totting-up system, and if his livelihood depends on his driving a car. Domestic cases can be mini-divorce suits, with harrowing glimpses into hatred-ridden, cat-

and-dog lives, unwanted children, and people too feckless to prevent the arrival of any more.

One is glad of a little light relief now and then, such as a quarrel between neighbours when Mrs Mudd pulled up armfuls of Mrs Mott's sprouts, Mrs Mott took revenge on Mrs Mudd's cauliflowers and Mrs Mudd set on Mrs Mott's dahlias – the gardens must have looked as if a bulldozer had run amok before a policeman arrived to calm matters down. Then there was a farmer at Minety, one of the sturdy, independent, old-fashioned pitch-fork sort, who tossed a Ministry inspector into the dung-heap. With great presence of mind the inspector kept his dung-encrusted jacket done up in a parcel until the case came on three or four months later, when it was produced in court as an exhibit, with its good ripe smell.

Over the years one learns a lot on the Bench, among other things how many unsuspected laws there are to break. For instance, lighting a fire within fifteen feet of a highway, shedding mud on a road from the wheels of a tractor, leaving the engine of the car running when one gets out, or failing to get a licence for a fishing rod. No one on our Bench knew about licences for fishing rods until a man was summonsed for not having one, and for angling in private waters.

The chairman at first refused to believe it, and a great deal of looking up in legal tomes went on. There it was, however, somewhere in the law of the land: a licence was needed, at the cost of one shilling. *Any* sort of rod? inquired the chairman; what about a boy who cut himself a stick from a hedge, tied on a bent pin and impaled a worm? Further legal consultation produced the answer that yes, strictly speaking, he should have a licence for that too. Both the chairman and his deputy owned unlicensed fishing rods. There was little the Bench could do but give the culprit an unconditional discharge.

Though our crime rate remains relatively low, types of crime are changing. More hooliganism, more youths getting drunk and roaming around breaking windows or smashing things in pubs, taking other peoples' cars and breaking into shops or houses to steal what they can find. We even had a drug case the other day, a bunch of teenagers caught with pot. All such cases are sent to the Crown Court.

Changes also impend in the composition of our Bench. Instructions from the top have suggested, if not demanded, a need for the appointment of magistrates with 'Labour affiliations', so as to reflect a cross-section of society. In other words, more working-class Justices and fewer true-blue Tories on the Bench.

In country districts, at any rate in ours, these instructions are harder to carry out than might appear. No doubt there is as high a proportion of working-class people in the country as in cities, but very few – in our area, none – have given any sign of wishing to take on this unpaid and sometimes time-consuming job.

One reason may be that there's less anonymity in a village. You know your neighbours, they know you, and if you have a share in imposing on one of them some penalty, bad feeling may arise. 'I'll mind my own business and you mind yours' is the general philosophy. And a long heritage of generation after generation having had to pull forelocks and drop curtseys to squire and parson and take the farmer's bidding, like it or not, has something to do with it. Administration of the law is a matter for Them, not Us; to join the Bench would be, in a sense, to go over to the enemy. And then, throughout the centuries, the more ambitious men and women have been drawn away into towns. Perhaps by now our country genes have become impoverished.

And then again Benches, like most institutions, tend to perpetuate their own kind. Justices used to be selected by a secret committee under the Lord Lieutenant, but now anyone who wants to be a JP can put forward his name. But most would-be candidates seldom do so unless approached by the chairman, and most chairmen of country Benches are more likely to know personally fellow classmates, so to speak, than members of the rural proletariat, other than their tractor drivers or the garage mechanic, who probably wouldn't welcome the idea.

The fact is that most people simply haven't got the time. Tractor drivers and mechanics, not to mention schoolteachers, publicans, shopkeepers, contractors, builders or whatever, can't drop everything for a day on the Bench without disrupting their concerns. So it isn't easy nowadays to find new recruits, especially as they have to be under forty if possible; retired people, who might have the leisure, are too old.

So there are still no shop-stewards on our Bench, though we have an uneasy feeling that there ought to be. On the other hand, we have no retired generals with deaf-aids, or port-drinking peers. We have an estate agent, a doctor's wife, a gentleman-farmer's wife, a vet, a tenant-farmer's wife and the sales manager of a factory making farm implements. And the chairman, also a gentleman-farmer, and myself.

A strong rural flavour; also a strong sporting one. In the room where we foregather before going on to draw the covert in the Town Hall, there's liable to be talk of good scenting weather, Cheltenham races or the Three-Day Event; and at the appropriate season someone returns from Scotland lean from crawling through the heather in pursuit of stags, or playing salmon in the Spey. We used to meet on a Wednesday, and so did the hounds; a conflict of interests, except in periods of hard frost or outbreaks of foot-and-mouth disease. In summer, it's mainly haymaking that exerts the counter-pull, except in periods of prolonged rain. Until our newest recruit (the sales manager) joined our ranks, I was the only member never to be seen following the Beaufort hounds.

18 April – THE MARTINS AT THE PARK

A cold wind still and still dry, and old Sid working in his garden as usual whenever weather permits; he's heavy now, corpulent, slower, but pretty sprack for eighty-three. His garden always looks tidy, the plants thriving and well-organized. He's a true gardener, but at his age – indeed at any age – ready to stop for a chat about the Government, the weather or the past.

Today he talked about the Martins, who lived at the Park before World War I and gave him his first employment, when he left school at thirteen, as garden-boy. The Park in those days employed much of the youth of the village, girls in the house and boys in stable or garden; naturally it became a sort of marriage bureau.

Mrs Martin was the last of the ladies of the manor to act as one. (Though technically she didn't hold this position; the Martins were tenants, not owners, of the Park.) She went among the sick and poor if not literally with soup, with things like beef tea and pies, and had coal delivered to the needy at her expense.

An old man called Moses Kent and his wife lived, Sid told me, in the cottage I now occupy. He had a weak chest and used to cough and spit. His wife would spot Mrs Martin coming along the road from the Park in her trap and call out to Moses: 'Here she be a-coming, Moses, get thee to thy bed quickly and cough and spit.' 'And how's Moses today?' Mrs Martin would call in to inquire. 'I'm sorry to tell 'ee, ma'am, 'e's had a little lapse.' Coughs and spits were heard off. 'I'm sorry to hear that, Mrs Kent. I expect he'd like a little invalid food.' And then a pie or pudding would come up from the Park, delivered by one of the grooms. Moses Kent lived on to a ripe age.

The cook who made the pies and puddings still resides at Eastcourt, well into her eighties. While in service at the Park she met and married postman Arthur West and together they kept the sub-post office and village shop for many years.

'A bit eccentric', Mrs West said of Mrs Martin. In what way? 'She was very religious.' Hardly eccentric in that day and age? She kept seven or eight maids, and it was no doubt eccentric to call them herself at six o'clock and make their tea, which they found waiting on the kitchen table.

Every Sunday morning, a procession set off across the fields to the church, headed by Mrs Martin with the maids, dressed in black, following behind in single file. Mrs West, then Annie Blackford of Malmesbury – her father, the Luces' coachman, was killed in a carriage accident – baulked at this compulsory attendance, not so much on religious grounds as because it was bossy. She had a show-down with Mrs Martin, who accused her of being too independent. 'So I was,' said Annie; but she was the cook, so in a privileged position, and got her way. In any case, I don't see how a cook could go to matins and still serve up a hot Sunday luncheon.

And what meals people had in those days. At least five courses every evening and three at lunch, cooked on a big coal-burning range difficult to regulate. Then eight or ten to feed in the servants' hall. Even when Mrs Martin was alone with her daughter, they changed into evening dress and were served by a liveried footman and two parlour-maids. Soup, fish or entrée, roast, pudding, savoury. Dessert and coffee. Yet people in those days seemed to be no fatter than we are today, if as fat.

Six or seven men and boys worked in the garden; they were paid five shillings a week to begin with and provided with a red cardigan; the head gardener's cardigan was blue.

Mrs Martin led the singing in church in a voice, Sid said, like a cross between a nutmeg-grater and a motor horn. A fine horsewoman, she rode boldly to hounds and drove a four-in-hand with dash and skill. She was a sister of Walter Long, at one time a popular Home Secretary who was responsible for the muzzling of dogs as part of a campaign to eradicate rabies. There was a dreadful moment when foxhounds appeared to be threatened by the ukase; the prospect of the Quorn or Pytchley Hunts pursuing their quarry in muzzles provoked enraged protests in the House of Lords and gave rise to a music-hall ditty which concluded: 'Should his order embrace the dogs of the chase, He would not be popular Long.'

Mrs Martin had a famous quarrel with the rector about re-opening the south door of the church, so as to save her procession the need to go through the churchyard to the north door on the other side. The vestry consented, the work was done, and Mrs Martin sent £20 to the Bishop to cover her share of the cost, the balance to be paid by the rector out of church funds.

Mr Faithfull, the rector, refused to pay. After a while, tired of rendering accounts, the builders took him to court and got an Order, with fourteen days imprisonment in default. This Mr Faithfull ignored. In due course, a bailiff arrived: a jolly character in a bowler hat, driving a pony and trap. Mr Faithfull welcomed him in and he stayed for several days at the Rectory, having an enjoyable time. (Mrs Faithfull and her daughter had turned the top floor into an aviary, full of branches and tree-trunks; bull-finches, waxwings and other birds disported themselves there.) The jolly bailiff failed to persuade the rector to pay up, and away they went to Gloucester gaol in the pony-trap. The news was carried round the village by Ted Dicks, the carpenter, in the words: 'There a'nt got to be no christenings, there a'nt got to be no weddings, there a'nt got to be no funerals; parson's gone to gaol.'

Within a week, back came parson. He summoned a parish meeting and gave a lively account of his experiences, swinging the big church key to illustrate his tale. Moreover he got the last word about the south door: when the Martins left in 1910, he had it blocked up again.

Entry through the south door, while it lasted, spared Mrs Martin's bevy of domestics the sight of the *sheila-na-gig* set in the north wall, which might have kindled wicked thoughts. Such small stone carvings are rarities in England, though in Ireland less uncommon; they're fertility symbols of Celtic origin, and ours must be considerably older than the church, which dates back to the early thirteenth century. It appears to represent a herma-phrodite figure with swelling bosoms and a very large male organ, and is said by some to be a relic of the worship of Priapus. How it got on to a Christian church is a mystery.

After the Martin affair, the Rev. Wyndham James Hamilton Faithfull grew progressively odder. Parishioners who called to see him would find him dozing with his feet on the mantelpiece, or talking to himself. He would open his confirmation classes with such remarks as 'What's going to win the Derby?', and give offence to the devout by declaring the Old Testament to be a pack of fairy tales. The war came, he had a son at the front and was no doubt worried; even so, his conduct was strange. He gave an order to the landlord of the Wheatsheaf to issue free drinks to customers to the value of £78, in the name of the Archbishops of Canterbury and York, to make up for the shortage of flour; and understandably gave offence when he went round the village saying that old people were to be sent to France to act as sandbags in the trenches. When taxed with this, in his defence he said that he'd been told the story by a pupil at the flying school and thought it 'an awfully good joke', and jokes were needed in times like these.

Higher authority could do nothing until the rector took to neglecting his duties. When the churchwardens found the church door locked at matins time on three Sundays running, they notified the Bishop, who appointed a Commission headed by a learned Judge. The members came to Oaksey in October, 1917, and heard evidence from parishioners in the village hall. The rector, as was to be expected, put up a spirited defence. (He was an Irishman.) On one of the Sundays in question, he had sent his daughter to the church to tell his would-be congregation that he couldn't take the service because he had rheumatism in the foot. This defence was torn to shreds, however, by a parishioner who'd seen him rolling his lawn that afternoon, and by two boys who'd observed him chasing a butterfly.

Parson's Freehold then reared its head; as the rector's moral life was blameless, he could not be sacked. The Commission found that he had indeed neglected his duties; not only had he kept the church locked but he had held no Sunday School, disbanded the choir, and failed to celebrate Holy Communion. He must have had plenty of time to devote to the aviary, and to collecting butterflies. The Commission attributed his negligence to 'mental worries working upon a nervous and excitable disposition', and the Bishop 'inhibited' him for a year. This meant that he could perform no clerical duties, and a curate from Malmesbury replaced him; but the Rectory continued to be occupied by him and his family, and presumably the birds.

The ecclesiastical authorities were by this time almost desperate, and kept on trying to get him to resign. At last he agreed, with a promise of a pension of £100 a year to be taken from the incumbent's meagre stipend. This meant that his successor had to manage on £150 a year instead of the £170 he had been drawing as a curate in Malmesbury. Mr Faithfull lived to be over ninety, still drawing his £100 a year.

29 April – INVASION

Now that my plan to reduce the garden has led to a small but significant increase in its size, my hankering for an asparagus bed has taken on a new force. Books say that crowns should be planted before the end of April, so there's no time to lose. I hurried off to buy two dozen three-year-old crowns from the local nurseryman, with instructions thrown in on how to plant them.

I've never seen an asparagus crown before; they look like crabs, though with many more legs. You spread out the legs and plant them five inches deep, but there's a problem: which way up? The legs, or roots, go sideways, not down, and the crabs look the same on both sides. Closer inspection revealed on some of them a tiny white shoot in the middle of the crab's body. Clearly this goes uppermost, but I couldn't find shoots on all of them, so went back to the house to get my spectacles. There was a car out in the road, and a man talking to my neighbour opposite over his hedge. Or, rather, Tom was talking to him, in fact shouting furiously: 'My rates are up a hundred per cent!'

The village is seething with rage about the rates, like all the other villages and towns. Suddenly, without a word of warning, everybody's rates have not just risen but leapt up in a single bound to twice their former level, or very near it. Meetings, speeches and hundreds, if not thousands, of telephone calls have expressed our impassioned feelings, and all to no avail. 'They won't pay no attention. It won't do no good.' In a democracy it *ought* to do some good, and we bang away but without hope, like people who go to church without believing in God.

'One hundred per cent,' Tom repeated, practically shaking his fist at the caller. Could it really be that 'they' *had* paid some attention? That someone from the Council had come to hear our views?

'Just say that again, will you?' the young man asked, motioning to two companions who had been lurking in the background. They moved forward, each carrying a grey metal object of indeterminate shape and blunted nose which they raised as they approached and pointed straight at Tom. He recoiled, and after a startled pause such as deer make when alarmed, made a dash for the house, shouting over his shoulder: 'You mind your business and I'll mind mine.' What had the rate-men got hold of now, some kind of computer? Foiled in their intention, they turned, caught sight of me, and advanced. 'We understand there's some feeling in the village about the rates. Would you give me your views?'

By now I had spotted the letters ITN on the side of their van so, despite the blunt-nosed grey weapons, stood my ground and said my views were much the same as everyone else's, what other view could one have? 'We've been through the village and people don't seem very articulate.' I could understand that. My hands and trousers were covered with mud, a strong-ish gale was blowing, gardening clothes taken unaware are far from television-worthy and my mind was on the asparagus crowns. But I stood obediently in the garden peering through a screen of gale-mangled hair at the two grey metal objects held by the crouching young men, and saying that we all felt very hardly done by, people in rural areas (as the countryside is now called) don't get the same amenities as people in towns so why should they have to pay more – for instance, sewarage rates on buildings unconnected to sewers?

That evening, there we were on the box. I could see what the young man had meant by people being inarticulate. He'd managed to catch Ruth peering out of an upstairs window, as if from the mouth of a burrow, clearly about to vanish into it like a startled badger. 'I tried to get round the back through the field when I saw them,' Ruth told me next day, 'but there was Charlie Todd's bull so I couldn't.' 'He's a very tame bull,' I suggested. 'Yes, he is, all the same I didn't fancy it. I thought they'd gone, looked out of my window and there they were.' They'd also captured her next-door neighbour in her garden with her retreat cut off before she could beat it. Everyone else had got indoors in time.

Back to the asparagus. Can a crown planted upside down turn itself round? It seems unlikely, although plants can do unlikely things, like thrust their way up through concrete, or come to life after lying dormant for centuries. In time, no doubt, we shall see.

May

14 May – CHARLIE AND ARTHUR

About once a year, you awake to a perfect May morning and then all is redeemed. Blossom foams over fruit trees, flowering cherries, almonds, shrubs; fallen petals drift across the grass and jump before the wind like tiny frogs. When the sun comes out it's all light, colour and a kind of song not only from the birds but from leaves, grasses, blossoms. Only for one day however, and this was it.

The ceanothus is garlanded from crown to root in powder-blue bobbles, the broom has exploded in pale gold, tulips shine like lanterns in the borders, tight-clenched lilacs are unfolding. As for the birds, they're singing their heads off. Blackbirds predominate, skimming low over the orchard and young green vegetables in rows that still look tidy. Pigeons are almost food-logged, their crops stuffed with juicy greenstuff. A pair of magpies struts about the lawn immaculate in dinner jackets, so handsome and so ruthless – they've destroyed two broods of moorhens on the Woodfolds pond, one after the other.

Charlie paused for a chat as he went by, limping. His knee again, and it all dates back, he says, to the time when a sow bumped into him. He had twenty breeding sows under his care and never missed a farrowing, day or night. Sometimes he was up half the night, putting each piglet under the infra-red lamp as it was born and getting the sow settled.

Charlie started work at thirteen at Court Farm for Arthur Rich, who employed his father George – the only employer George ever had from leaving school till he retired at seventy-seven, and died a fortnight later. On a wage that rose over the years to a peak of thirty shillings weekly, plus little sums the children earned, George and his wife reared thirteen children in the old cottage next to the church, now modernized and occupied by a retired London couple. It had two bedrooms upstairs, two rooms down. Boys slept in one room, girls in another with the parents in a corner partitioned off by a blanket. The ceilings are too low for a six-foot man to stand upright, windows small, the walls thick, so it kept snug and warm in winter.

'Hard work never harmed anyone' is one of Charlie's maxims and seemingly it never harmed his mother. Thirteen children (plus two who died in infancy) in that tiny cottage; water drawn by a bucket from a well in the garden and heated in a copper in a lean-to wash-house; coal carried for the kitchen range which was cleaned and re-lit every morning; an outside privy; lamps and candles; so much ironing on the kitchen table with an old-style flat-iron; and all on thirty shillings weekly at the most; how did they manage?

They grew all their own vegetables, including potatoes; kept a pig and hens; snared and ferreted rabbits. A big black cooking-pot hung on a chain over the kitchen range and everything was cooked in it at once – everything there was, as a rule mainly potatoes. Charlie and his brothers often went to work on a crust or two of bread and a scraping of lard. When they killed their pig the lard was melted down and made to last till the next pig was fat.

Charlie was at the farm by six o'clock to feed the horses and harness them ready for the men who came an hour later to take them out to plough, sow, drill, cut corn or whatever operation was in season. For harrowing, men and horses went out at seven and worked through till three, non-stop. Then the horses were brought in and fed and the men went back for their dinner to return afterwards for other tasks. Charlie's was to rub down the horses and see to their bedding. Every evening he and one of the brothers still living at home did a spell in the garden before they were free to go off with other lads to roam about the fields and hedgerows throwing sticks at birds or netting them, and, later on, courting.

Since we are what we eat, you might have expected Charlie to be spare and puny; he's thickset, sturdy, ruddy-complexioned, strong, and did a steady eight-hour day at seventy-two. His mother lived to be eighty-seven. He worked for thirty-nine years at Court Farm for Arthur Rich and then for Arthur's nephew, Tom, and then came to Woodfolds. So he's spent his working life on two farms, instead of on one like his father.

Arthur Rich has passed into the folklore of the village. Some liked him and some didn't; no one was neutral. Everyone who knew him (he died in 1943) remembers him, and when his name is mentioned generally smiles, gives a shake of the head and says, 'Ah, Arthur.'

Arthur swore at everyone, he cussed and shouted and was a bully, but underneath the bluster was said to beat a heart if not of gold, possibly of bronze. He helped more people than he hurt, after swearing at them. He lived well. Joints of beef would come almost every day to his table where he'd carve his own liberal portion, a smaller one for his housekeeper Miss Chambers, and then say to the maid-of-all-work who'd brought it from the kitchen: 'Take it away, don't let me see it again.' Often it went round to George Butcher. Sometimes one of his men would drop off a sack of potatoes at George's cottage. But never coal – that had to be paid for, so fell into a different category.

He was one of four brothers, all well-to-do, all farmers, all robust and well-built men, all well known throughout the West Country. Arthur's bark was worse than his bite but he could bite too. Miss Chambers was an excellent housekeeper, economical – she had to be – and a first-rate cook who took special pride in her baking. After church on Sunday Arthur would ask two or three friends in to drink a glass of port. On one occasion she had placed an appetizing sponge layer cake with chocolate icing next to the decanter. He picked it up and bellowed 'What's this bloody muck?' Miss Chambers burst into tears.

She must have been a much-tried woman. Once, returning from a morning's shopping, she found the dining-room and sitting-room stripped bare of every bit of furniture. The Murrays, who had just arrived at the Park, had asked Arthur if he knew of anyone with furniture for sale to supplement their own. 'Dessay I could find 'ee some.' Next day, he had all his front-room furniture loaded on to a farm wagon and taken to the Park.

Church on Sundays was a ritual. A visiting parson once took the service in an unfamiliar cassock with a coloured hood. As he approached the altar a stentorian whisper 'Damme if parson ain't wearing Lord Ellesmere's colours!' rang through the nave.

There was no better judge of cattle in the West Country. He used to go to Ireland, return with drafts of young beasts as wild as hawks, and fatten them on the rich pastures of Court Farm. Then Charlie would drive them, single-handed, to Tetbury or Cirencester markets, sometimes all the way to Gloucester, about twenty-five miles. No cattle lorries then. 'An open gate and they were off, for miles sometimes, and they didn't wait to see an open gate neither, used to leap like race-horses over the hedge and be gone.'

Did he lose any? 'Never one,' Charlie said. But once, when he got back from Gloucester market, he found a bullock missing, and took Bill Harris back to help him find it. A man hoeing roots said they'd never catch it, the beast was wild as a mad dog and leapt like a steeplechaser. Charlie and Bill ran after it for four hours, scrambling through hedge after hedge, struggling across ploughland. At last it fell backwards trying to leap a hedge, and Bill and Charlie brought it home quiet as a lamb, one hand resting on its flank all the way.

Arthur died in his seventieth year and left the farm and part of his fortune to a nephew, who was young and gay and handsome and as wild as one of his uncle's Irish beasts. In seven years everything was gone: the fortune first, then the cattle and implements, finally the farm. It was said that a rumble could be heard at nights in the churchyard as Arthur, cussing and swearing, rotated in his grave. The epitaph on his tombstone reads: 'A friend to many and an enemy to none.' Sums it up, most people seem to think, pretty well.

19 May – CRICKET

When I woke the sky was stormy and the early morning sun coming at an angle lit up everything dramatically, like a powerful floodlight. The foliage of the trees glowed, especially the may at the bottom of my little orchard; planted only three years ago, it's now quite big and loaded with deep-pink blossom. A pair of fat wood-pigeons, so full they could scarcely get themselves airborne, perched in a branch of the may tree which sagged under their weight. Blackbirds ran about the orchard chattering, darting like insects or fish. In the field the magpies strutted and beyond were heifers black and white too, sleek with young grass. The wind has dropped, everything is calm, still too early for the aeroplanes to tear the peace to shreds. Everything is bone-dry and hard as rock.

Frederica cut out a skirt, Jos pulled a teacloth rail out of its socket, Isis the black cat brought a poor bedraggled fieldmouse upstairs. The sky was full of clouds and it was cold.

Charles played cricket. 'I expect you had a slap-up tea,' I remarked on his return; Oaksey had been playing the Royal Agricultural College, one of their grander fixtures. Everyone supposes the students to be rich and upper-class, with fast cars and glamorous girl-friends. 'No, it was bloody awful,' he said. 'Thick slabs of dry bread, a bare scrape of butter and half a jar of seedy pips going by the name of raspberry jam.' Disappointing. 'If my missus gave me a tea like that I'd throw her over the allotments,' one of the Oaksey team had remarked. 'These posh people don't eat half as well as we do,' said another. 'My dad used to work for the Whosis and said he'd be ashamed to sit down in our kitchen to what they had for dinner. Bloody great Rover in the garage, he said, and left-over scrag-end in the fridge.'

Catharine does the Oaksey teas in our village hall and they're excellent. 'Nice thin-cut sandwiches, two or three kinds, cucumbers and tomatoes as well as jam,' Charles observed. The Oaksey XI preened themselves not only on their teas but on their prowess: much to their surprise, they won the game.

20 May – CROWN COURT

My turn for the Crown Court at Swindon. The back door which magistrates generally use was locked, but as I turned away a porter with a large bunch of keys appeared.

'Security,' he said, shaking his head. He was in a philosophic mood. 'God gave the world to man,' he remarked, rattling his keys, 'and said, you can make a hell of it or you can make a heaven. It's a beautiful world – the trees, the wind and sky, the birds, the flowers. God said to man, do as you like with it, it's all yours, you can make it a hell or a heaven.' He locked the door behind me. 'Made a hell of it, that's what we've done. Fighting, murdering, torturing, pollution. It didn't used to be like that, not when we was children. It's the way the parents bring up children now. They leave God out and then what happens? In comes the devil. It's the devil's world now.' He put me a bit in mind of the porter in *Macbeth*, though he didn't get on to drunkenness.

The most interesting cases, as well as often the most tedious, are the defended ones that go before a jury and thus enable barristers in their fancy dress to display their somewhat overblown histrionic talents. But the majority concern convicted offenders up for sentence from the lower courts, because their past record demands a stiffer sentence than those courts have powers to inflict.

Today, for instance, there came into the dock a young woman caught stealing a turkey from a supermarket while under a suspended sentence for previous offences of the same kind. In theory, if you offend again while under a suspended sentence, you should go straight to gaol; but it's not automatic, the Court decides. Shop-lifting is rife; to go on putting people on probation or giving them suspended sentences can make a mockery of the law; obviously the sentence she received ought no longer to be suspended and off to prison she should go.

But what a mess her life has been. She started off with a baby at fourteen. Since then she's had four more, by various fathers. One of the fathers married and then deserted her, she lives on Social Security and, so far as one can tell, always will. The social inquiry reports said that she's a good mother, has a council house and keeps a tidy home. One of the children was taken by its father and one adopted, so now she has three at home: a brand-new baby and two boys.

The boys, it seems, are happy and doing well at school. What would happen to them if she went to prison? the Recorder asks. The two boys would have to be taken into care, she would lose her council house and no one seemed quite sure about the baby. A problem. By letting the law take its proper course and justly punishing one offender, you would very possibly create two future ones in the shape of the boys. We all agree that prison would be futile, the Recorder gives her a stern warning (not the first I'm sure), the Probation Officer takes over and everyone hopes, not too hopefully, for the best.

The glimpses one gets into the lives of some of one's more disorganized fellow citizens provides a constant, if melancholy, interest to the proceedings. George, for instance, came up yesterday accused of obtaining money by fraud. He leads a peripatetic, gipsy sort of life largely on caravan sites and in seaside resorts, and always has a lot of ready money, if not in his pocket then under a carpet or in some other unusual place.

People seem to lend him money readily, although he is, as his counsel said, a rough diamond. But the 'reasonable doubts' which must be totally excluded crept in, and the jury found him not guilty. Doubts are so readily kindled in the often-bemused minds of jurors that I sometimes wonder how anyone ever gets convicted at all, unless several reliable witnesses have actually seen the crime committed before their eyes. What the Bench knew, in this case, and the jury didn't, was that George had more than half a dozen previous convictions for exactly the same kind of offence. This time he got away with it, guilty as hell.

<h2 style="text-align:center">24 May – GLADYS AND KITTY</h2>

In a very small, very old cottage next to the Wheatsheaf dwell two sisters, Kitty and Gladys: Kitty, the eldest, is eighty-ish; Gladys, a few years younger, is a pillar of the church choir and has just retired as secretary to the parish council. They're the only ones who didn't marry out of eight children born to the wife of Mr Chambers, gardener and coachman to Robert Warner who owned four farms in the parish: Church, Street, Okewell and Sodam, as well as a considerable number of cottages.

I get the impression that Robert Warner (who died in 1930) was respected rather than loved. Sid says he was called behind his back 'Old Proba'ly' because he prefaced every remark with that word. 'Probably you'd better start to hoe the roots tomorrow,' to his foreman. 'Probably the mare's cast a shoe.'

At Church Farm he kept eight Shire horses, and Gladys remembers their going out to work every morning at seven sharp, or eight o'clock in winter, with harness jingling, coats shining, and hooves polished every day. At haymaking time each of the women he employed as casual labour armed herself with a heavy kind of spring-time rake called an ell-rake, and went out to the fields to sweep the hay into rows for the men to load with pitch-forks into wagons. The women worked from eight till four and got a shilling a day. Now and again Gladys earned a penny for taking bunches of grapes from Mr Warner's hot-house down to the Park.

The Warners kept a flock of eight ducks and a drake. There was a pond near the farmyard, but for some mysterious reason the ducks rejected it in favour of another pond along the village street. So every morning, led by the drake, they could be seen proceeding past the Wheatsheaf, turning left into The Street, and so to the favoured pond; and marching home again at dusk in the same order.

When Gladys was a child, in the early 1900s, the school had about twice as many children as it has now. Whether they got twice as good an education I couldn't say, but certainly people of that generation write a clearer hand, do sums more correctly, and have a wider vocabulary than the young. Of course they used to read much more, by their oil lamps and candles, in the absence of television; and every cottage had its Bible.

At thirteen, Gladys left school to go into service. Four of the Chambers girls – there were six – trod this road, starting at £12 a year, finding their own uniforms. After two or three years, if a girl worked hard and learned her work properly, she could better herself substantially. 'Mother was lucky, if you come to think of it,' Gladys said. 'All four of us in London and all came home safely, not one of us got into trouble.'

Their parents were strict. Both were alive when I came to the village; Mrs Chambers lived to be ninety-five and I remember her doing fine needlework, without glasses, and by lamplight, almost up to the time of her peaceful end. Her two unmarried daughters looked after her until she died, then moved to the cottage where they live now. 'It was a happy, carefree village then,' Gladys said, implying that it isn't so any longer.

June

5 June – CHRISTENING PRESENT

To Chipping Campden to collect the goblets commissioned last October
as christening presents for the twins. My third visit so I know the way now,
the workshop is practically impossible to find the first time. You turn off a
side street into a little passage leading to a builder's yard, and if you can
find anyone there, he will direct you to a doorway opening into a pitch-dark
bicycle shed. If you hunt about among the bicycles in the darkness, you
will find an old, unsafe-looking naked stairway, more of a ladder than a
stair. Two flights up, you see an arrow chalked on the wall and the word
HART.

You push the door open and find yourself in the upper storey of a warehouse with ancient rafters overhead, bare planks underfoot and a welter of
benches, rickety chairs, tools, papers and nameless bits and pieces lying
about all over the place. I located a man (this was on my first visit) seated

at a bench absorbed in his task. 'Which is Mr Hart?' He looked up benignly. 'We're all Mr Harts.' 'All' meant three, Mr Hart senior and two sons. Until recently there was a fourth, the grandfather, who continued at his bench until he was eighty-three, then found his sight not so sharp as it had been, reluctantly retired, and died quite soon afterwards.

I explained my need and Mr Hart conducted me to a cubby-hole constructed in a corner of the warehouse, opened a drawer and pulled out piles of sketches on odd bits of paper; sketches of spoons, inkstands, coffee-pots, jugs, candelabra, chalices and so on. We decided on goblets. There were many sketches and we chose a combination of a couple of them. Could I actually see any examples of his work? Mr Hart looked round the workshop and said regretfully that there was nothing there at the moment. Some pieces of communion plate had gone off to California the day before.

He added in a fatherly way 'Leave it to me,' and with this I was content. An entry was made in pencil in a kind of ledger. I asked 'How long?' This was in October. 'Come back about Easter time.' It was no good thinking of the telephone, there wasn't one. Letters could only waste the time of one of the finest craftsmen in England. I admired his filing system; it consists of spikes suspended like stalactites from the beams overhead on which are skewered wads of letters, invoices, receipts and the like. 'How do you get at the ones at the bottom?' I enquired. 'It's not the bottom you have to worry about, it's the top,' Mr Hart replied. I could see what he meant. The bottom of each pile was at the top of the skewer.

A wonderful day, June at its best. Green and white: hedges white with may blossom, hedgerows white with tall, delicate cow-parsley, fields green with young corn and grass. Clear sunshine, sharp shadows, a strong gusty wind rippling the corn and mowing grass, and provoking trees to lash branches smothered in fresh greenery. The white candles of the chestnuts are just going over. Clouds scudding, ewes with their lambs like big white daisies on green pastures, big grey barns and farmhouses looking as if they had grown there like trees out of the earth. On top of the Cotswolds you feel as if you were at sea with green waves and white spume billowing away in all directions.

About a month after Easter I found my way back to Mr Hart's, not really expecting anything much to have happened. There was Mr Hart sitting at the same bench peering over his task. He looked up, beamed and led me without a word into the cubby-hole where I half-regretted to see changes: a telephone had appeared. There were the goblets, just unpacked. 'They came back this morning,' he said. 'Must have known you'd be coming along.' Back from the assay office in London where they'd been stamped with the Hart mark, and with the lion, leopard's head and symbol that dates them. They were not quite ready for me to take.

I had brought a spoon with a crest, to be engraved on the goblets. A twisted snake designed, I believe, by Thomas Henry Huxley to commemorate his service as a naval surgeon in HMS *Rattlesnake*, and since worn on signet rings by his descendants; the twins are his great-great grandsons.

Another fortnight, and I came to take them away. They're pleasing goblets, solid, honest and at the same time light and elegant; like many other goblets, yet unique. Extravagant, perhaps; but when the barbarians arrive they can be buried, to be dug up and enjoyed a couple of thousand years hence as much as they will be today.

9 June – A DOYENNE

Marjorie to supper: we've known each other for thirty-five years and live half a mile apart, yet scarcely ever meet. Preoccupied. In her case with thirteen grandchildren always needing to be ferried from one place to another, or having half-terms, or being put into aeroplanes to join parents abroad, or just turning up to stay. Marjorie lives in an atmosphere of vicarious crisis and rises to each emergency like a yacht with her bows into the wind, breasting every wave with confident ease.

When we came first to Oaksey, the Lawrences were already old inhabitants. Geoffrey Lawrence bought Hill Farm before World War I, but as a busy barrister couldn't make his home here even after he married in 1920. (They met at a tennis party at Hankerton; Geoffrey asked a neighbour 'Who is that girl?' and made up his mind on the spot; he pressed his suit, as people used to say, and they very soon became engaged.) After they'd had four children fairly quickly, Hill Farm became more and more their home.

In those days village women expected, and were apparently content, to be organized by the gentry; soon Marjorie was president of the Womens' Institute, an energetic and active getter-up of church fêtes, as well as bringing up her family and entertaining masses of guests. There never seemed to be less than fifteen or twenty people sitting down at their long dining-room table at weekends, all certain of an excellent meal. By the time we came to Oaksey, Geoffrey was already Sir Geoffrey and a Lord of Appeal. World War II followed and then the Nuremberg trial of Nazi criminals at which he presided, then the peerage when he took Oaksey for his name.

In the war Marjorie joined the ATS and became a Colonel; her three daughters joined too. Once, when all on leave at the same time, they came to see us, entering the room in order of rank: Colonel Marjorie first, then Elizabeth the eldest who was a Captain (and later a Town Major); then Corporal Rosamund; finally Jennifer the youngest who was still a Private. It was an impressive sight.

Everyone in the village liked and respected Geoffrey. Courteous, friendly, gentle in manner, he was interested in everything around him – the farm, the village, racing, his friends' opinions, above all his pedigree Guernseys. As a keen theatre-goer, at one time he shared with Gervas an admiration for a rising young star called Dorothy Tutin. Geoffrey, not content merely to admire from a distance, boldly wrote and invited her to lunch. Evidently the occasion went off well. Gervas was not only envious but a bit put out. 'It wasn't fair,' he said. 'Geoffrey gave her lunch at the House of Lords.'

Geoffrey also had an eye for pictures, furniture and *objets d'art* at a time when they could be bought for very modest sums. I asked him how he had come by their long mahogany dining-room table. As a young man, he said, he used to drive down from London very early on a Saturday to hunt, and breakfasted at Slough in a pub with a long cloth-covered table where everyone sat. One morning he ran his finger under the tablecloth along the table's bevelled edge and recognized its quality; it was a fine piece of Chippendale. The innkeeper was glad to sell it to him for a few pounds and there it was at Hill Farm, shining like silk and set, on party occasions, with beautiful silver and glass.

The perfect end, Geoffrey used to say, was that of his uncle, who was drowned while salmon fishing at the age of ninety-two. He himself lived to be ninety. A memorial in the church records his office as 'Churchwarden of this parish', and nothing more.

12 June – A CRAFTSMAN

That memorial to Geoffrey in our church is remarkable for the excellence of its lettering, and of the carving of the coat of arms (which includes a pair of rampant Guernsey bulls) and ornamental surround. They're the work of Simon Verity who lives a couple of miles away at Minety, also surrounded by bulls, though not Guernseys but Devons, and not rampant but contentedly recumbent and placidly cud-chewing, and not his but those of his landlady, Betty Crocker who owns the cottage.

How peaceful it looked when on this fine afternoon I looked in, with Frederica and the three grandsons, to be greeted on the lawn by two lively kids and two equally lively children, Tom still at the crawling stage. Judith brought us mugs of tea and slices of the wholemeal bread she makes from flour fetched from a mill near Bath, where wheat is ground by millstones and creaking machinery that have been in use for centuries. The children drank goats' milk. This family lives mainly on home-grown food not as a gimmick, but because it tastes better and costs less.

Their old farm cottage is crammed with every kind of tool for every kind of craft: carving, etching, ironwork, book-making, anything you can name, they make it. Simon is a jack-of-all-trades but master of several, especially lettering on stone. He doesn't toil away unrecognized; a recent commission was to carve the lettering in Canterbury Cathedral on the spot where Thomas à Becket fell. In lighter vein he made a pair of sprightly unicorns to adorn Count Badeni's garden gates near Malmesbury. There's no question of looking for work; he's offered more commissions than he can undertake. With his dark lively eyes, white skin, gentle medieval profile and tousled hair he might have stepped out of an altarpiece or stained-glass window, discarding as he did so the wings and halo of an angel.

The sun shone, a yellow climbing rose was flowering against the grey stone cottage wall, a heavy scent of beans in flower mingled with those of hay and of the drowsy munching red Devon bulls; the children played in a sand-pit or squirmed about on the grass. The kids were curled up asleep on the roof of their shed. For a moment, time halted in this oasis of content.

16 June – TOMBSTONES

The rector has all but mown off a finger with his rotary mower, trying to keep the churchyard tidy. One of the occupational hazards of a parson nowadays, I suppose. When you see him hurrying along The Street, the unforgiving minute at his heels, you half expect him to break into a run. Not only does he have two parishes to look after but he's become a Rural Dean. Spare and lightly built, he looks and speaks like a young man but has three grown-up sons, each with a scientific bent. Friendly to all, he's well liked in the village but that doesn't normally swell the small band of faithful worshippers on a Sunday.

Although inscriptions on the older tombstones are too time-worn to be deciphered, there's still a lot of history in the churchyard, and some enigmas. Here lie six of the Hanks family who had Dean Farm before World War I and are something of a legend; of ten children born there, three were deaf and dumb. There seems to have been no hereditary weakness to account for this, but, probably because of it, not one of the ten married, so the family died out. The eldest, Anna, was born in 1857 and the last, Lizzie, lived on till 1949.

They were well liked, and a number of people in the village picked up the deaf-and-dumb finger-language so as to be able to converse with the afflicted Hanks's. One of them, Lizzie, used to go to whist drives and play a good hand. Two of the three met their end because of their infirmity. One of the brothers became a forester; he failed to hear the warning shouts and was killed by a falling tree. Lizzie was run over by a car; she was seventy-seven years old.

Another family with a tragic history lies together in the churchyard. Their name was Vizard. A whole family of five was wiped out in one year, 1834. First a baby, in February. Then a daughter aged eleven in March, and a son of twelve in May. The mother, Sarah, died in August aged forty, and finally the father John, also forty. The hand of God must indeed have seemed to have struck at that single, probably inoffensive family in that single year. In the parish register, John Vizard is described as a yeoman.

I've found no trace of any other Vizards in the village, and no legend to account for the holocaust. But the other day when I encountered Gladys by the church and mentioned the Vizards she said: 'I do believe that I once heard Mother say something about it. I believe it might have been typhoid.' Gladys' mother lived to be ninety-five and died in 1965, so *her* mother might have known this unlucky family.

20 June – BIRD-WATCHING

Back to Middle Gaer for another brief visit between lets to 'see to things' – how I hate everything to do with the trade of landlady. I ought, no doubt, to think more of the pleasure the place brings, I hope, to jaded city-dwellers, and less of my own reluctance to hand it over to them, for which of course I get paid. So far I've been lucky in my tenants, but I feel it can't last for ever, and one day there'll be a horrible family who'll break things, scrawl on the walls, dirty blankets and carpets, and leave the whole place in a mess.

Meanwhile between bouts of washing, polishing, tidying up outside and so on, I have another go at bird-watching of an ultra-amateur kind. There's no one to ask so I must rely on books. Bird books are all very well, but first you must have a long, close, unimpeded look at your bird, which must be prepared to stay put while you describe its markings in a notebook. Then you must roughly classify it before you can decide which chapter to look it up in.

It's all those anonymous little brown birds that are the trouble. They're divided, in my experience, into two classes: those that fly out on the other side of the tree or hedge as soon as you approach, keeping the foliage between you and them; and those that sit tight, so well concealed that you never see them at all. There remains their song, if any, but they fall silent on your approach (except nightingales, I'm told, which accelerate), and anyway I can't tell one cheep from another. (With at least one exception, reminding me of a story Gervas used to tell about one of Queen Victoria's daughters, I forget which, who, finding herself in close proximity to his grandfather, inquired: 'Do tell me, professor, what is the name of that bird one often hears in springtime that makes a silly noise something like "cuckoo, cookoo"?')

Books are no help as regards cheeping. My only hope is to have at all times an expert at my elbow. I should like always to have John Buxton, but alas I cannot. I know, because he told me, that the little birds which fly up from under your feet at the last moment out of the bracken, all over the hills, with a trace of white on them, are meadow pippits, and that the ones you see sitting on a fence post on top of the Gaer, if not blackbirds, may be redstarts.

Only too frequently, John puts me to shame. Sitting one sunny April day on our little patio, I remarked that I wished I could find a bird's nest. 'There must be dozens round here,' I said. 'There are three within fifteen yards,' he replied coldly; a thrush in a may tree, a blue-tit in the wall and a chaffinch in a hollow in a decrepit old apple tree about five yards from our chairs. The hen chaffinch emerged as he spoke with a derisive flutter of her wings. And John has only one eye.

Today I heard the sweet song of a wren in a hedge and was actually able to see it. It was surprising to hear so much music out of so small a musician, wrote Dr Livingstone, when a tree-frog about half an inch long sat on a leaf in a drenching downpour in the depths of an African forest and sang to him. I felt the same about the wren.

Often you see ravens wheeling and croaking above the cliff face across the valley on the side of Hatterall Hill. Probably they nest there. Egg-stealers are said to be more active than ever, equipped with grappling irons, ladders, ropes and fast cars. Crazy prices are being paid for eggs of rare or semi-rare species, and egg-collectors are no longer schoolboys but well-organized professionals.

The hills are very dry. Ewes look as ragged and as thin as scarecrows, and are continually being butted by fat lambs as large as they are, who have to go down on their knees to get at the udders. Their sharp teeth must punish the mothers who wear a pained, long-suffering and half-rebellious expression (and no wonder) that reminds me of a camel's.

Everywhere bracken is thrusting through the short-cropped turf its tightly clenched fronds, bronzy under fresh green. Each frond has the look of a ram's head in miniature, its ears erect between a pair of long, crinkled, down-drooping horns. Foxgloves are beginning to unfold their speckle-throated trumpets, a sign that we are past the crest of summer though not yet past the longest day.

Coming home fairly late, the sun red and slanting, I skirted a small field of wheat on the hillside and a big hare stood on his hind legs, ears pricked, red-brown in the evening light, then loped into the corn and disappeared. A single hare only, I wondered if he had a mate. You see so few hares round here now, they are so much hunted.

On the other hand you see plenty of grey squirrels, despite a war continually waged against them by the Forestry Commission. Every man's hand is against the grey squirrel. 'Only rats,' people say, which of course is more or less true, morphologically speaking. Yet, looked at objectively (which no one does), they are charming little animals. One ran along the wall just outside my door yesterday, pausing now and then to sit up, the better to inspect its world with bright little eyes; the evening sun turned its coat silver; it looked so alert and nimble.

The real trouble with grey squirrels is that they aren't red squirrels. Everyone loves red squirrels and believes that grey squirrels, which are foreigners to boot, turned them out of their territories. So the guilt-ridden, blame-obsessed human species (how often has one heard the phrase 'who do you blame for that?' on radio or 'box') burdens the poor grey squirrel with the guilt of not being what its maker, or natural selection, or whatever, never intended it to be, a red one of a different species.

Of course, grey squirrels do destroy young trees. It is their nature so to do. So do men destroy trees; they make fortunes out of it, and are honoured for printing lies all over the resultant pulp.

23 June – HILL FORT

Sunday: so I clambered up the Gaer to see the archaeologists who are digging up the Twyn-y-Gaer, an Iron Age fort they've been excavating for over ten years. All are amateurs, but by now they've learnt so much that they're professionals in every way except for the fact that no one pays them.

This hill fort covered about four-and-a-half acres right on top of the hill, with an inner and an outer earthwork. So far, three large gateways have been excavated, each with post-holes; also some neatly built stone walls and round declivities lined with stone which were no doubt sites of houses. Alan Probert, leader of the small team, told me today that they have at last received a carbon-14 dating of about 400 BC. The fort may, of course, have been in existence before then. There are no traces of occupation in Roman times.

Finds in Twyn-y-Gaer have included bits of pottery made, the archaeologists believe, on the Malvern hills, where there was a pre-Roman pottery. They've also dug up various iron tools: spear-heads, iron plough-tips, several brooches, and a modern-looking file. Slag has been found, indicating the practice of smelting, and animal bones; but no human ones. Here is a mystery: what happened to the dead? No traces have been found of graves, no barrows, no indications of cremation. Dead men's bones seemed to have vanished into thin air. Mr Probert wonders if bodies might have been sunk in pools, rivers or boggy places. Only speculation, he said, but their bones must lie somewhere, or their ashes.

These hills must have been much more densely populated then than now, and quite a lot of corn grown in the valleys. The people kept sheep and cattle and, contrary to some popular ideas, weren't rudely clad in woad and skins but had woven garments – spindles have been found – and cooking-pots and ornaments.

How cold they must have been in winter on this hilltop, how unenviable the task of women hauling water from springs down below – perhaps from the very spring that supplies my cottage – in the gales and downpours you get on these hills. I can scarcely manage the climb without using my hands, and there's no heavy water-skin sloshing about on my back. Perhaps, in the dead of winter, they stayed in their huts and melted snow.

You have to be really dedicated to be an Iron Age archaeologist. No chance of a rich hoard of coins or silver plate awaits you, no jewellery, no votive statue, least of all a tasselated pavement, those fat prizes of Romano-British sites. Iron Age specialists, sustained on masonry and post-holes, are the puritans of the trade. 'You need the eye of faith,' said Alan Probert. Helped by his wife, his son Simon, a few friends and the spaniel Jack who keeps off sheep drawn by curiosity, bit by bit he's uncovering the outline of the whole fort, or encampment. Self-taught, self-directed, independent, to him life in an Iron Age hill fort must often seem more real than the small family business in Abergavenny that provides the family's livelihood. He's earned, and now enjoys, the respect and friendship of eminent academics. In his round pork-pie hat, shirt open to the waist, constant cigarette and constant energy he bestrides the hilltop like a captain on his quarter-deck.

And when he raises his eyes, what a green ocean confronts them. Away in all directions roll the cloud-patterned hills and tree-patterned valleys, here and there a white cottage or grey barn-roof in the nearer valleys, pelts of dark forest on distant mountains, wind-blown clouds sailing overhead. Who would live anywhere except among hills? A snatch of a Chinese lyric translated by my neighbour Duncan came to mind.

> These only last, the far hills,
> The misty cloud-hung hills,
> The dark-at-dawning hills.*

* From *A Folding Screen*, translated by Duncan Mackintosh and Alan Aylward, Whittington Press, 1974.

Written a thousand years ago and ten thousand miles or more away, the poet Su Shih might have been standing beside me today on Twyn-y-Gaer.

25 June – A HAMPSHIRE HOWDAH

Back in Oaksey, and walking up to the shop (why must something always be forgotten?), Jim and Renée passed and stopped for a brief greeting. They're just back from a couple of days in their Dormobile, camping, and fishing in the Test, bringing back a three-pounder and a nice little story told them by the bailiff of the estate on which they camped.

In his early days, he said, back in the thirties, the landowner used to communicate with his agent by means of memoranda which were filed in the office. One such, in particular, is carefully preserved. A hare shoot was being organized. 'My brother', it ran (Jim quoted from memory) 'will be home on leave from India and wishes to take part. The only shooting he has ever done has been from the back of an elephant. Kindly station a combine harvester in a suitable position for showing him good sport with the hares.'

July

2 July – A HAPPY LIFE

Out early picking the first raspberries. A pigeon was cooing from a hedge creamy with fat elder blossoms. Presently it lumbered off to sit in the holly. The sun emerged from behind a low bank of pink-tinged grey cloud and slanted across the fields in long shafts, lighting the elder blossoms and heavy foliage of the midsummer trees. Blackbirds chattered and whistled. At six o'clock the chimes of Hankerton church came limpidly across the fields, seeming to make the quiet air quiver and dying softly away. A car came down the Park road, a van scurried along towards Eastcourt. The village slept. It was so peaceful, and the raspberries delicious.

I called yesterday on Mrs Harris who's lived for sixty years in the same cottage since her marriage to Bill who was first groom, later chauffeur, to Arthur Rich. Her grey stone cottage has changed very little save for the advent of electric light. The same ornaments, the same open grate, the same furniture that were here when she married. Now she shares the cottage with her daughter Nellie.

She told me that she came from Crudwell, one of seven, and at thirteen went into service: not a grand house like the Park but maid-of-all-work for a farmer. Those were the girls who had it really tough.

Churning butter in heavy tubs, cheese-making with big vats and presses, carrying buckets to calves, feeding poultry and all the housework as well. Up at six every morning, seven days a week, to cool the milk, the first job of the day. Slush and mud and in winter with long skirts and stiff boots, no wellingtons. Cleaning lamps, scouring pots, carrying pails, washing mud-caked garments, pumping water. 'Hard work, but I was strong, I had to be. I enjoyed it mainly.' Wages? Half a crown ($12\frac{1}{2}$p) a week. After a year, she had a rise to three and six. After another year she said she really must find a job with better pay, so she went to a place near Swindon where she got nearly double, £12 a year. Two years after that, she went to Arthur Rich at Court Farm.

That was the hardest of all. It's a big house, damp and inconvenient in those days. Arthur Rich was very strict and his housekeeper Miss Chambers stricter still. An old termagant, who lived to be 101. If 'the girl' was five minutes late of a morning, Miss Chambers would be banging at her bedroom door. The girl did all the cleaning, carrying coals, scouring a whole range of old-fashioned copper pots and pans, sweeping, dusting, washing. By twelve noon she had to have changed into a black uniform with starched white cuffs, and then to serve the meal; Arthur Rich and Miss Chambers sat down together. If there was a plate smeared or a glass not nicely polished Arthur would let fly and use shocking language. She'd be on duty all afternoon, cleaning silver or something of the sort. Arthur dined late and there was often company; horse dealers from Ireland, or buyers of his horses, and one or other of his brothers. They would sit late over their meal and then there was all the clearing up to do. Nothing was left till next morning.

It was a hard life but she thrived on it and was walking out with Bill. They married in 1914. The cottage they got for half a crown a week. On £16 a year she'd saved a bit, and on fifteen weekly shillings they managed.

'We never had a cross word,' said Mrs Harris. 'Never?' 'Not once. He was a good husband.' On Saturday nights, while she bathed the two children, he went up to the Wheatsheaf, had a pint, and came back with a twopenny packet of biscuits for the kids. This was their weekly treat.

Bill Harris worked for thirty years for Arthur without a holiday. It became too much for him and got on his nerves, especially the cussing and swearing, so he went to work for Geoffrey Lawrence at Hill Farm. The job itself was the same but not the atmosphere. Geoffrey Lawrence, by then a risen barrister, was a quiet, kind, considerate master occupying a hospitable and well-organized home. Bill's chief claim to fame was that he taught the now famous son John to ride.

I asked Mrs Harris what had been the biggest change she'd seen in sixty years. She paused before replying: 'I've lost my good neighbours.' She has nothing against her successors but they're of a younger generation and it's not the same. 'So many new people,' she added. Older folk feel unsettled by all the faces they don't recognize in The Street. 'It's been a happy life,' Mrs Harris said.

10 July – VILLAGE BENEFACTOR

Everything about the house at Church Farm is Victorian and solid: thick walls, big windows, gables, pointed stone, polished pinewood banisters and a lot of smallish rooms awkward for cleaning. There was even a baize door, not green but red, until a cat scratched off the baize. The house was built by old Mr Warner, Robert Charles, when he married in 1884.

Robert Charles built this capacious nest for his expected offspring and entailed the property to the eldest son. Tempting the gods: there was no son, no children at all, in fact, to occupy all these rooms. So when he died in 1930 the farm, being entailed, had to come to a cousin whom he'd never met, nor apparently wished to, though Frank was farming no further away than Tewkesbury.

It was Robert Charles Warner who gave the village its water supply. He had a borehole sunk, a water-tower built and pipes laid through the village and people could draw all the water they wanted from standpipes free of charge. This put Oaksey in a very favoured position, until Mr Warner handed the system over to the council and there were rates to pay. 'He gave the water to the village with a spoon,' commented Arthur Rich, 'and he'll get it back with a bucket' – meaning that the value of his own farms had been considerably enhanced by the piped water.

But he never laid the water on to his own house. When the Frank Warners came forty-five years ago there was a bathroom but only a hip-bath in it, an earth closet outside, and a pump in the old kitchen.

How large and empty these Victorian houses appear to today's small families and ageing owners. Both senior Warners are around the eighty mark but, with Molly, keep the garden spick and span, full of colour, lawns smooth and mown, without outside help. For tea we had strawberries – beautiful firm, fresh-picked strawberries. A silver teapot, thin porcelain cups, even thinner bread-and-butter and a splendid iced chocolate cake. Anyone on the other side of the ex-baize door? 'Only me,' said Molly.

15 July – PERCY'S POLLY

We used to have a bee-keeper in the tall, thin shape of Percy who lived with an ancient aunt behind a screen of conifers and surrounded by hives, in an ugly little house opposite Court Farm. There I used to visit him sometimes, especially during the war, on a shameless quest for honey. He would much rather have sold me one of the wooden salad bowls, trays, or candlesticks with twisted stems that he turned on his lathe in the garage.

On the lawn stood a telescope through which I would sometimes gaze at the moon. Percy was knowledgeable about the heavens, perhaps attracted to them by his relationship to Sir Bernard Lovell, a cousin by marriage.

With great patience and forbearance he looked after his aunt, a woman of uncompromising standards, formidable character and, in her old age, demanding habits. Once, in the war, when Gervas went to see her, she told him she was busy with her war-work. Picturing knitted comforts for the troops or hospital pyjamas, he inquired its nature. Watching the blacked-out trains, she replied. (The house commands an excellent view of the London to Cheltenham line). 'When I see a light, I notify the authorities.'

Proof of the need for this unremitting vigilance came when Oaksey was bombed, in her view because of the carelessness, if not worse, of an offender in the village who had allowed a chink of light to penetrate a black-out curtain. One night a stick of five bombs – mini-bombs by modern standards – straddled the village. One fell near the railway bridge and another set fire to a small tree in a field. The Home Guard turned out with buckets, carried across two fields from the nearest pond. Oaksey's pride in having been an enemy target excited bitter jealousy among the citizens of Crudwell, who took some solace in the thought that while the bombs might have fallen on (or near) Oaksey, they had been released over Crudwell.

Polly, as she was generally called – I don't know why, her real name was Louisa – a white-haired lady clad always in black, lived to be well over ninety. She was proud of her ancestry; in the eighteenth century the Hawkins family had owned much of Oaksey. Their name occurs in many old deeds, and in the parish register from 1676 onwards, and there are several Hawkins' in the churchyard. Percy's great-great-grandfather, Thomas Hawkins, owned Court Farm.

Polly is dead; Percy married late in life and lives now at Minety where today I went to visit him and his wife Elizabeth. At the age of seventy he has a workshop and sub-contracts in light engineering. He told me much I hadn't known about his aunt, and it's an odd story.

Percy was the youngest of eight. His father had studied the chemistry of brewing; too much sampling was his undoing. The combination of eight children one after the other and their father's intemperate habits became too much for his mother; one day she walked out of the house without a word or note and was never seen or heard of by her family again. To this day he has no idea of what became of her.

He was three at the time. His father's sister Louisa (Polly) took charge of the children. Percy's father emigrated to America where all the children joined him except Percy, who was too young. His aunt brought him up herself in Bath. In 1926 she bought a plot of land opposite the old family home in Oaksey and built on it that ugly little gabled house from whence she could keep a resentful eye on Arthur Rich, owner of the property she believed should have been hers.

19 July – THE OAKSEY BOWL

Twenty-four years ago, Geoffrey Oaksey presented a cup to be competed for among local village cricket teams, with a limit of twenty overs per side. The native eleven won it once, in 1953, but then cricket languished to such an extent that Oaksey ceased even to enter for the competition. Gradually cricket started to revive, thanks mainly to the efforts of our young butcher and sub-postmaster Rodney, and this year our team got through to the final.

It was a classic finish, like something from a film. Oaksey fought it out with Minety, their traditional foe. Minety went in first and were all out for 84, Rodney taking three wickets. Oaksey followed full of confidence but the opening pair were dismissed for eleven and nine. Gradually the score mounted until the last over, when Oaksey wanted five to win.

Richard Hiscock and Geoff Boulton faced the bowling. Three runs came off the first two balls and then Richard's wicket fell. The last batsman came in with two balls to go and two runs to make. Terrific tension. Geoff Boulton, luckily, is a pretty stoical type. He hit the last ball of the match for four; and so the Bowl – 'after twenty-one years of itineracy among the bastions of local cricket,' in the words of the *Wilts and Gloucestershire Standard* – came home. 'A celebratory jig across the ground by a peer of the realm' was its description of John Oaksey's reaction. It was all almost too good to be true; even the weather stayed fine.

The evening's celebrations apparently made local history too. Habits of restraint – by and large the Oaksey eleven are a fairly sober lot – were thrown to the winds. Some of the visitors didn't get home at all that night and heads were thick next morning. But then such a game may never be seen again.

25 July – PROBING THE COURT

A week or two ago I met the schoolmaster exercising his dogs and we spoke about the buried castle in a field behind the church. All you can see are two grass mounds beside the Minety lane, a shallow dyke and bank curving across the western part of the field, more earthworks on the northern side, and a small pond with a hard stone bottom, said to have formed the courtyard of the castle – perhaps not actually a castle, more of a Court or manor house, from which Court Farm perhaps derived its name. Local legend says that it belonged to John of Gaunt.

About a year ago, when a sewer was being put in, a mechanical digger cutting across a corner of the field brought to light fragments of pottery. John Lucie suggested that we might embark upon a little amateur archaeology. So today we sallied forth with two thin steel rods, a measuring tape and squared paper, marked out on the ground a square covering part of one of the mounds, and started to prod into the turf along two parallel lines a yard apart.

The probes struck stone everywhere, five to nine inches below the surface. This is fairly stony ground but not as stony as that; clearly we were prodding at the remains of a building. It must have been a big one; the two mounds are seventy yards apart, the whole site about three acres. No archaeologist has explored it and it has no name on the map. About a mile due north, at Dean Farm, there's a mound with a moat, marked on maps as Norwood Castle. There must have been some connection. John Aubrey wrote of the building we are now probing that 'there are yet to be seen, the ruins of an old seat of the Duke of Lancaster's, and a Chapell'. That was around 1670, so evidently the Court had not by then been wholly demolished.

By the beginning of the nineteenth century it was all gone. In a *Description of the County of Wilts* published in 1814, John Britton wrote that 'in a field south of the church is a square area inclosed by a deep moat and embankment, and having a large mount at its north-east angle', as well as several other square enclosures, formed by slighter banks. There were no surviving walls.

There is no mystery about what happened to these walls. They were used to build most of the village – a convenient quarry with the stones already shaped and faced. Over a mullioned window in a block of cottages known formerly as the Rucketts is a stone carving of a flower, seemingly a tulip, set between two sprays of thick leaves. And on an angle of the roof-top is a lion couchant, wearing that half-amiable, half-puzzled expression common to the faces of heraldic lions. These must surely have formed part of the decoration of 'John of Gaunt's castle'.* Sometime between, presumably, the defeat of the Spanish Armada and the English Civil War, the village must have been entirely rebuilt, mainly with stone from the medieval court or castle

Was it ever John of Gaunt's? I've been digging not only into Church Woodfalls (the name of the field), but into the records to try to trace the history of the court. At the time of the Doomsday Survey (1086) the manor

---

* Oswald Brakspear, the distinguished architect and expert on old Wiltshire and Cotswold buildings, thinks not, at least as regards the tulip between sprays. He thinks the work too coarse to have graced a castle; more likely that a local mason was indulging his fancy.

of Wochesie belonged to a Saxon thegn called Brihtric and was part of the honor of Trowbridge, an honor being a number of manors, not necessarily contiguous, owned by one baron. The headquarters of the honor was probably at Trowbridge Castle.

Wochesie was a smallish manor, assessed at ten hides. A hide was the amount of land that could be tilled by one plough-team in one year, and could support one household. There was no standard size, which in terms of acres varied widely from one part of the country to another. Some Anglo-Saxon historians estimate an East Anglian hide at about 120 acres, but in Wessex at as little as forty. Other estimates put a much higher value on the Wessex hide, which doubtless varied even within the kingdom; on the King's Heath near Malmesbury it was 116 acres.*

Like most Saxon nobles, Brihtric lost his land to the Normans. The honor of Trowbridge went to Edward of Salisbury, who was High Sheriff of Wilts in 1081. In the first half of the twelfth century his great-granddaughter Margaret married Humphrey de Bohun, taking the manor of Wochesie, along with many other manors, with her. Their son, another Humphrey, inherited our manor; he was followed by a third Humphrey, first earl of Hereford of the second creation; then by a fourth; and so on until the male line ended.

One of the de Bohuns, earls of Hereford, must therefore have built our Court or castle: which? The earliest record I have so far found is an inquisition on the will of Humphrey, the third earl, held at Calne in 1299. This earl died 'seised in his demesne as of fee of the manor of Wockesygh with a capital messuage, garden and curtilage' worth twelve shillings a year and a dovecote worth two shillings. This clearly indicates a manor house, supplied with pigeons, and standing in the midst of well-populated and cultivated land which comprised four caracutes covering 300 acres and worth one hundred shillings a year; eighty acres of meadow valued at four shillings; and thirteen virgates (a virgate was a quarter of a caracute or hide) held by free tenants. In addition there were ten virgators bound to their lord to work for him every day throughout the year except Sundays and feast days and the weeks of Christmas, Easter and Pentecost, 'or shall give for each day ½d.'

Then there were eighteen half-virgators bound on the same terms plus

* According to a survey made in 1591 by the Duchy of Lancaster, the manor of Wokesey then embraced 1,448 acres. The boundaries may, of course, have been altered between 1086 and 1591, but as the manor remained for the greater part of that time in the hands first of the de Bohun family and then of the Duchy of Lancaster, it seems, on balance, unlikely that any substantial changes were made. In that case, the Wokesey hide would have been approximately 140 acres.

a due of 3s 9d; thirteen cottars each to pay 12d a year at the feasts of St Michael, the Nativity and St John the Baptist and on the gule of August; and six cottars paying 10d on the same terms. The manor embraced a wood, a windmill, pannage of pigs worth two shillings and 'pleas and perks worth 6s 8d yearly, because they are only held twice a year'.

If you add up these different classes of tenant you arrive at a figure of sixty, and this takes no account of the considerable manorial staff that certainly existed, but had no rights to land. These sixty men were heads of families; allowing five to a family you reach a figure of 300, or say 350 with the landless families, for the population of the manor in 1299. This is very little less than the population today. A half-century later, it would have been drastically reduced by the Black Death.

Altogether, Humphrey the third earl's will reflects a going concern at Wockesygh, and suggests that either he, or more probably his father, to whom the manor had come in 1220, built at least the nucleus of the Court, which may have been added to later. Capital messuage means a piece of land with the owner's dwelling on it, so the Court was certainly there in 1299.

In December, 1253, this Humphrey and his eldest son jointly held a licence from the King to hunt hare, fox, cat and other wild beasts (but not deer) in the Forests of Braden and Savernake. The bounds of Braden lay less than half a mile from the Court at Wockesygh. (There were many spellings of our manor: Wochesie, Wockesheye, Wockes, Oxhay, Woxy, Okssey, Oxey, Ocksey and finally Oaksey; 'ey' or 'eye' indicated an island and the word is said to mean Wocc's island, so described in *Wocce's Seat, Cartalorium saxonicum*, 1080, published in 1885/93.) So the most likely dating for the Court seems to be between 1220 when the second earl of Hereford inherited the manor, and 1253 when he and his son were hunting in Braden; this is guesswork, of course.

The fourth earl of Hereford, yet another Humphrey, who hunted with his father and inherited our manor in 1299, married a daughter of King Edward I, so from early Norman times Oaksey had a royal connection. The last Humphrey de Bohun and seventh earl died in 1373 without male issue, leaving two co-heiresses, Elinor and Mary. It was Mary who, in 1380, married Henry Bolingbroke, son and heir of John of Gaunt the Duke of Lancaster, to be crowned in 1399 as Henry IV. She took as her portion an enormous number of manors of which ours was one. Thus it was that Oaksey became part of the great Lancastrian empire which went with Henry Bolingbroke to the Crown. This empire continued to be administered separately by the Duchy of Lancaster, while other Crown lands were administered by the Court of Exchequer; the King owned them all.

Small and unimportant though it may have been, our manor is mentioned by name in the Treaty of Troyes of 1420. When Bolingbroke's son Henry V married Katherine de Valois, this treaty secured to her 10,000 marks and the revenues of part of the Lancastrian lands. (Henry got most of northern France.) To her were secured the cities and castles of Leicester, Melbourne, Knaresborough and Hereford, together with a great many manors, of which Wockesey was one. So, for a time, the citizens of Oaksey paid their dues and fiefs and fealties to the French. This made no difference to the ordinary ceorl, villein, virgator or ferlingman, for the manor continued to be administered by the Chief Steward for the South Parts of the Duchy of Lancaster, with reassuringly native names like Sir Thomas Hungerford (the first, appointed in 1375) and Sir Thomas Skelton.

No doubt they put up at the Court when they, or more probably their deputies, rode round to see how things were being managed by their bailiffs, reeves, constables, scriveners and stewards, and enjoyed some hunting in Braden Forest at the same time. Later, the Tudors are said to have used Wockesey Court as a hunting-lodge for sport in Braden Forest and there is no reason to doubt it, but no proof, either, that they did. They had plenty of alternative accommodation.

When was the Court abandoned to be used as a quarry? There are no records. Some of the stone was probably incorporated into its successor, built near the Swill Brook less than a mile away after the architectural revolution of Tudor times replaced the needs of defence by those of domestic comfort and display as the prime object of the building exercise.

Now and again our manor received a subsequent mention in the Duchy records. In 1443 Henry Gairstang was granted the trees of Wokesey for repairs, and later he got the herbage of the Park for life. About that time Robert Willoughby, Lord de Broke, was appointed Steward for life of Trowbridge, Aldbourne, Wokesey and Poole, and lieutenant of Braden Forest. He died in 1502. Gradually the various kinds of tenant became confirmed in possession of their lands, and at the end of the sixteenth century the manors of Oaksey, Kemble and Poole, along with several others, passed into the possession of the Pooles.

After an hour or so probing in Church Woodfalls we fetched spades and dug a small trench, revealing stone a few inches down and, after sifting through the earth and rubble, two or three small pieces of pottery. These might be medieval or they might not. There's a legend in the village that a golden coffin is buried under one of these mounds. I have far more respect for the citizens of Oaksey than to suppose they'd have let a golden coffin lie buried on their doorstep for all those centuries, so we didn't expect to light upon it, but kept in mind Aubrey's statement that at Norwood Castle 'Farmer Earle ploughed up a sowrd'.*

The church clock struck twelve as we walked back to the school-house, while John told me that the school had been reprieved. About three years ago, the County Council issued an edict that it was to be shut down and the pupils transferred to Crudwell. There were many protests. A village without a school loses its heart. Not, I think, because of the protests, but because of some ebb or flow of policy in the mysterious, amorphous organism of authority that inhabits County Hall, or perhaps Whitehall, the decision has been reversed and we are to keep our school for the time being. The future is obscure.

26 July – POTTERY

More digging. This time we tried the other mound. Keith Wilson, who owns the field, has turned his heifers into it so we had a fascinated audience sniffing at our feet and crowding round with sweet-smelling, grassy breath and large, dark, trusting eyes. John Lucie put down beside us the squared paper on which we had started to map our explorations. Soon there was a distressed cry: 'They've eaten our plan!' And so they had, neatly removing the top sheet and reflectively chewing it.

After tea I took our pottery fragments to a young potter who works at Minety. He's been exploring the Roman brick-kiln on Jim Woodhouse's land beside the Swill Brook, and showed me bits of tile marked with swirling patterns, and one with the clear imprint of a dog's paw. He said that the kiln was sunk about six feet into the ground. This, of course, invited flooding, and he thought the kiln wasn't in use for many years for that reason. Probably the bricks were loaded on to barges on the Swill Brook, taken to the nearest road and thence to Corinium, where the demand must have been insatiable. The native workmen may have lived in huts in the forest or perhaps there was already a mud-and-wattle British village on

---

* 'In this Parish, about half a mile northwards, is the remains of a little Citadel, with a keepe hill, both moated round. In the ground near this place, Farmer Earle ploughed up a sword. This Citadel is called by the name of Norwood Castle, a place of defence, no question, for the Duke of Lancaster. Mem: In a close, adjoining to the Church, are yet to be seen, the ruins of an old seat of the Duke of Lancaster's, and a Chapell, it is now called Court and Chappell Close....' Aubrey and Jackson, *Wiltshire Collections*.

the ridge at Wockesic, and they lodged there. Possibly they belonged to the Dobunni tribe, whose capital at Bagendon was nearby.

As for our pottery fragments, he washed one and explained how it could be roughly dated. In medieval times, techniques were crude and unreliable, and pots were over-baked on the outside and under-baked in the middle, like a joint of meat 'sealed' by frying in hot fat before being put to cook slowly in the oven. And as techniques advanced, clay was refined by a series of rinsings until only the finer particles were used.

Once they had been washed, it was easy to see that our fragments have a dark crust and consist of coarse particles, and are therefore medieval, or even earlier. Almost certainly there would have been a pottery at Oaksey in medieval times, David Llewyellin said.* There was one beside the church at Minety, and others all over the place. This is good potting clay, though not as good as that at Purton, where it can be made into vessels almost as fine as porcelain; he showed me a bell he'd made from it which tinkled beautifully.

28 July – PARISH REGISTERS

I've been looking at the parish registers from 1670 on, to find which names recorded three hundred years ago remain familiar in the village today. One of the earliest is Henry Sparrow, baptized in November 1670. Until about ten years ago Walter Sparrow lived in the cottage next to the one I now inhabit. Whether he was a descendant, of course I don't know. He used to catch our moles, and many other people's moles, and use their skins to make moleskin waistcoats. George Todd still treasures such a waistcoat, made from forty moles caught on Dean Farm.

Walter was a widower when we knew him, doing for himself in his old stone cottage and presenting something of a hazard when you walked up to the shop. Coming to his gate, he'd invite you in to eat a slice of cake. His cakes were a labour of love but not up to the standard of the Women's Institute; Gervas broke a tooth on one of them. Poor Walter, he had an unpleasant end; he cut a corn clumsily, the place turned gangrenous, and

---

* He was right. About twenty years ago, alterations being carried out to a cowshed at Woodfolds brought to light pottery fragments which found their way to the museum at Devizes. After talking to David Llewyellin, I looked up a note about them in the *Wiltshire Archaeological Magazine* for August, 1951. An article by J. B. R. Andrews of the Cricklade Historical Society gave a dating for these fragments of 1150–1200, and surmised that they had been fashioned in the field behind the cowshed, which has some likely looking mounds. No further exploration has been made.

his leg was amputated. He managed for a year or so with an artificial limb but then died. One of his sons lives in Bendybow so there's a Sparrow in the village still.

Oatridge is another familiar name. The first Oatridge in the register appears in 1678 and Sid Cook remembers the last of the line, two spinster sisters living in a cottage on The Street. Now the name is extinct in Oaksey but is commemorated by Oatridge Farm on the Eastcourt road.

The following year, 1679, sees the first mention of the Boulton family. Mary, a widow, was buried without an affidavit, then required by law, to certify that she was 'buryd in woollen only'. Then, as now, the Boultons were prolific. Soon afterwards a spate of baptisms was recorded: Elizabeth, Mary and John, offspring of Richard and Joanna, born between 1702 and 1708. Boultons have figured prominently in the parish registers ever since.

Happily, there's no prospect of the family dying out. When we came to the village, old Tom Boulton was the senior member, but Sid remembered his father Will'um, and can render well his broad Wiltshire accent, a speech all but extinct.

Will'um worked on the railway. Coming home one evening along a narrow footpath beside the road, he met a horseman, a stranger. He didn't give way. 'Get 'ee off the pa-a-th or I 'its 'ee with my girt whip, 'ee says to mee' Will'um recounted. 'Get 'ee off the pa-a-th oo-self or I 'its 'ee with my go-oa-oa-oat stick, I says.' And Will'um triumphed. 'I dunno what sort 'ee was,' Will'um concluded. 'Ee warn't a canna varmer, nor 'ee warn't a canna gentleman, 'ee were a canna bum townee.' 'Canna?' I inquired. It meant 'kind of'. People used to call him 'Canna Boulton' just as Robert Warner was known as 'Old Proba'ly'.

Sid has another story, not a very kind one and possibly apocryphal, about 'Old Proba'ly'. Moses Kent (my predecessor here) lost his pig – in those days to lose your pig was to lose your whole winter's meat supply. A subscription was got up, a penny or two all round, to buy another. Old Proba'ly Warner, the squire of the village then, was approached. He pulled his ear-lobe and said: 'Proba'ly, if Moses can afford to keep a pig, proba'ly he can afford to lose it.'

August

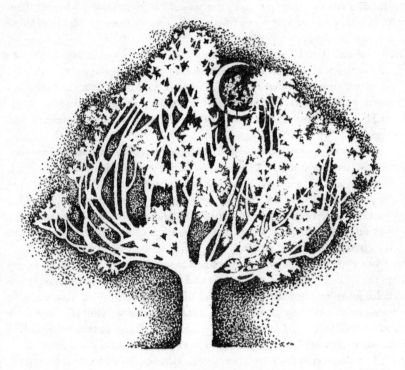

4 August – THE BOULTONS

Old Tom Boulton and Priscilla had eight children, raised in a tiny cottage at Earl's Corner, one of three in a row which have been turned into one. How so many people, like the Butchers and the Boultons, squeezed into these tiny cottages, each with two tiny bedrooms, is almost a miracle.

Tom was a plate-layer on the railway and had to give up work for good when he was under forty. There was no Social Security or sickness benefit, only parish relief with a maximum of ten shillings weekly. They reared eight healthy children on that.

The burden, of course, fell on 'Scilla. In my mind's eye she sits surrounded by feathers in a small dark outhouse, plucking fowls for twopence a time – good pay when she had a large order and plucked forty a day. Hers was a strong, lined, wide-cheekboned face with very blue eyes, ice-blue almost – a Scandinavian face, I know a Swedish woman much like her

(Bathe was her maiden name). In their small garden she generally managed to grow extra vegetables for sale. She cleaned the village hall for a few shillings weekly. In September, she picked blackberries and wheeled them in an old pram into Cirencester, seven miles, to sell to a man who used them for making dyes.

The children helped as they grew older. Ruth won a scholarship to Malmesbury Grammar School and used to cycle in, seven miles each way, on a machine provided from a Trust left by Robert Warner. After tea she'd go blackberrying, work in the garden, or settle down to fowl-picking, according to the season. I don't know how the homework was fitted in.

Once a week, Ruth or one of her siblings walked to Somerford Keynes to pay the rent to two old sisters, half a crown a week. When they died, a message came through a lawyer from a brother in America that the Boultons could have the cottage 'for as much as they could afford'. This couldn't have been much, certainly well under £100. So after that there was no rent to pay, and virtually no rates since there was no water laid on, no garbage collection, no sewerage.

None of the family went hungry or unclothed, several won scholarships to the Grammar School, all married and had families, not one turned into a delinquent or layabout, and several of the grandchildren have risen to substantial positions in the world. One, in London, is a JP; another a schoolmaster; a third an archaeologist of repute. They've raised themselves by their own bootstraps, so 'Scilla's fowl-plucking wasn't in vain.

The Boulton males have always been athletes. 'We could field a cricket team,' Ruth said. They used to walk to Tetbury (seven miles) en masse on Saturday morning, including old Tom who umpired. His brother was an athlete too. On the evening before the Oaksey steeplechases, held every Whitsun at the Park, he used to run round the course jumping every fence – stiff fences too, which next day generally brought down a number of well-trained horses.

Five of this family of eight, old or middle-aged now, have never lived away from the village. Tom, the eldest, lives down Minety Lane, half-crippled with arthritis but working his garden still. In the next cottage lives his widowed sister, mother of the archaeologist. Farther down still lives Charlie, the youngest, with a family of five. It's a kind of Boulton enclave.

Dick, a railwayman like his father and grandfather, lives in Bendybow with four. Two of the next generation are in the cricket team and there are plenty more coming on. It looks as if there'll be Boultons entered in the parish registers for quite a while to come.

4 August – OATRIDGE FARM

In 1678 Mrs Robert Oatridge contributed one shilling towards the building of St Paul's Cathedral. Madam Poole, the lady of the manor, led off with ten shillings; the rector, Robert Dalton, and his wife each gave five shillings. Robert Driver, John Smith and Mrs Robert Oatridge each one shilling, John Manby gave sixpence and the rest ranged from fourpence to twopence. Oaksey's total contribution to the fund was 37s 10d.

When did the Oatridge family cease to own the farm that bears their name? They were there in 1773, when an agreement was drawn up on the occasion of the marriage of Ann Oatridge to the Rev. John Lloyd. By 1880 it was theirs no longer but the property of Captain Arthur Randolph of Eastcourt House.

Next to Dean Farm, which follows a later and more sophisticated architectural style, I think Oatridge Farm house is the comeliest here-abouts. Long, solid, beautifully proportioned, it was built of dove-grey stone in the sixteenth or early seventeenth century and, unlike so many ancient houses, has been little altered or restored. It basks calmly amid the trees, smiling at gales, under its roof of Cotswold stone tiles. Stone-flagged, oak-beamed, rambling cheese-rooms and dairies occupy the back of the house, never again to be used for their true purpose.

Oatridges must have lived here until well into the nineteenth century. The churchyard holds the record of a family tragedy. In 1842, Richard Oatridge died at the age of seventeen. Three years later his wife Elizabeth died, also at the age of seventeen, so she can't have been more than fourteen when she married. A shot-gun wedding, clearly. In 1843, the year after her boy-husband's death, a son John was born to the fifteen-year-old widow.

There were plenty of Oatridges around then, well-to-do and respected, so despite this family scandal the orphaned boy would not have been homeless; but he emigrated to America and died, aged twenty, at Fort Leavenworth in Kansas, in 1863. It must have been these shady Oaksey trees and lush meadows to which his last thoughts turned from those distant, parched or frost-gripped prairies as he died, perhaps of wounds or sickness as a soldier enlisted in another's quarrel, the final victim of this village tragedy.

7 August – EARLES OF CRUDWELL

Oatridge, Boulton, Sparrow – another name that often crops up in the parish registers is that of Earle. The first is William Earle who was buried in 1775 – he could have been the Farmer Earle who ploughed up a sword at Norwood Castle, according to Aubrey. Today the name lives on in Earl's Corner by the butcher's shop.

In Crudwell there were plenty of Earles, starting with Margaret who married the rector in 1591. In 1633 Thomas Earle presented the church with a new bell. He could afford to, for he it was who founded the fortunes of this branch of the family by succeeding as a merchant in Bristol. His son, Giles, became MP for Malmesbury and built a mansion, Eastcourt House. This branch thrived, but most of the Oaksey Earles stayed where they were as yeoman farmers.

In search of Earle monuments, I went to Crudwell to explore the church. This wasn't as easy as it sounds. A notice on the locked door instructed visitors to call for the key at Mr Wiggins' next to the school. At the end of an overgrown and jungly path I found his cottage but no Mr Wiggins. A child in the next-door garden said he was out on his tractor, and a young woman emerging from another cottage suggested that I might find the key in a leather bag hanging outside Mr Wiggins' door. I found the bag but no key, and retreated to the road to encounter Mr Wiggins in person, driving a very old, wheezy, vintage tractor.

Once inside the church, saying 'hang on a jiffy' Mr Wiggins disappeared into the vestry, to emerge ten minutes later sweating profusely and panting like a long-distance runner. What had been going on? Winding the clock; it's a stiff 'un and needs winding twice a week.

Meanwhile I had found a plaque, complete with scrolls and cherubs, commemorating 'Thomas Earle, mercer', and put up by his widow and a son (evidently not Giles) who died in 1715 and was, according to the church pamphlet, 'a rather notorious vicar of Malmesbury'. There's no hint of the reason for his notoriety, but a linked tendency to take the cloth and have woman-trouble was nothing new among the Earles.

A century earlier, in 1631, the rector of Oaksey, Thomas Earle, importuned the Justices at Salisbury to release his son, Thomas the younger, a clerk in holy orders, from a bond to be of good behaviour, notwithstanding young Thomas' 'foule offences and misdemeanours', on payment of £10 to Richard Plumer in compensation for the seduction of his wife. The petition was backed by John Poole of Oaksey Park, who assured the Justices that 'Thomas Earle the younger hath made twoe sermons expressing his conversion and repentance, and if att any tyme he shall returne to his vomitt which I persuade myself hee will nott, you shall be sure to heare thereof'.

The Crudwell Earles prospered throughout the eighteenth century but then vanished from the records, and today there is no one of that name living either in Crudwell or in Oaksey.

8 August – DUNCAN PRUNING

Duncan came over to prune my eight fruit trees. He considered the future of each branch and twig with the same meticulous care and consideration that he no doubt gave to fitting each man and woman into the right niche in the great international organization of which he was personnel director, and to the VSO after that. His head cocked slightly to one side, secateurs or saw in hand, he addressed each tree with great politeness, not telling but advising it what to do: this branch would prosper better if it grew in that direction; this other one, most regrettably, is getting in someone else's way and will have to go.

Sometimes a sterner note creeps in; it's time that tree thought more of having children and less of romping irresponsibly towards the sky. If an amputation must occur, the wound is smoothed carefully over with a clasp-knife and sealed with black ointment to keep out infection. One feels that, if he could, he'd give the tree an anaesthetic. But when he encounters an earwig curled up in a leaf, or a hairy caterpillar, that streak of ruthlessness which must lie somewhere beneath the surface of every successful man of business shows itself briefly. Enemies are deftly eliminated.

At night, this week, Woodfolds is lit up like a bingo hall and in every room music-makers are busy. There are twenty-four teenagers camping in tents in the orchard or sleeping on mattresses indoors, and even one sub-teenager, aged twelve. All shine with enthusiasm, and enjoy as well as music the fiesta atmosphere, the fresh air, al fresco meals, a scent of roses and honeysuckle and the gaiety and youthful confidence of this unusual camp. The week has its culmination in a performance by all the children in Malmesbury Abbey.

Yesterday Duncan regaled the campers with Chinese stories told in his dry, dead-pan way and had them howling with laughter. Biddy, laying by her 'cello, heroically cooks three hearty meals a day for thirty hungry mouths on her four-plate cooker, which to me is a miracle. This is the third year of the camp, so soon it will become a tradition if Duncan and Biddy can stay the pace from seven a.m. till after ten at night, ending with cocoa. It's a nice change to have music instead of ponies as the purpose of a children's camp.

10 August – HAUNTED GATES

Today I heard from Percy Hawkins a variation of the legend of the haunted gates of Nether Lypiatt, a legend I first heard many years ago from John Gwynne who inherited the house, found there little happiness, and quitted it with relief, believing it to be touched by some sort of curse.

The manor house, built in the time of William and Mary and standing high above the Stroud valley, belonged first to Judge Coxe, who'd earned a reputation as a 'hanging judge' like his near-contemporary Jeffreys. One evening, so the story goes, Judge Coxe dined with a neighbour and admired a handsome pair of newly erected wrought-iron gates. 'The smith who made them,' said the neighbour, 'came before you yesterday and you sentenced him to be hanged.'

'If he'll make me another pair of gates as good as yours, I'll reprieve him,' said Judge Coxe. Here Percy's story differs a little from John Gwynne's. In Percy's version, the Judge allowed the smith a year to make the gates but, try as he would, the smith couldn't finish them, and so was hanged. In John's version, the smith completed the gates, they were hung, the Judge greatly admired them and said: 'There's only one thing that would improve them.' 'What is that?' asked the smith. 'To see you hanging from them.' And there and then, the smith was hanged.

These gates hang today at Nether Lypiatt, so obviously they're not the same pair as those formerly in the possession of Percy's aunt Louisa (old Polly). She believed hers to be the ones from which the smith was hanged. Percy said that his aunt bought them from a builder who did repairs at Nether Lypiatt. Clearly there must have been a second, smaller pair. Even so, the gates brought unhappiness. Percy refused to hang them because of the legend, so they became a bone of contention, 'creating disharmony' he said. After Polly died, he sold them back to their original owner for £50, and shortly afterwards had a motor accident which cost him £50 in repairs. And soon after that, the lady of Nether Lypiatt manor lost her life in a road accident. So that smith is still taking his revenge.

To Percy and Elizabeth, who are Jehovah's Witnesses, the explanation is simple. When Lucifer was thrown out of heaven, a lot of lesser demons went with him and over-ran the world. They're cunning, powerful demons who can possess certain people, and attach themselves to certain objects, such for instance as the Nether Lypiatt gates. It is they who are at the root of all our troubles. Demons are in the torture-rooms of police states, demons in the Kremlin, demons loose all over Ulster on both sides, demons egging people on to batter babies, rape small girls and bash old women on the head, demons planting bombs, hijacking aeroplanes and kidnapping hostages, demons everywhere. Only too many demons it appears.

If, at the moment, demons seem to have got altogether out of control, Jehovah's Witnesses are not unduly worried because the demons' days are numbered. This year, next year – probably next – Armageddon will engulf the world and that will fix the demons forever, as well as nearly all the rest of us. After Armageddon comes the millennium when the survivors, those who have seen the light, will live in peace, bliss and harmony for a thousand years, and then enter into eternity. Witnesses don't insure their lives, make wills, or accept blood transfusions, lest some of the demons should get into them from a contaminated donor.

Percy brought some old newspaper cuttings, from which I learned that in World War II our blacksmith, Robert Hall, used to shoe oxen kept by the Bruderhof at the Park, and 'each beast had to be fitted with eight shoes of an unusual design.' The beasts must have been of an unusual design also.

I also learnt that on the outskirts of the village was an 'Incroachment where the Stocks formerly stood', let to John Gardener for 4½d a year. This was near the small village pond and was probably a sort of 'punishment corner', where the ducking of scolds also took place. Many villages possessed a cucking stool, from which any unfortunate woman who had incurred her husband's displeasure, or the dislike or jealousy of others, was tipped into the pond amid the jeerings of her fellow-citizens.

What scope this gave for spitefulness, tittle-tattle and malice. How easy to work up feeling against a rival and see her ridiculed and half drowned. Some villages improved upon the cucking-stool as a discipline for scolds, and possessed a device called a brank or Scots bridle. One of these was in use in Marlborough in the reign of William III, at the dawn of the Age of Elegance; here is its description: 'Like a Crown, it being of iron, which was muzzled over the head and face, with a great gap or tongue of iron forced into her mouth, which forced the blood out.' That for answering back. Men, of course, could beat their wives unmercifully, and did, without incurring public disapproval.

And still do: but at least it's frowned on nowadays. There are subtler

ways of bringing wives to heel. One local husband, angered by his wife
(he's a nasty-tempered man, she a most hard-working, kind-hearted
woman), tore down the line on which she'd just hung out the family wash
and trampled every garment, over and over again, into the mud. Another,
who believed that hard work never hurt any woman, came home to dinner
to find his wife wrestling with a sweep's brush stuck in the chimney. She
was heavily pregnant and asked him to tug it out for her. 'You got the
bloody brush up there, you can get it bloody out,' he said, and sat down to
his dinner.

13 August – OLD SID

A real soaker of a day. Rain kept on steadily from dawn to dusk, the sky
like a heavy saturated blanket, gardens sad and sodden. Sid was bound to
be indoors and so he was, in reminiscent mood. Born in Oaksey in 1890,
Sid has an enviable memory for bygone events and a talent for unhurried
story-telling.

In his youth, the village had a Silver Band which won an open competition for the whole of Wiltshire. Thomas Locke was bandmaster, and they
practised in the village hall.

'Now do 'ee run dru the muzic,' Thomas told his men, 'while I goes
outside to listen how she sounds.' He rushed back into the hall beaming
with delight. 'Wonderful, marvellous, you could zinc into the earth!
Come on out, you fellows, and hear how she zounds.' Out they poured
into The Street to listen. Silence. Gradually it dawned. 'Why,' said a
downcast Thomas, 'there's no one left inside to play the muzic.'

Oaksey Races are always a popular topic with those whose memories
reach back before 1914. They were run over Park Farm and the course,
Sid says, was three-and-a-half miles with very stiff fences. Riders used to
come from far afield with their best horses. Jack Anthony, a famous
gentleman rider who won the Grand National several times, was one.

It was Oaksey's big day. Stands were erected by the tenant of Park
Farm, who paid for their putting-up, taking-down and storage and
received in return the money paid by carriage-owners to drive on to the
course. For days beforehand, women were busy making pies and buns for
sale, and anyone with a shed or yard offered to put up a horse. The landlord of the Wheatsheaf reckoned to make his year's rent on that one day
alone.

It must have been a stirring sight, Oaksey Races. Carriages with postilions rolled down to the Park with a 'trumpeter', as Sid called him, standing behind on the box. Ladies and gentlemen in fine clothes, the men in top hats; picnic baskets unpacked by the postilions and spread on white cloths on the grass. (It must have rained sometimes surely, even snowed, but no one remembers that; Oaksey Races live on, bathed in spring sunshine.) Fritillaries, cowslips, buttercups coloured the pastures under the horses' feet. And the riders in their brilliant colours, on horses lean from a winter's hunting and fighting fit, had a martial brilliance about them.

There was a remembered tragedy: one of the riders was killed, a Captain Faber. Dolly recalls his body going down The Street in an open carriage, with his jockey's cap and whip on top of the coffin. The last race-day was at Whitsun, 1914.

When Sid left the Park gardens he did a bit of farm work but never liked it, for an unusual reason. 'I don't like to see animals hurt. You've got to be brutal on a farm.' He also didn't like animals to hurt him. At Woodfolds he wouldn't cross the yard if a goose was sitting on a manger in a loose-box on the other side; she was liable to hiss and charge. If he saw a wasp, he took off his cap and flapped it. He kept well away from cows. Cats, however, he's devoted to. Kit told me that she couldn't get him to bed if the big white cat they adored (it was eventually run over) was curled up on the blankets, because he wouldn't disturb it.

In August, 1914, Sid had no regular job and before long enlisted in the Gloucestershire Hussars. Sid had so many wartime stories that when he was looking after our garden at Woodfolds (by this time World War II had come round) we used to call him Sidi Barrani.

One embodied a truly classic remark. In a draft of reinforcements coming up to join his unit was an old acquaintance and fellow Wiltshire man. Taking a look round at the unpleasantness that plainly was to be their lot, he concluded: 'Sid, this is no place for an honest Englishman.' Soon afterwards his rifle went off, accidentally damaging his foot. Next time Sid encountered him, back at the base, he was a quarter-master sergeant.

Now and then there were compensations. When billeted in a Macedonian village, Sid observed the peasants going out to labour on their small-holdings and watched with interest the progress of a patch of succulent melons. When he judged them ripe enough, he and a mate crept out by moonlight and swiped the lot.

Here on his home ground Sid would no more lay hands on another's property than swim the Atlantic. 'What would you have said if American soldiers billeted in Oaksey had swiped your cabbages?' I inquired. Sid looked blank. 'Well, they was foreigners, wasn't they?'

When Sid came back, unscathed, in 1920, jobs weren't easy to find and Sid didn't find one. There was no dole then and he lived on savings till they ran out. In just about the nick of time, a job as a part-time postman came along, at fifteen shillings a week. He made extra money by doing odd jobs, when he could get them, after tea.

His round started at Hankerton, thence to Minety, up the Common, back by Tidling Corner to Flagham and Clattinger, across to the Dean and Sodam nearly to Poole, then back to Hankerton with the outgoing letters. This he did twice daily on his cycle, a good forty miles a day, winter and summer, with plenty of water and mud.

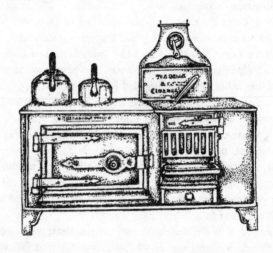

The Rucketts, as Sid's cottage used to be called, was very cosy on this grey dripping day. It's one of the oldest dwellings in the village; tradition has it that, before the Dissolution, it was a hostel for pilgrims making their way to Malmesbury Abbey. Kit's brass fire-guards and -irons glow like gold; she polishes them daily, and blacks the old grate though blacking's getting hard to find. There's always a fire burning. Two brown enamel kettles sit on top of the stove. There's no cat now, but two budgerigars in the parlour. In the kitchen there's a television, immersion heater and electric cooker, so there's comfort and security in old age after a life of ups and downs. Kit said: 'I go out first thing every morning to see what's come out in the night.' Even in mid-winter, there's always something happening, even under frost and snow.

15 August – A CORNER–STONE

Continual rain has thwarted our digging operations, but today we resumed and, about a foot down, came upon a large flat stone shaped by hand and surely part of the foundations. Perhaps a quoin? Encouraged, we worked round it carefully, trying to avoid murdering worms, but didn't manage to free it before the time came to walk back to the school-house for our cup of tea. John expects to dig up at any moment if not the golden coffin, then at least a ring, bracelet or medieval coin.

When he came here ten years ago, he told me, he heard two Oaksey women in a bus queue in front of him in Cirencester discussing the new headmaster. 'I expect he'll be like the rest of them,' one said. 'Go to church on Sundays and have no time for the likes of us all the rest of the week.' A schoolteacher hovers uneasily in a limbo between Them and Us, not truly one of either. It's a lonely life, a tight-rope stance.

Although a small but faithful band of Us go to church, by and large the Church as an institution belongs to Them. 'I used to walk past the church, all lit up of a Sunday evening, on my way home from milking,' one of Us told me in recalling his start in life as a farm boy fifty years ago. 'Raining pouring very likely, I was wet and cold and hungry, and there they was snug and warm inside bellowing hymns and praying for their own salvation, never thinking of the likes of I. They can keep their church, I said, I'll never go inside it and I never have.' Except, he might have added, when his children were baptized.

Like most of my fellow citizens I'm not a churchgoer, never have been. Yet one retains a certain sense if not of guilt, then of defensiveness. Illogical. To stand up and repeat 'I believe . . .' and then a whole string of things one doesn't believe in must be hypocritical. We're all hypocrites but shouldn't, surely, feel defensive about, for once, abstaining from hypocrisy. Perhaps it stems from a residual, long-buried fear of persecution as a heretic or atheist. At least, today, one runs no risk of that. Greater tolerance, or just indifference? The latter I fear. Society is tolerant only when it doesn't care much one way or the other.

A perfect ending to the day, the setting sun an enormous red-gold ball resting on a sharp horizon against a forget-me-not-blue sky. A few trailing wispy clouds stained a deep apricot colour. Oaks and ashes black against the skyline.

A summer day ending in glory can work its magic even on aeroplanes. One or two, climbing steeply, left long silver plumes across the blue. Scarcely plumes, more like the clean swoop of a scimitar slashing through the sky. Then the edges start to blur, the scimitar widens and dissolves into fluffiness, its hard silvery white turns to a pinkish grey.

A slender moon appears between the branches of a young apple tree. I must make a wish. But what wish? So many spring to mind, ranging from the moral kind – to be more patient, less irritable, give more to good causes and less to self-indulgent ones – to the more immediate, practical variety: to acquire the strength of mind to cut out nibbling between meals, to learn to identify trees, put off things less, stop losing everything, get the windows painted, ask that nice, but talkative, old friend to stay – resolutions, rather than wishes. The result of all this indecision is that nothing gets wished at all.

Those destined to achieve their purpose know exactly what to wish and wish it firmly, with no strings, every time they see a new moon, or eat their first strawberry, or mouthful of Christmas pudding. I haver, and am lost. 'Infirm of purpose, give me the dagger.'

And yet, however firm of purpose, circumstances can be too strong. After darkness fell the peace was broken by a bellowing heifer which paced to and fro along my garden fence, throwing out her desperate appeal across indifferent fields whence no bull will return his answer. She's firm of purpose enough, in all conscience. Her wish is plain. It won't be granted. Tomorrow will come a man with a slim glass tube to thrust up her own tubes and after that she will be silent. She went on crying through the night.

16 August – DOLLY

Today Dolly started her annual fortnight's holiday. She never goes further than Coates, about three miles, to stay with her married niece. They go together for a day trip or two, perhaps to Weston-super-Mare; Dolly cleans the silver for a family living in the village; otherwise her holiday is uneventful. She doesn't seek out events. She's almost the only person I know who is truly contented. If it's pouring and blowing a gale, she walks to work from the far end of the village in her gumboots, old mac and little old hat (very faithful friends these) and says she enjoyed the blow. If it's fine she cycles, still in the same mac and hat, and enjoys the freshness of the morning. I don't think I've ever heard her complain, nor say an unkind word about a neighbour.

The secret, of course, is to have what you want and not want what you haven't. Dolly at rising seventy-five has, I think, all she wants. Her own cottage, with its well-kept garden small enough to manage. A bicycle. The niece at Coates with two children. Membership of the church choir. Excellent health. The pension, which she thinks more than adequate; she's always been a saver. The respect of the community. She could have a television if she wanted but she doesn't. Not even a daily paper (though she has a radio).

Dolly's lived all her life in Oaksey and the only time she left was in the war, to work in a factory in Stroud. She was born at Sodam, in a farmhouse tucked away on its own at the end of a lane. Her father, Markwell Jennings, was for many years Robert Warner's bailiff and later the tenant of Church Farm. There were five children, all born there and brought up to farm skills. Dolly can milk a cow, feed a calf, make butter, pluck and draw a fowl. Of her three brothers, one was killed in World War I, one managed a big farm in Cambridgeshire, and the youngest, Frank, was for many years bailiff for George Todd at Dean Farm.

After the war she came to work for us at Woodfolds and has been with us ever since. Next year, she'll complete (God willing) thirty years' unbroken part-time service in our household, and when I say unbroken, that is what I mean. In all that time she's never once, quite literally, missed a morning (three a week) or been a minute late. On the contrary, she's generally ten minutes early and stays long after she should have gone. She'd no more go home leaving a job unfinished than fly to the moon. This, beyond doubt, must be a record, and I wish it could be fittingly marked.

The day Dolly retires will be (if I'm still alive) a dark one indeed. She's part of our lives as we are of hers. The house won't be the same without her small, spare, scurrying presence – she does her work almost on the run, and always thoroughly, keeping her mind on the job. Even when she has a cup of coffee, she won't sit down. Without her, I'd never be able to find anything; she's the only one who remembers where things have been put away. She never gossips in the tittle-tattle sense, but knows exactly what's going on in the village. While her own standards of behaviour are as high as the Himalayas she is never censorious, never condemns. Altogether, Dolly is a marvellous person. She likes a joke, too.

In fact she presents only one problem, virtually insoluble: her Christmas present. There must be something she wants, or at any rate would like to have, but I've never been able to discover what it is. In this respect, she's no help at all. And so the annual head-scratching goes on.

23 August – JACK AND RAY

Like Tweedledum and Tweedledee, the brothers Jack and Ray with their wives live side by side in two identical cottages, sharing a vegetable garden which is always fully under control. All four look much alike: shortish, squarish, amiable, unhurried, red-cheeked except for Jack, keeping their own counsel but *au fait* with everything that goes on. All staunch church-goers; Ray is in the choir and his wife plays the organ, Jack's a sidesman; they seldom break the routine.

Ray's wife was working in her garden, and over the wall we discussed what happens to butterflies when the buddleias are over. Cabbage whites are always with us, but the peacocks, tortoiseshells and red admirals that suck the buddleia blooms seem to vanish as suddenly as they appear. She thinks they go on to the sedums and always grows some, largely for that reason.

Jack and Ray, unmarried then, were living at Woodfolds when we bought it; their father had been first carpenter, then bailiff, for the Oaksey estate, and the tenant of a sixty-acre farm. I was told that he possessed the enviable, if hazardous, talent of being able to go to sleep when up a ladder. His wife I remember as an apple-cheeked, white-haired old lady who lived to be ninety. Their four sons had been born nearby at Manby's Farm whose house has crumbled away into the earth; little remains but a chimney, ivy-smothered and propped up by elder bushes, and some derelict sheds. Thrushes and robins nest among rusty bits of ancient implements and among clotted cobwebs and old rotted manure. A wagon has disintegrated into the nettles which smother the old rickyard. A cat used to rear her broods up there and once we saw her leading a procession of kittens across the fields, to take up residence among the hay bales in our Dutch barn.

Jack and Ray were still working the farm with horses when we came: Duke, Smiler and Kit the mare, whose stables became a back sitting-room and a boiler-house. They milked by hand a herd of old-fashioned red-and-white Shorthorns in a dark, low-raftered cowshed full of cobwebs, sitting, with their caps back-to-front and heads pressed deep into the flank of the cow, on three-legged stools. No fuss in those days about tuberculin tests (Brucellosis wasn't even heard of), sterilizing in the dairy or clean white overalls. Every evening I put a jug on top of the gatepost and next morning retrieved it full of fresh, frothy milk, containing I am sure hundreds of thousands of bacteria for which none of us was ever the worse. The water, whether used for drinking or to wash the dairy utensils or for any other purpose, was pumped by hand from a well situated underneath the pig-sties. (The trough by the pump now houses a camellia.) The well never ran dry and the humans flourished.

27 August – BRIHTRIC

Three of the fattest missel-thrushes I've ever seen were pecking in the orchard first thing this morning, in grass silvered over with dew. The faint mistiness presaging a fine day in early autumn made them look bigger, like battleships looming out of a fog. Then a flock of starlings landed aggressively and the thrushes, with dignity, went away.

A day to be out of doors, but as I had to go into Malmesbury I did more delving in the library and was electrified to learn that a former lord of the manor of Oaksey was more or less responsible for the Norman Conquest. Brihtric, it appears, was no ordinary rustic Saxon thegn, he was a great landowner, a diplomat, and evidently a charmer. Edward the Confessor sent him as ambassador to Baldwin, Count of Flanders, and the Count's daughter, Matilda alias Maude, fell in love with him. He didn't reciprocate, and when she married William, Duke of Normandy (on the rebound?) she 'is supposed to have urged him on' to the conquest of England out of pique, according to E.J. writing in *Wiltshire Notes & Queries* in 1893. Having accomplished the Conquest, Duke William then, adds E.J., deprived Brihtric of his lands and shut him up in a fortress.

However, S. Grose of Melksham, writing in the next issue, pointed out that twenty years after the Conquest, in 1086, Brihtric was still in possession of his Wiltshire lands, as testified by the Doomsday Survey, and twenty years is a long time to nurse one's pique; in any case, Matilda died in 1083. 'She was a young lady whose flirtations were much talked of,' Mr Grose remarked in the best William Hickey manner; so the handsome Saxon may not have broken her heart. Nevertheless the Continuator of Wace (Wace was a twelfth-century Anglo-Norman chronicler) states that, by Matilda's influence, Brihtric was imprisoned at Winchester until his death, when the King divided up his lands.

For whatever reason, Brihtric did meet with a miserable end. It chills the mind to think of this vigorous Saxon noble, the friend of kings, with lands from Wiltshire to Cornwall, eating his heart out behind castle walls until death released him. In the library, I came across this old ballad about our thegn who so unwisely spurned Matilda.

À lui la pucele envela messager
Pur sa amur a lui procurer
Mees Brihtric Maude refusa
Dunt ell mult se coruça;
Hastivement me pursa
E à William Bastard se maria.*

This episode raises the question of whether Brihtric was free to marry the forward Maude, or Matilda. There is a record of a marriage settlement between Brihtric and Earl Godwine's daughter in 1016–20; he gave her a pound's weight in gold, some land and thirty cows, ten horses and ten slaves. Matilda espoused the Bastard William in 1059. If it was the same Brihtric, by the time Matilda set her cap at him he must have been in his late fifties or early sixties, and by the time of the Doomsday Survey, when our Brihtric was still alive, he'd have been well over eighty. Also, the Brihtric who married Godwine's daughter came from Kent; 'every trustworthy man in Kent and Sussex, thegn or ceorl,' was called upon to witness the terms. All our Brihtric's lands seem to have been in the West Country: 6,800 acres in Wilts and other manors in Devon, Cornwall, Dorset, Gloucestershire and Worcestershire. So it looks as if there were two, overlapping, Brihtrics.

I'd like to know whether our thegn had a dwelling on his Oaksey manor, and walked, or rode, two thousand years ago, along the path between the church and the site of the medieval Court which may later have been built on the foundations of the earlier Saxon castle: the same path which John Lucie and I follow with our spades and trowels to prod away at the ancient stones.

---

* I submitted this to an erudite friend, Colin McLaren, who kindly supplied the following rough translation:

> The maid sent him a messenger
> In order to procure his love
> But Brihtric refused Maude
> Therefore she was greatly enraged;
> And hastened to cross the sea
> And married Bastard William.

Matilda and Maude were the same person.

September

3 September – THE QUEEN'S HEAD

A great gale blew last night and is still blowing. Rain pelts down, skies are black and menacing, gladioli lie like fallen soldiers in scarlet uniforms prostrate on the grass. Runner beans with their canes have been punched sideways. Here, deep inland, the gale punishes trees and gardens but at sea it punishes people. Evening bulletins carried news of the destruction of Ted Heath's *Morning Cloud* with two men drowned.

I set off in driving rain and had the windscreen wiper going all the way over the border into Wales, when the clouds lifted a little; then out came the sun. I'm sure the sun doesn't shine more in Wales (probably less) but it seems to, just as people seem to be more friendly and polite and helpful.

At the bottom of the Queen's Pitch leading up the mountain to my cottage stands the Queen's Head, a small pub beside the Honddu which manages to support, more or less, a lot of people. Mrs Lowe is always the same, placid and unruffled, a little slow of movement these days, attending not only to the customers but to a ninety-year-old mother in the back room. There's often a nephew around, sometimes a girl who's some kind of relation, and then there's Philip who runs the pony-trekking. Oddly enough, Philip is French, although you wouldn't know it. He was left here when on a holiday from London and here he's remained, grown up to be a prop and stay to Mrs Lowe and as Welsh as the next man in this valley.

Up the Queen's Pitch in low gear and into my lane, just wide enough for a car and no more. Large stones often roll into the lane and you have to stop to remove them, but the problem is that in many parts it's too narrow to open the door. Some timid souls prefer to leave their car at the bottom and walk, but once you know it, it's perfectly all right. Hedges and trees meet overhead, their drooping branches and creepers brushing the car as it pushes a way through. Sheep flee ahead with agitated bleats and tail-waggings to scramble over low places in the wall.

What you notice most, when you get here, is the silence. No outbursts of Red Arrows, no thump of balers or whine of circular saws, no horrible Concorde overhead. Occasionally the distant hoot of a train comes faintly up the valley. Sometimes you can hear the ravens over the Gaer, often the woodpeckers' yaffle and the harsh cry of a jay. In spring, ewes and lambs bleat, but now the lambs are weaned and they are silent. There are not even dogs yapping – sheep-dogs do their work in silence, and Ken when he comes up to see to his sheep doesn't shout much to his dog.

6 September – GROSMONT

Hitherto castles have bored me, just lumps of masonry, but since digging at the roots of one I've seen them in a different light. So today I went to Grosmont, its Norman name incongruous among all the Welsh-titled villages like Llanvihangel and Pontrilas, Llangattock-Lingoed and Llantilio-Pertholy.

Though the gale is over it's wet and stormy and I was the only sight-seer. Not a soul to be seen in the village save three children in brilliant red jackets walking up the street. It's a tidy little village with a curl in the middle, low white cottages with slate roofs and dark gables, and a profusion of flowers in front gardens.

You could drive through the village and miss the castle, which stands above it yet escapes notice until you walk up a narrow lane and see it in front of you behind a huge green moat, thirty feet deep I should say, and partly screened by trees. Its stones were glowing in the evening light with a burnt-brick colour. The walls so high, so thick, so immemorial and dominant. It must have been awe-inspiring when it stood there in its full might, one of a trio – Whitecastle, Skinfrith and Grosmont – guarding the Welsh marches above the river Monnow.

Inside, how dark it must have been in the great hall with window-slits no wider than the length of my finger. Day and night it must have needed torchlight, and how cold despite a huge log fire at one end, where the chimney still stands. Henry III built it to keep out the Welsh, and here, in 1300, was born his grandson Henry of Grosmont, first Duke of Lancaster, who married his daughter Blanche to John of Gaunt. Their son Henry Bolingbroke acquired, through his marriage, our Court or castle, so there's a link between Oaksey and Grosmont on the Monnow.

It's hard to see how so great a fortress as this, its walls so high and thick, its position so commanding, its moat so wide and deep, could ever be taken, unless by treachery, by men armed with swords and cross-bows. Yet Henry III himself was driven from Grosmont Castle by Llewellyn the Great, and his wife with him; they were obliged to flee in their night-shifts and only just escaped annihilation. Nearly two centuries later the tables were turned and one of Owain Glyndwr's supporters was driven from it by Henry of Monmouth; and that was more or less the end of Owain Glyndwr. Henry garrisoned the castle with a single constable and six archers, to whom he paid fourpence a day, and that seems to have been enough, for it was not attacked again.

A sign reading: 'Refreshments: Walk down drive' led me through an orchard to a house called Athelstan. Why is our Wessex hero thus commemorated in Gwent? The lady who brought me a cup of tea said she had no idea, but the house had formerly belonged to the Mayor and she thought he had so named it. Mayor of what? Villages of two hundred people don't have mayors; on looking it up, I found that Grosmont was a full-blown borough until 1860. A fire destroyed three parts of the village and it was never rebuilt. But it still has a Town Crier; at least there's a picture of him in the current *Abergavenny Chronicle* dancing in the street, accompanied by his dog, during a Victorian Festival.

'A conservation storm is brewing', says the newspaper. The village has been chosen as one of nineteen 'conservation areas' by the new Gwent County Council. Its inhabitants don't want to be 'conserved', they want to be developed: new houses, more 'amenities' and so on. Not surprisingly, the anti-conservationists are headed by an architect and the schoolmaster. Grosmont is full of history and still 'unspoilt'. It's other people's villages we want to leave unspoiled so that we can go and look at them, while we develop our own.

13 September – NEAUDD

I saw an animal today I've never seen before. Under a pile of dung and straw Bonzo, the ebullient and approval-seeking spaniel, discovered what Bridget assumed to be a rat. A terrific struggle ensued. Bonzo at last dragged forth his vanquished opponent: a dark-brown creature with white markings, about ferret-sized or larger, which stank. A polecat, rare in these parts. Under the straw, in a kind of nest, was a lamb's head.

There's a new crop of Welsh Mountain foals, no larger than sheep, all legs and bounce. Twenty mares with their foals, and a sorrel stallion, need some looking after; then there's seventy or so ewes with their lambs, twenty or thirty cattle, as well as ducks, dogs, the vegetable garden, cooking, goodness knows what else, for Bridget to deal with; and in summer, all the pony shows and sales.

As soon as father William is back from his office in Newport he's out on the tractor, or dosing lambs in the yard, or feeding calves, or heaving bales about, according to the season. At the moment he and Bridget are building a cattle shed. Joan paints the spiny structure of the mountains, the brilliance of flowers, creatures of the sea, twisted tree-trunks, and when she sells her paintings gives the money to the ancient little church of Patricio, or Patrishow, hidden among the hills, from whose friar's cross Archbishop Baldwin preached the Third Crusade.

Neaudd hums with activity but there's always time for a cup of tea. In fact it would be a strange Welsh farmhouse where a cup of tea wasn't always handy, and pressed on anyone who comes to the door.

Back by Ty-coch where a lamb, evidently reared on the bottle, followed at my heels expectantly, supposing every human to be its mother. It bleated indignantly when I climbed a gate and left it behind.

Another gale in the night. I was woken by a demonic yowling and shrieking outside. There on the window sill was a big spotted cat baring its teeth and not asking but demanding to be let in. Spotted like a lynx. Could it be a feral cat? Or just lost? Its teeth gleamed in the darkness, it looked enormous, its claws like razor-blades, its nature ferocious, its demands urgent. Should I let it in? I should have I suppose, but what could I have given it to eat? There was no meat in the cottage – no dead meat that is. Only me. It yowled for hours, but in the end went away.

15 September – EARLES OF ESTCOTT

By self-invitation I called at Eastcourt House, sheltering in a grove of trees beside Braydon brook, to be boisterously greeted by three spaniels, with more reserve by a caged parakeet, and hospitably by Colonel Tim and Cynthia Pitman, who've lived since immediately after World War II in this fine house built by Sir Giles Earle of Crudwell, son of a successful Bristol merchant, between 1648 and 1662. He bought the land, and a hamlet then called Estcott, off Sir Nevill Poole of Oaksey. Probably, like Robert Warner more than two centuries later, he hoped to fill it with a numerous progeny and to found a line of landed gentry. Like Warner, he was disappointed; his heir was a nephew, Thomas, who made up for his uncle's ill fortune by rearing a brood of thirteen.

Above the fireplace in the panelled dining-room is a plaque depicting Sir Giles standing beneath a canopy in a wide-brimmed hat, baggy breeches and long curls, one arm akimbo and one resting on the head of a kneeling gentleman, presumably his nephew Thomas. On his right, reaching barely to his elbow, stands his wife with a swaddled baby, which must have died in infancy, in her arms. The figures are surrounded by a lush baroque design of curling leaves and dangling tassels, enclosing a coat of arms bearing the three escallops of St James of Compostella.

Sir Thomas died in 1678 and his eldest son, another Giles, carried on the family tradition of representing either Malmesbury or Cricklade in the House of Commons. He's the only member of this branch of the Earles to achieve a mention in the *Dictionary of National Biography*. By no means a favourable one. His biographer makes no attempt to conceal his dislike for Sir Giles, whom he depicts as a toady and sycophant.

Through the influence of the Duke of Argyll he was appointed Groom of the Bedchamber to the prince who became George II, and then given the lucrative post of Commissioner for Irish Revenue. When the Duke fell out of favour Sir Giles immediately deserted him, and pursued his own interests with a single-mindedness that excited comment even in that age of political corruption and place-seeking. 'His readiness to do the minister's bidding ingratiated him with Walpole,' says the *DNB* contributor, 'and the coarseness of his humour made him an acceptable companion in that minister's happier hours of social life.'

Pride went before a fall; his 'covetous disposition' and 'strokes of wit which he had frequently exercised against the Scotch, turned into hatred the disgust which they [Parliament] had always regarded his abandonment of the Duke of Argyll'. In 1741 he lost by four votes an election for the chairmanship of the committee of privileges and elections. This marked his downfall; he dropped out of politics and died at Eastcourt, aged eighty, in 1758. His 'broad jokes', according to the *DNB*, were 'set off by a whining tone, crabbed face, and very laughing eyes'. 'A facetious gentleman,' Lady Mary Wortley Montagu called him, adding that his favourite toast was: 'God bless you, whatever becomes of me,' apparently the only example of his wit – hardly a coruscating one – to survive.

If he failed in politics he succeeded in marrying an heiress and in begetting an heir, another Giles, born in 1732, who married another heiress, through whom Giles the younger inherited an even grander country seat than Eastcourt, Benningborough Hall. Then followed the last of the Earles to live at Eastcourt, William Rawlinson, who died in 1764 leaving the house and forty acres to his wife for life and then to his son, another Giles, together with property in London, Dorset, Hampshire and Northampton. William also left £500 to erect a memorial to his parents in Hankerton church, but he himself was buried in a family vault at Hendon.

17 September – THE FORGE

As I saw a glow coming from the smithy I stopped and had a word with Cyril Hall, who was standing exactly as I remember him thirty years ago, in the same leather apron, one hand working the bellows, the other holding the tongs, deftly lifting each strip of red-hot metal on to the anvil to be hammered into a horse-shoe, and holes tapped for nails.

'Here's one thing that hasn't changed,' I said, looking round the grimy old shed hung about with rusty horse-shoes and bits of iron of all shapes, and things that had just stayed where someone had thrown them. There's a hearth at each end, and Cyril's son Robert stood at the other. The only difference was that thirty years ago, indeed forty, Cyril's father Bob Hall would have been hammering away at this end of the smithy and Cyril at the other, instead of Cyril at this end and *his* son Robert at the other. 'I wonder how long the place will stand up?' 'I wonder too,' said Cyril.

Old Bob, now in his eighties, bought the business here in 1910, coming from Cirencester. No one knows how long there's been a smithy on the same spot. Cyril joined his father, and now one of Cyril's three sons has joined him.

A lot of farriers abandoned the trade after World War II when horses disappeared from farms and were thought to be dying out. The Halls went through hard times but made a living by repairing farm implements and converting them from horses to tractors. So there was just enough business to get by on but it was up-and-down.

Then the use of horses started to revive and soon they engulfed the countryside. Fox-hunting is more popular than ever, nearby is Badminton with its Three-Day Event, pony clubs proliferate on all sides, there's polo at Cirencester Park and hunter trials are constantly held. The horse is 'in' at all levels, and on the roads one's constantly having to slow down and scrape the hedge to pass equestrians who politely touch their caps in response – a ritual, like the courtship of birds, since the equine race has long since adapted itself to traffic as a condition of survival.

So now Cyril and his son are never idle, mostly out in their van equipped with a mobile forge. When Cyril started work in 1929 the cost of a set of shoes was fourteen shillings; now it's about six pounds. A regularly hunted horse may wear out a set of shoes in a fortnight, and at the best will need a new set every month.

Cyril solved one minor mystery for me: the eight shoes of the Bruderhof's oxen. His father shod them in the ordinary way to start with, and they'd cast the shoes before they got out of the gate. Then he learnt to do it the German way. He made two half-shoes for each hoof, leaving a gap for the cleft in the middle. This worked better, but was always tricky. So each ox had eight shoes. Were these the last oxen to be shod in England? People can remember ox-teams ploughing on the Bathurst estate, but they were given up between the wars.

20 September – THE POOLES

Pouring with rain all afternoon, skies grey as winter, so I went to Sapperton church to see the tomb of Sir Henry Poole. The door was unlocked, and on it were pinned instructions as to how to latch it properly so that birds wouldn't get trapped inside.

Sir Henry and his wife Anne are worthily commemorated. They

kneel face to face with his knight's helmet in between, hands joined in prayer, beneath an elaborate Jacobean canopy in marble picked out in gold.

'These both loved and lived together many Years, Much given to Hospitality. He was always Faithful to his Prince and loving to his Country, True to his Friends and Bountiful to his Servants. Being 75 years of Age Deceased A D 1616.' The same year as Shakespeare. How pompous and complacent are these seventeenth-century tombs, how exemplary the virtues of the deceased and how certain their salvation. How fruitful too those Jacobean wombs. Three sons are listed on the tomb, Devereux, Gyles and Henry, and four daughters, all of whom were married to knights: Elinor to Sir Richard Fettiplace, Dorothy to Sir John Savedge, Ann to Sir Theobald Gorges and Frances to Sir Nevill Poole of Oaksey.

The Pooles were a large and prosperous family typical of many here-abouts who made their fortunes out of wool in the fifteenth and sixteenth centuries, married into the aristocracy, bought manors, established seats, sat unobtrusively in Parliament and on the local Bench, and in general ruled the English countryside, not unsuccessfully, until the Industrial Revolution combined with social reform eroded away their foundations.

The Pooles of Oaksey were a junior branch of this clan. As with most families, their lineage is complicated and I didn't sort it all out on one wet afternoon in Sapperton, but I give the story here in one piece, so far as I've been able to fit it together, to avoid even more confusion than must inevitably arise in genealogical matters.

The family came originally from Cheshire, and the first to settle in these parts was Richard, who leased the 'scite of the manor of Poole' (among others) from the Duchy of Lancaster in 1515, and died two years later. (The connection between the name of the family and that of the village of Poole Keynes is fortuitous; the village of Poole was mentioned in Dooms-day Book long before the family was heard of, and the 'Keynes' was tacked on to it after the elder daughter of Sir John Maltravers, who held the manor in 1327, married Sir John Keynes, one of the old family of de Kaines who held various offices under the King in the royal Forest of Braden.)

Richard Poole's eldest son Leonard (1477–1537) married Katheryn Brydges and in his will, proved in 1538, left her his 'manor of Staperton and all my lands and tenements in the countie of Glouc. and Wokesey in the countie of Wilts', the remainder going to his second son Henry. So evidently, in the first half of the sixteenth century, our manor of Wokesey was one of a number, including Poole, Kemble, Minety and various others, leased from the Crown through the Duchy of Lancaster by the Poole family, whose seat was at Sapperton in Gloucestershire. Later, the two branches of the family, headed respectively by Leonard's sons Sir Giles and Henry, were to divide.

To deal first with the Sapperton branch: Leonard's eldest son Sir Giles (or Gyles) married Elizabeth, daughter and co-heiress of Thomas Whittington of Pauntley, who took that manor, together with others, to her husband. Sir Giles died in 1588 and was succeeded by his son Sir Henry (1541–1616), the one under the marble canopy in Sapperton church.

No wonder the inscription is complacent; he became immensely rich and at his death held sixteen manors, as well as great areas of land round about, the seven hundreds of Cirencester, a great many hamlets, mills and orchards, a thousand acres of woodland, fairs and markets in Stroud and Cirencester, and goodness knows what else besides.

This rich Sir Henry's heir, another Sir Henry (there were far too many Henry's for clarity) must have been a younger son, for he was baptized in the same year, 1590, as the death of his brother Devereux, who, 'being of tender age, was for his worthyness and valour knighted in France by Henry IV the French King after his owne Order, and there ended his dayes, and was there buried'. This is recorded on a plaque beside his parents' tomb in Sapperton church. It was his sister Frances who married Sir Nevill Poole of Oaksey, born in 1592 and died in 1651, her second cousin once removed.

To come then to the Oaksey Pooles: they descend from Leonard's younger son Henry, who, on his mother's demise, inherited the manors of Minety, Kemble, Poole and Wokesey. He made a grand marriage into the family of Nevill, one of the oldest and most powerful in the land, descended from Maldred, a brother of Duncan, King of Scotland; Jane, Henry's bride, was related to the Lord Abergavenny of the day. They settled at Poole, whose lease from the Duchy of Lancaster Sir Nevill obtained in 1587–8, his father and grandfather having had it before him. (Providing that the line continued and no trouble arose, leases from the Crown seem to have been renewed more or less automatically, and were assigned by the holders to their heirs.)

This Henry's heir was Edward, who married Margaret Walton and died young in 1577, expressing the wish that he should be buried in the church at Poole 'beside my good father there'. His lands he left for life to Margaret, with instructions to bring up their children 'in vertuous education till twenty-one'. Besides a daughter Eleanor, who married another Nevill (another Henry, too), he left two sons, both of whom matriculated at Trinity College, Oxford, in 1578, aged respectively fifteen and sixteen. The younger, Walton, got the manor of Ewen, while the elder, Sir Henry (1563–1632), not to be confused with his cousin and contemporary Sir Henry of Sapperton, inherited Kemble, Poole and Oaksey, with several other manors.

In 1614–15 Oaksey's Sir Henry was granted by the Duchy a lease of 'Westwood in Wokesey'; Westwood is to this day the name of a field adjoining the Park. In his will, proved in 1633, he was 'seized in his demesne as of fee of the manor of Kemble' and of other manors, including 'Woxey alias Okesey and of the manor of Poole; of Okesey Park and its capital messuage'. All this went to his wife Griselda for life and then to his son Nevill, whom he appointed sole executor, enjoining him to 'be careful, loving and kind to his brother and sister, and to be good unto my tenants, suffering them quietly to enjoy their several estates'.

So the new manor house, to replace the disused Court, had been built at Oaksey by 1632; most likely soon after 1614–15 when the lease was granted. It was an honest, unpretentious, three-gabled building with fair-sized rooms – baronial halls were going out of fashion – and an unusual octagonal room jutting out over the porch. To the south stood a long row of stables; there were servants' quarters, kennels, barns, granaries and other out-buildings; a long avenue was already noted for its fine oaks. A survey of the Duchy's manors made in 1591 has this to say about Wokesey.

It standeth somethinge highe in a verie wholesome aire, well furnished with woode, having fertile corne fields, and well stored with goode meadowe grounds, and also large scope of common, iiij miles east from Malmsburie. And mitch beautified by the parke and fair okes therein.

It sounds almost as if a dwelling was already there by 1591; if not, one was evidently intended, since a park had been established to surround it.

Sir Henry must have been away from home a good deal; he sat in every Parliament between 1604 and 1626, either as Member for Cricklade or as a Knight of the Shire. A letter he wrote in December, 1620, to Edward Gore, observes that owing to the 'untimely' dissolution of Parliament 'the Countie who chose me to be one of the Knights of the Shire lost my service and I my attendance and charge'; an election was to be held at Wilton and Sir Henry requests Edward Gore's support for himself and for Sir Francis Seymour.

Professor S. T. Bindoff, writing in the *Victoria County History*, concludes that Sir Henry was 'the outstanding Wilts parliamentarian of the reign of James I' – not perhaps very high praise since the rest were 'a silent and inactive' lot. Subsequently most of them – 21 out of 29 – became anti-Royalist, though moderate in tone. Sir Henry was a fairly frequent speaker, described by a contemporary diarist as 'merry', and a moderating influence when tempers rose. He was evidently a kindly, tolerant family man and we may hope that under his aegis the citizens of Wokesey, following his lead in putting up better and more modern houses with the aid of stone removed from his unwanted old castle, were able 'quietly to enjoy their several estates'.

21 September – THE BATTLE OF MARLBOROUGH

Sir Henry's eldest son Sir Nevill was the only other Oaksey Poole to make a mark, albeit a faint one, on his country's history. Born in 1592, he was knighted at Newmarket by James I at the age of twenty. James had taken to selling knighthoods, and fining those who refused the accolade, so probably Nevill had little choice in the matter. Two years later he was returned to Parliament as Member for Malmesbury. He transferred to Cricklade in 1623, and to Cirencester three years later.

When the Civil War came, he declared for the Parliament. This must have caused family ructions, since his brother-in-law and cousin, Sir Henry of Sapperton, was a staunch Royalist. Sir Nevill raised a troop, no doubt pressing into service Oaksey stalwarts who would much rather have stayed at home, and in November, 1642, found himself defending Marlborough against Lord Digby, who advanced upon it with 400 Royalist cavalry.

From the Royalist ranks emerged a Mr Vincent Goddard; Sir Nevill came forward in the name of the Parliament; a parley followed which Sir Nevill managed to prolong until some seven hundred 'countrymen coming to market had been induced to take up arms'. One wonders what arms they took up, surprised in the market with their pigs and cheeses. Pitchforks? Cudgels? Defied by Sir Nevill, the Royalists withdrew to Aldbourne and during the night were attacked by Sir Nevill's forces, who captured Mr Goddard and marched him off in triumph. This gentleman, a former High Sheriff of Wilts, was a son of John Goddard of Upham at Clyffe Pypard, seat of the senior branch of this powerful clan, so Mr Goddard was a rich prize.

This was not his first mishap; six years earlier Thomas Hopkins, a shepherd, was arraigned at Quarter Sessions on the charge that he 'threw his pronge at a greate Fatt Gentleman, meaning Mr Goddard, that he mist him but verie narrowlie, and that he bowed his pronge, and that he had killed his dogge'. Mr Goddard had been out hawking. Thomas Hopkins' fate is unknown.

The inhabitants of Marlborough appealed for help to the Earl of Essex, Lord Commander of the Parliament's forces, then at Windsor, who sent a Colonel Ramsay to fortify the town. More or less in the middle of it was a 'Mound' on which stood the residence of Lord Seymour, a Royalist, then occupied by his wife and daughter. Colonel Ramsay filled the castle with musketeers and the two ladies (quoting from James Waylen's history of Marlborough) 'found themselves prisoners of war'.

On 3 December 1642, Lord Digby advanced from Wantage with 4,000 men and on the following day a grand assault took place with horse, infantry and heavy artillery. The guns were so inexpertly handled that a three-hour bombardment did practically no harm, the balls going over the roofs of the town. At last, however, a barn was fired, next a house, and then the Royalist soldiers burst in and ran amok. 'All discipline was at an end.'

Sir Nevill Poole withdrew with his halberdiers and pikemen to Lord Seymour's Mound, and had two dummies, dressed in white aprons and black hoods to look like women, hoisted on top of the Mound. He then sent word that if Digby's men stormed the Mound, the ladies would be put to death. The Royalists, however, were too busy looting to stop for any Mound-storming. Houses were burnt and smashed; oil and cheese, wine and treacle, flour and spirits, all went up in a great blaze; £50,000 worth of damage was done and next day there were two hundred of the King's men to be buried. Lady Seymour and her daughter were unharmed.

Lord Digby tied his prisoners together two by two and marched them barefoot to Oxford, an action which later drew strong protests in Parliament from Sir Nevill, who had evidently got safely away and retired to Oaksey. We hear no more about him as a soldier. He died in 1653, and according to Aubrey 'lies buried in this [Oaksey] church: no Monument, only a little Coate which is Poole, impaling Poole of Sapperton'. No trace remains today of this 'little Coate'.

Sir Edward Poole, Sir Nevill's eldest son (1618–1673), succeeded him, and kept out of trouble; at the Restoration no question seems to have arisen of confiscation of his lands. He carried on the Parliamentary tradition, representing in turn Wootton Bassett, Chippenham and finally Malmesbury. It was he who entertained John Aubrey at Oaksey in 1670. Sir Edward, Aubrey noted, 'hath this privilege, that nobody can be arrested in this manor without his consent'. I have found no confirmation of this.

The best oaks in the county were those in Oaksey Park, Aubrey observed, adding a typical comment. 'When an oake is felling, before it falles, it gives a kind of shreikes or groanes, that may be heard a mile off, as if it were the genuius of the oake lamenting. E. Wylde, Esq., hath heard it severall times'.

He also referred to the 'wich-hazells', a local name for wych-elms. 'There are two vast wich-hazell trees at Okesey Park, not much lesse than one of the best oakes there'.

Sir Edward's eldest son, another Nevill, was born in 1636 and in 1670 married Elizabeth, daughter of Maximilian Bard of St Bartholomew in London. Bard was a City alderman and twice, in 1652 and 1663, Master of the Girdler's Company, one of the smaller of the ancient City guilds whose members had, in medieval times, made the belts and garters worn by every gentleman of substance. After the Restoration the craft died out but the Company lived on, as it still does. Elizabeth Bard no doubt brought a satisfactory dowry to the Pooles, as in the case of so many other unions between the wealth of the City of London and the status of the landed gentry.

In six generations of Pooles of Oaksey, Elizabeth Bard is the only member of the family to have a tablet, or a tablet that's survived, erected in her memory in the church, and she didn't even start or end her life as a Poole. Sir Nevill predeceased her, and she married John Strange of London. She died at the age of fifty-eight, having, in 1672, produced an heir, another Henry, who in 1692 married Elizabeth, one of the thirteen offspring of Sir Thomas Earle of Eastcourt. When their son and heir, also called Henry, died in 1726, the male line of the Oaksey Pooles ended.

This last Henry left two daughters, Finetta and Elizabeth. In 1713 Finetta married Benjamin Bathurst, a younger brother of the first Earl Bathurst and son of Sir Benjamin, Governor of the East India Company and Cofferer to the consort of Charles 1, the first of this family to settle near Cirencester and to become lords of all they surveyed. The unfortunate Finetta bore him twenty-two children. Understandably expiring after this, she left him free to marry again and beget fourteen more. (I think of them sometimes when assured by opponents of population control that, as peoples' standard of living rises, so do their families shrink; the Bathursts were scarcely in want, and nothing stopped *them*.) Oddly enough, of Finetta's enormous brood only one, a daughter, appears to have had surviving issue.

It was this Benjamin Bathurst who, in 1732, sold the manor of Oaksey. As Finetta's sister Elizabeth was unmarried and her trustees dead, an Act of Parliament had to be passed to enable him to do so. The buyer was Sir Robert Westley, dismissed by Britton as 'an army taylor', who bought at the same time the manors of Kemble and Poole, then also in the county of Wiltshire.

22 September – LORD MAYOR OF LONDON

From the little I've been able to find out relating to Sir Robert Westley, he seems to have been something of a Dick Whittington figure (without the cat). A village boy from Barminster in Wiltshire, he was apprenticed in 1689, at the age of nineteen, to a London tailor, and six years later admitted as a freeman of the Merchant Taylors' Company. If Britton is right, presumably his fortune was amassed by making army uniforms, and no doubt augmented by his marriage to a lady, Elizabeth, who acquired eighteen houses in Bond Street, Albemarle Street, St Christopher Street and Piccadilly.

His own investments in property were considerable. By 1738, when he made his will, he had land in Essex, Hertford and Eastham as well as his three Wiltshire manors, and property in Cheapside, Long Acre, Cannon Street and elsewhere in the City of London, not to mention plate, jewelry, furniture, a library (at Kemble), coaches, horses and other appurtenances of a rich man. All this was left to his wife for her lifetime and then to be divided between his three children, Alice, Elizabeth, and John.

He was no less active as a public figure than as a merchant tailor. In 1737 he became Master of the Merchant Taylors' Company; he was an alderman and sheriff of the City of London, and president of the Irish Society, which looked after those dragons' teeth, the plantations of Protestants in Ulster for whose support contributions had been wrung from the reluctant City Companies, almost ruining some of the smaller ones in the process. In 1744, he was knighted and became Lord Mayor.

His term of office wasn't uneventful. In March 1744 he paraded through the City with trumpeters, constables and sheriffs armed with javelins and halberts to proclaim the declaration of war against France. By royal command he supervised a house-to-house census of all 'Papists, Reputed Papists and Non-Jurors' who were summoned before the Justices to take the Oath of Allegiance. Towards the end of the year, violence and disorder had reached such a pitch that he and his court of aldermen addressed a petition to George II. 'Numbers of evilly disposed persons, armed with Bludgeons, Pistols, Cutlasses and other dangerous weapons' were committing many outrages 'upon the persons of Your Majesty's good subjects', and a plea for quicker and more severe execution of justice was made.

A year after completing his term of office, Sir Robert died, desiring in his will that he should be buried at Kemble – born in Wiltshire, evidently his heart was there – and that, should his son John die without lawful issue, Kemble and Poole should pass to his daughter Elizabeth and Oaksey to his daughter Alice. John survived his father by only three years and was evidently childless, since his sisters inherited the manors as their father had wished. Alice (the elder) had by then married Benjamin Adamson of Henley-on-Thames, and Elizabeth become the wife of Charles Coxe, a descendant of the hanging judge of Nether Lypiatt.

23 September – THE ADAMSONS

I've had a very limited success in discovering anything about Benjamin Adamson. He was evidently a man of substance, since he lived with his family at Phyllis Court, that handsome dwelling, now a country club, whose gardens slope down to the Thames and provide a perfect vantage point for watching Henley regatta.

He wasn't the owner, however. In 1771 a claim was made by Sambooke Freeman of Fawley Court on behalf of his tenants, Benjamin Adamson included, for exemption from militia tax. And in the same year a sale was advertised of Adamson's goods at 'Philip Court his late residence'.

Did the Adamson family then take up their residence on Alice's manor of Oaksey? Possibly; nine years later (1780) the list of land tax assessments gives the names of Benjamin Adamson and his son Robert as joint owners and occupiers of the manor house. Three years later the *Gentleman's Magazine* noted, with no details, the death of Benjamin Adamson of Oakly, Wilts.

Son Robert became a Member of Parliament for one of the briefest periods in history. An inglorious period, too; elected for Cricklade in the summer of 1784 in partnership with his cousin Charles Westley Coxe of Kemble, he was unseated in the following February, together with his running-mate, as the result of a petition presented by the two defeated candidates, which alleged that thirty-two fraudulent names, plus those of forty paupers, had been added to the voters' register. The investigating committee not surprisingly concluded that the returning officer had been 'partial' to Adamson and Coxe.

Even by the standards of the eighteenth century, Cricklade was renowned for the corruption of its electoral practices. In 1872 an Act of Parliament 'for preventing of bribery and corruption in the election of members to serve in Parliament for the Borough of Cricklade in the County of Wilts' had received the Royal Assent. Like so many other Acts of Parliament, its excellent intentions were thwarted by the dogged determination of the English people to go on doing wrong. To what extent Robert

Adamson of Oaksey was personably responsible for the skullduggery of
1874 there is no way of knowing. The debate of the investigating committee was 'acrimonious, prolonged, and completely inconclusive', according
to Dr T. R. Thomson's *Parliamentary History of Cricklade.*

During his brief parliamentary career, Robert Adamson made no
speech and cast no vote, so it seems unlikely that a potential Prime Minister was addled in the egg at the age of thirty-two, when he was obliged to
retire into the perhaps not uncongenial life of a country gentleman. He
never sought re-election. Four years later, he put his Oaksey property up
for sale and vanished from the scene.

24 September – GARROWAY'S COFFEE-HOUSE

On 7 November 1787, the manor of Oaksey was offered at auction in
separate lots at Garroway's Coffee-House in Change Alley, London.
'Particulars of the Sale', preserved in Swindon's public library, show the
freehold property to have comprised 1,314 acres, with a rent-roll of
£1,521.15s per annum, plus another £293.15s due on 178 acres let by
'copy and lease'. There was also the Rectory with its glebe, valued at £250,
whose 'perpetual advowson and next presentation' went with the 'genteel
small mansion house', having ten bedchambers, a dining parlour, hall,
drawing-room, kitchen and other offices; there was also stabling for twelve
horses, a walled kitchen garden, a coal house, servants' quarters and lofts.
A small property as things went.

Evidently the lord of the manor, Robert Adamson, didn't live there, for
the tenant of the mansion was James Hawkins. John Burgess had Park
Farm with its 'new built farm house' and John Hawkins, a brother of
James, held the lease of 'Clottengar' Farm. Dean's Farm had a 'new built
dwelling house' with Thomas Darke as tenant.

I find myself greeting as old friends these Oaksey names when they crop
up in old documents. William Earle, aged seventy-five, was living in a
cottage with two tiny paddocks – perhaps on Earl's Corner? There were
several Oatridge's, also Lucian Manby (of Manby's Farm), Mrs Pill (Pill
bridge over Braydon Brook?), Richard Boulton and Widow Hawkins.
Woodfolds was leased for £180 a year to John Dore.

What struck me most about the particulars of this sale was the very high
farm rents, then a good deal higher than they were to be a century and a half
later, despite changes in the value of money. Clattinger Farm, for instance,

was let in 1787 for nearly £4.50 an acre. When we came to Woodfolds in 1938 the annual rents of farm land were mostly under £3 an acre, and it wasn't until the 1960's that they bounded upwards. In the last ten years, they've risen by a factor of four or five.

Unfortunately the catalogue gives neither the prices fetched on that November day at Garroway's Coffee-House, when the manor was broken up for the first time since the Doomsday Survey, nor the names of the buyers. But a sizeable portion of it, perhaps about half, passed into the possession of James Harris, a distinguished diplomat, who was raised to the peerage in the year following the sale and, two years after that, created first Earl of Malmesbury.

James Harris's home was in The Close in Salisbury. At the time of the sale he'd probably have known of his impending enoblement, and may have been looking round for a suitable title; Salisbury was pre-empted, Malmesbury had a pleasing sound and here was a nice little property with Malmesbury as its market town. Or it may have been the other way round; he may have bought the property as an investment, and its postal address inspired his choice of a title. He bought the 'mansion house' itself and four of the farms: Park, Woodfolds, Dean and Manby's; the others went to different buyers, in some cases probably their tenants.

Whether James Harris bought this property at the sale, or later, there is no way of knowing. Oaksey rent-rolls preserved among the Harris papers begin with the half-year ending at Michaelmas 1795; but earlier ones may well have been lost or destroyed, since a new agent, Francis Webb, took over probably in that year, and may well have started a new set of books. The half-yearly rents in 1795 amounted to £550.15.6d and remained stable until Lord Malmesbury sold the property in 1801. The buyer was his agent and next-door neighbour in Salisbury Close, Francis Webb.

That Lord Malmesbury never occupied his Oaksey manor-house seems certain; he was constantly abroad on diplomatic business – a kind of eighteenth-century Kissinger – and had a London house as well as his family residence in Salisbury Close. The running of the small estate was left to his agent, and James Hawkins continued for some years as tenant of the Park.

25 September – GODDARDS OF SWINDON

Before the Great Western Railway engulfed it, Old Swindon must have been an attractive little hilltop village, with a wonderful view down across

the vale, a prosperous market, gardens and farmland intermingled with
shops and houses, coppices, a fine parish church; little did it dream of the
fate that lay in store.

My aim was to inspect The Lawn, or rather the site of The Lawn, for
the house, like so many others, has been demolished. This was the residence
of the Goddard family, grandees of Swindon since the fourteenth century,
and the house where our Kitty Cook was in service with the last Goddard
to live there. Halcyon days, in her recollection; she was young and pretty;
The Lawn retained much of its former splendour; she recalls a long
mahogany table set with silver candelabra when she was parlour-maid to
Major Fitzroy Pleydell Goddard, who died in 1927.

The house has gone, but there remains the chancel of a little chapel
dated 1154, and a sunken Italian garden. The Swindon Corporation, as it
then was, preserved the gardens, which were laid out by a pupil of
Capability Brown. In it are some wonderful old trees now showing their
age; a huge beech rests one arm on the ground in the reclining posture of
a Roman *bon viveur*, while a neighbouring beech leans over it with a
motherly air. Wych elm, holm oak, ilex, sycamore, chestnut; all sorts of
evergreens; spruce, fir, hemlock, a great variety. And then far below – you
stand as on the quarter-deck of some gigantic vessel – stretches away the
vale which once was open country and has now become a vast conglomera-
tion of houses, houses, houses, patterned by radiating roads. Beyond lies
the crisp outline of the Marlborough Downs.

What a site and what a view. The public library preserves photographs
of a dignified greystone mansion of the period of George II, its façade
topped by a balustrade set with a row of pineapple finials. Below lay a lake.
In the days of the Goddards the eye would have skimmed over it to take in
a green uncluttered vale, most of which belonged to them.

While beautiful to look at, the house was inconvenient to run. Kitty
remembers scurrying down long corridors miles from the kitchen, bearing
plates and dishes. Didn't the food get cold? 'The cook didn't allow it to.'
'But she could hardly have prevented it.' 'You should have felt the dishes
when I picked them up, they scalded my hands.' 'Didn't you ever drop
one?' Kitty smiled, forgiving this insult to her expertise. 'Never.' There
were thirteen servants living in, plus butler, housekeeper and a man they
called 'the second horseman'. Mrs Goddard, a great huntress, kept her
horses in a row of stables which still stands, across a narrow lane called The
Plank. Meets were held sometimes at The Lawn, with footmen taking
round stirrup-cups. Gamekeepers in green velveteen breeches would come
to report on the state of the coverts. Right in the middle of Swindon.

There was a dark tunnel, Kitty said, running from The Plank to the back entrance of the house, and after nightfall, when the girls were returning from their afternoons off, the footmen would swathe themselves in sheets and scare the girls out of their wits. 'Young beggars,' Kitty said with affection. The girls would run away screaming and 'one of them ran all the way to Wroughton' – about four miles. 'We had a good time in The Plank.'

Although the Goddards did not hold the manor of Swindon until 1563, they owned property in the neighbourhood long before that; there survives a deed dated 1346 concerning their acquisition of a tenement in Newport Street, High Swindon, from Constance Dolyn. Their fortunes were made by a Welsh marriage resulting in a gift to Thomas Goddard by Rice ap Owen of Pembrokeshire and William Watkyns of Llangorse, Brecon, of the reversion of the manors of Nether and Over Swindon, including 60 messuages, 40 cottages, two water-mills, one dove-cote, 100 gardens, 100 orchards, 600 acres of land, 200 acres of meadow, 120 acres of pasture, 30 acres of wood, 100 acres of heath, also the fair and market of Over Swindon (up on that hill). Almost the whole of modern Swindon, in fact. Later, they acquired also the manor of Wanborough.

From the Thomas of 1562–3 followed a long line of Thomas's and Ambrose's. In 1691 the Thomas of the day had in his custody arms sufficient for more than a hundred men. Starting with an Ambrose in 1741, each Goddard of the next three generations sat in Parliament as Member for Cricklade. In the nineteenth century the Empire called several young Goddards to its service. Some perished tragically. Major Ambrose of the 14th Light Dragoons died in the Punjab campaign at the age of thirty-two; when the news reached Swindon, on 7 July 1854, a notice was posted on the doors of the theatre cancelling that evening's performance. John Hesketh, when serving as a midshipman in the Royal Navy, leapt aboard a pirate vessel to grapple with a man about to fling a lighted torch into the hold; he was too late and was blown up together with most of the pirates and eight of his men.

The decision of the Great Western Railway, made in 1840, to establish its works here and house its workers at the bottom of the hill signed the death-warrant of Old Swindon, The Lawn and the Goddard way of life. Their name survives in the Goddard Arms, an attractive old inn, in Goddard Avenue, and on deeds of lease, sale and mortgage of their former messuages and meadows such as Eastcott Mead, Oxenlease, Brockwell, Trulocks, Walcott, Mudge Close, Shortland Furlong, Fludwell, Lapwings, Two Lights, Peake's Hay, Okus Grounds, Small Gains. Many of these deeds record the occupations of the artisans and smallholders who were party to them: brazier, glover, quarrier, feltmaker, fellmonger, waggoner, cordwainer, buttonmaker, roughmason, shearman, husbandman, barber, sackmaker, joiner, clerk. Swindon's only industry before the nineteenth century was the quarrying of limestone.

The last of the line to live in Swindon was Kitty's employer. She cherishes a photograph of a white-haired, white-moustached old gentleman with a bird perched on his shoulder and a kindly expression. Birds fed from his hand and flew about the house. He had the old-fashioned, courtly manners of his generation and was – truly, Kitty says – liked and respected by all. He lived to be nearly ninety.

26 September – MIGRANTS

This is perhaps the saddest day of the year, when you wake up to see the telephone wires bare as winter trees. No more swallows. Yesterday they were sitting wing to wing on the wires (electricity as well as telephone wires, and I used to wonder why they didn't frizzle until someone explained that they'd need to have one foot on a wire and one on the ground to be electrocuted); today, there isn't one.

For several weeks the clusters have been thickening: restless little gatherings, taking off for short flights and returning to the wires to wait, but not serenely – keyed up, somehow. To wait for a message that the moment has come to start on that tremendous journey over continents and seas that will end, for the survivors, five thousand miles away in southern Africa.

How does the message come to them? Is there a leader who gives the signal, or does some corporate urge build up to a climax in those small pulsating bodies? At what hour did they leave?

Fortunately, swallows don't deal in statistics; a little book about them that I bought because I liked the picture on the jacket tells me that two out of three who start from England will never arrive. And what a journey. A bird ringed in Johannesburg on 11 April 1956 was caught thirty-four days later in Siberia, 7,500 miles in a bee-line – and swallows don't follow a bee-line but fly further. Most of ours from England, apparently, fly right down to the Cape, but aren't in so much of a hurry in the autumn as they are in spring.

Some of those who took off last night were doubtless born under the rafters in the old cowshed at Woodfolds, where two or three pairs nest every year. One morning this summer I watched about half a dozen young ones playing just outside my window: swooping, banking, darting, soaring with that superb effortless ease that gives a lift to the heart. They spun through the air as swiftly as bullets, enjoying the exercise of their new-found skill, their total muscular control, the freshness of the morning and each other's company. They looked so clean and shining in their new-fledged plumage, white and steel-blue.

Scientists can get men to the moon and rockets to the planets, they can tell us what goes on millions of light-years away, but they can't explain why those little birds took off last night from those wires, how they are at this moment navigating by day and night across Europe and Africa – the young go first, so it can't be memory – and how the survivors will find their way back next spring to the shed where they were born. Personally I hope they never will. Let's keep some mysteries.

27 September – CLATTINGER FARM

Clattinger lies off the Somerford road, along a track running at first through briars and brambles, then across an open pasture. 'You'll always find Odys living way out in the middle of a field,' Harold said. He and his wife work this 157-acre farm single-handed.

What's more they do so in an out-of-fashion, non-labour-saving way. There aren't many farms left nowadays like Clattinger, which has got into scientific journals and last year was visited by thirty-five scientists from all over the world. Why did all these learned individuals converge upon this level, Thames-side stretch of grassland that floods every winter and grows no crops? Precisely that, because it grows no crops and so these pastures have never been ploughed.

Never, certainly, within living memory, and Harold believes the 'never' to be strictly accurate. 'These are the original pastures,' he said. 'We've got the grasses, the wildflowers just as they used to be. The old-fashioned wildflowers.' Cowslips, buttercups, orchis, cuckoo-pint, purple scabious, yarrow, great burnet, snakeshead fritillaries. This is because he's never used a chemical spray and (one feels) would rather die than do so.

There's only six or seven inches of top soil on these fields, and then gravel. The Odys could make a fortune any time by selling to the extraction companies. 'But we don't want a fortune,' they said. 'We want the farm. There've been Odys farming in North Wilts for five hundred years.'

Not, however, at Clattinger, which once belonged to an ancestor of Percy Hawkins' known as Withypole because he was tall and gangling, and had planted a bed of withies for the better baking of his bread. The shoots, tied in bundles, burnt to a fine white ash that could be swept cleanly from the oven. The withies are still there. Withypole led a troop of Wiltshire yeomanry to Bristol in 1831 to help quell the Chartist riots.

Harold's father farmed near Dauntsey, and until he was twenty-three Harold and his brother drew no pay and had no holiday. If they needed pocket-money their father gave it to them, but they needed very little, Harold said. Their father had been brought up in a hard school. When he was twelve, *his* father had been thrown from a pony-trap and killed; as the eldest boy, he had to take on a man's responsibilities and, with his mother, run the farm and provide for the education of his younger siblings. All got a good schooling and did well in life.

It was a hard struggle, and Harold's father learnt to count every farthing. He'd go to London to buy cab-horses which could be had for a song, then build up their physique and sell them at a handsome profit. He never had his horses shod, but would file their hooves so level that shoes could be dispensed with. He bought other horses on the far side of Wales, and walked them to Cirencester market tied head to tail, twenty in a string. This went on into the early 'thirties.

When he'd got together enough money, Harold's father took the tenancy of a larger farm, Idover, from Lady Meux, whose husband had lost both legs, but used to shoot snipe from a wheel-chair. Lady Meux ran the estate with authoritarian efficiency. There's a moat at Dauntsey Park. Lady Meux carried a gold-headed cane. One day she said to her bailiff: 'Will you fetch me my cane?' 'Yes, m'lady.' With that she threw the cane out into the moat. The bailiff plunged in, fully clad, retrieved the cane and brought it to her, like a dog. What did she do that for, I asked? 'To test his loyalty.' She was a good landlord, Harold said, and after some years his father was able to buy his own farm and, as times went on, several others, including Clattinger.

Harold doesn't take his tractor from its shed for three months every winter, because of the harm it would do to his flooded fields. He has no covered yards, but winters his cattle in the fields and carries out each bale of hay to them on his back, using a prong. Four thousand bales last winter. Hard going for a man in his fifties. 'What happens if you fall ill?' 'You don't.' An aspirin and a nip of whisky keeps you on your feet.'

He's never bought a bag of fertilizer, he says, nor a ton of cattle cake; the cattle spread their own dung; no need for expensive machinery. It's a natural cycle. One year, they picked seven hundredweight of mushrooms by the brook. I could scarcely credit it – over seven hundred pounds of field mushrooms, which in many parts have disappeared. Such a crop has never come again at Clattinger and Harold doesn't know why it came in that particular year.

He makes the old-fashioned, sweet-smelling, soft meadow hay which he believes to be much more nutritious than seeds hay made from modern leys, as well as more appetizing; there's so much more variety for the cattle – twenty or thirty species, possibly, of grass and herb, instead of two or three. He'd like to make hay as his father did, without machinery, handling every bit with a prong, but that's too old-fashioned even for Harold. He can hardly call out half a dozen women with sun-hats and ell-rakes for a shilling a day. He remembers his father running his hand down the side of a rick and releasing a shower of tiny seed-pods of ladyfinger, a vetch whose seeds are rich in protein. Machinery would knock all these seed-pods out.

Clattinger was mentioned in Doomsday Book and there was a farmhouse here in the fourteenth century; traces of it remain in the present house built in the seventeenth; there are workmen's initials carved on a beam and dated 1635. When the Odys came, the house was in a very dilapidated state; bit by bit they've done it up themselves, spreading the work over thirty years and restoring it, so far as they were able, to its original condition with modern comforts added. There's a big cheese-room under the roof above the bedrooms, and a circular oak staircase so steep that when Mrs Ody was taken seriously ill she had to be slung in a blanket to be carried down, since it was impossible to use a stretcher.

When Harold had to repair the roof he bought some tiles off an old farmhouse at Foxley, and was told that they had come, in turn, from the ruins of Bradenstoke Priory. There was a legend attached to this Priory concerning a novice who fell in love with a monk said to be seven feet tall. When workmen were pulling down part of the ruins, they came upon a walled-up skeleton. It was seven feet tall.

One of Ody's predecessors at Clattinger was William Morse, depicted in an old photograph wearing a bushy beard, a kind of skull-cap and a shrewd, sceptical expression. Percy Hawkins tells a story about him. Refreshing himself on market day in the Black Horse in Cirencester, William observed a very tall stranger enter the bar. Speaking loudly in broad Wiltshire, William began to brag about a row of beans growing in his garden. 'I'll bet any man a pound', he said, 'however tall 'ee be, 'ee can't stand upright and touch the top of they beans with 'ees hand.' 'However tall 'ee be?'

inquired the stranger. 'However tall 'ee be, and if 'ee has the longest arm in England, 'ee won't stand upright and touch the top of they beans.'

The tall stranger took up the challenge and accompanied William in his pony and trap to Clattinger Farm. 'Now, where be they wonnerful beans of thine, as I can't stand upright and touch with me ha-a-and?' William Morse led him to the kitchen garden and pointed to a row of dwarf beans.

Today, less than a mile from the farmhouse, amid a waste of mud and chewed-up pastures, monster gravel excavating machines are dragging the guts out of these Thames-side water-meadows, ringing Clattinger as if poised for the kill.

October

3 October – JOS SCREAMS EVERY DAY

Halfway through ordeal by grandson, seen by his parents as a period of breaking-in to get the old grey mare accustomed to future duties.

'I scream every day,' Jos says complacently to neighbours who inquire how we're getting on. How right he is. How often we all feel like screaming and how fortunate he is not to have to worry, just go ahead and scream and unload frustrations. And how many frustrations there are. Bringing up children consists almost entirely of imposing more and more, in order, if possible, to turn them from egocentric savages into at least the semblance of a human being. No wonder Jos screams every day, let him scream while he can and make the most of it.

The question of how to deal with Jos is the same, in essence, as the question which currently preoccupies our political leaders, of how to deal with the nation. Basically there are two methods; appeasement and confrontation. Naturally one leans heavily, like Mr Wilson, on appeasement. Jos wakes up early. I mustn't get him up at six o'clock, partly in my own interests and partly in those of his parents, who eschew early rising. On the other hand confrontation at 6 am is uncongenial; and it's all right for Jos to scream every day, but not *all* day.

So this morning I tried a banana: you can have a banana if you go back to bed. Jos agreed to this but of course only for so long as it took him to eat the banana. The social contract was then thrown to the winds. Jos is now around on the upstairs landing. I hear ominous thumps and bangs and he's probably catching a cold, but on the other hand he's still upstairs and isn't actually screaming. So appeasement has more or less worked so far.

But of course there's a limit. Today one banana, tomorrow two bananas? Three? Breakfast in bed? Jos at two-and-a-half has long ago caught on to the principles of blackmail, which follows on appeasement as the night the day. There comes a time when Wilsonian tactics simply must give way to Heathian confrontation. My tone changes from cajolery to a barrack-square bellow. Orders are given. Intimidation is tried. All right, kick the door in if you like, it hurts you more than it hurts the door. (I hope: the doors are only made of hollow veneer; once, when we sawed a bit off the bottom of one, we found the inside to be stuffed with egg-cartons.) The screaming becomes demonic and continues unabated for what seems like hours and one hopes it's true that tots don't die of apoplexy.

Confrontation does work if one holds out, but then one has full command of all the resources; Jos can't picket the boiler or dismantle (as yet) the fuse-box. But confrontation is extremely exhausting. It certainly exhausts me more than it exhausts Jos.

I wonder how the myth originated that people want leisure. The very last thing any child wants is leisure and children don't turn inside out when they grow up. Doing nothing for an instant is anathema to Jos, and grannie's problem is to find a non-stop supply of things to do for at least twelve hours a day. In few of life's aspects is failure more swiftly punished. Even a moment's silence from the next room, one quickly learns, is ominous.

Today I took him out to tea with Richard, and while his mother and I lingered for a minute or two in the kitchen, the boys ran off and, for a short and welcome interlude, no screams rent the air. They were busy. We found them in the sitting-room, with wood-ash that had accumulated in the big open fireplace strewn all over the room. The only formula for relative peace is constant activity.

9 October – BLACK DEATH

All the elm trees are coming down along the Eastcourt road; every evening the screech of a saw jars the ear; in every hedge you see bleak, leafless skeletons awaiting their turn. The disease has been creeping in for some time from the west and this summer its pace has become a gallop. The disappearance of the elm may turn out to be the greatest change to come over the English landscape since the enclosures.

I was hoping the farmers would replant with other species, but apparently this is too risky because of honey-fungus, which attacks the stumps and spreads to young trees planted near them.

The timber from infected trees can't even be used to make furniture, it goes for firewood. How sad these giants look lying on their sides, done for in their prime, like men killed in battle. What will the rooks do? The've always favoured elms for rookeries. I asked John Buxton and he replied, in his matter-of-fact way, 'They'll go elsewhere. Birds are very adaptable.'

But it's an ill wind. . . . One of the Boultons, a nephew of Old Tom's, has started a one-man business near Minety making bird-tables. So long as new housing estates continue to go up, demand seems insatiable. No semi is complete without a table in the garden. He's been able to stock-pile cheaply enough elm to make thousands of bird-tables.

10 October – POLLING DAY

The radio said that polling was slow in the west of England because of drenching rain. I walked up to cast my vote in cloudless sunshine, encountering old Tom Hicks slowly walking his labrador, the little gnomish Dickie with his fag-end, as always, between his lips, and a tractor loaded with straw bales. At the school Molly, checking in the voters, said that it's been very quiet. In the schoolroom two men sat in silence at a desk without even a crossword to beguile them.

Further along The Street I saw one poster, yellow, in a window, and another red one on a telegraph pole. This didn't, as I'd expected, exhort me to vote Labour, but to attend a Dance with Discotheque on Saturday at Minety.

It was such a lovely fresh October afternoon with warm sunshine that I walked towards Sodam Farm, and didn't meet a soul. There are blackberries still in the hedges. Old 'Scilla Boulton used to say that the devil spits on them after the first of October. Despite this I ate some and they were sweet. On my way home no one was going in or out of the polling station.

Governments come and governments go but the Women's Institute goes on if not for ever, at least for a great deal longer, and this evening the Oaksey branch celebrated its fiftieth anniversary. What's more its first president, Marjorie Oaksey, was there to receive congratulations from present members. There was a splendid buffet supper with red and white wine and a conjuror who kept everyone in stitches. Some speeches, but these were short, friendly and dignified, which is a great deal more than can be said for those we've been treated to in recent pre-election weeks. The evening ended with euphoric farewells rather than with gloom, false hopes and fierce vituperations.

16 October – ALONG THE ISIS

When I had a dog to exercise I used to take her sometimes along a foot-path beside the infant Thames from Neighbridge at Somerford Keynes downstream to Ashton Keynes, passing through a small wood. Level water-meadows, green at any time of the year, lay on either side. In spring these were spattered with fritillaries; you might see a kingfisher, and there was (and is) a heronry on the left bank.

I hadn't been this way for several years until today. A shock: no more water-meadows. In their place, on both sides of the stream, flooded gravel pits. At one point the Isis has been reduced to the condition of an aqueduct, flowing between two narrow strips of bank with a lake on either side. A rutted lorry track has come into existence beside it, and discarded plastic jerricans lie among the dry, brown grasses. The water is a hard dark blue, the western sky indigo, shafts of slanting sunlight illuminate wind-torn trees smothered in ivy, every one of them neglected and dying.

On the gravel strip blooms one solitary poppy. Out of season, out of place, rather strange. How evocative is the poppy, how tragic and symbolic. Nearby, a bird sits all alone, like the poppy, on the withered inflor-escence of a giant hemlock. An orangy buff breast with a pinkish tinge, brown elsewhere save for black bars on the crest, black legs, a small, neat bill; about the size of a robin. It flies silently away. A bunting of some kind? What kind? In my book, the drawing that seems most to resemble it is that of a rock bunting, which has been sighted in Britain only six times.

Scarcely that. Oh for a pocket Buxton, instead of an inconclusive pocket book.

On the gravel pits the seagulls bob about, a piercing white against navy-blue water, mingling with black tufted ducks that show white flashes as they dive. A solitary swan moves silently downstream on crystal-clear water. No sound but for the ugly clank, muted by distance, of earth-raping machinery engaged upon its task of destruction.

On the outskirts of Ashton Keynes, the Manor Farm house that over-looks the Isis has given up hope. Dilapidated, deserted, it doesn't look reproachful, merely dead. In the overgrown orchard some caravans, like waiting scavengers, have gathered under the trees.

Thirteen hundred years ago, the monks of Malmesbury owned all these Thames-side water-meadows; Aldhelm, their first Abbot, built a chapel at Somerford Keynes for local folk to worship in. One of its Saxon doorways survives, built into the wall of the much bigger church which replaced it. The stone remains: but the soil by which the people lived has vanished or is vanishing. Gravel won't make milk or meat. One day we'll find ourselves with a lot of splendid roads, and not enough to eat.

18 October – CO-EXISTENCE

I looked out of my window first thing to see a mist half-concealing the fields; moisture glistened on drooping leaves, tree-trunks looked like masts rising above a motionless grey sea. An autumn smell of dampness permeated the air. Immediately beneath my window, mysterious dark shapes were weaving about on the lawn and leaping like porpoises from a silent ocean.

I couldn't at first make out what they were – long, lithe shapes rising and falling in graceful parabolas over the shrubs and over each other, to and fro, in and out, as if to form a kind of cat's cradle in the mist. So lightly did they leap, no shadow of a sound broke the stillness.

Three young foxes, this year's cubs, at play. Mist beaded their fur. Away they bounded into the orchard, disappeared, then were back under the window: slim as eels, faces sharp as arrow-heads. They played like this for ten or fifteen minutes, then leapt the post and rails and flowed away until the mist swallowed them.

Will the hounds snuff out those gay young cubs before Christmas? I hope not. I'm of the same way of thinking when I see young rabbits popping in and out of the wood-pile, and hear pigeons cooing from hawthorns in the hedge. But it's not at all the same when I survey my demolished broccolis and beak-shredded cabbages.

Co-existence with wildlife, except in very limited fields, is impossible. Admitted that other species have as much right to the planet as we have, if not more—they don't, like us, exploit and ruin it—nevertheless we are stronger, and much more ruthless. If the beasts of the field follow the law of the jungle, we debase it.

Pigeons. . . . A few days ago a fat one, grown over-confident, pecked round my red oak sapling just beyond the garden, less than ten yards away from where I was standing. Well, I thought, I'd better get the gun; he'll be off for sure as soon as he sees it.

I found the gun, a little ·410 with which Charles used to bang away at starlings, and then a cartridge, and tried to remember which way to push the safety catch. Back I went and there was the pigeon, still foraging in the grass. Taking aim, I pressed the trigger and nothing happened; I'd been wrong about the safety catch. The pigeon still paid no attention while I fiddled about with the mechanism. Resolutely thinking of a whole row of ruined cauliflowers, I pressed the trigger for a second time and, with a flurry of feathers, the bird expired.

So handsome it looked, so plump, with its soft, pastel-tinted plumage, greys and pinks and mauves so gently blending; irridescent, as when a drop of oil spreads over a puddle. Who was I to destroy it? By destruction we live. The spade severs the worm, the ear-wig is washed out of lettuces, the lettuces themselves are alive when we cut them. There stands the aerosol spray in wait for flies, the tin of anti-slug pellets. Self-interest justifies all. 'We've got to live, haven't we?' The great unanswered question is, Why?

A mole is tunnelling away under the cabbages, avoiding the trap which is old and rusty. On one of the many scraps of paper I leave lying about the house with notes on them to remind me what to do and get, I write 'mole-trap'.

> All but blind
>   In his chambered hole
> Gropes for worms
>   The four-clawed mole.

But not too blind, very often, to see (or perhaps smell) a trap. A more modern and efficient method is to dig some worms, poison them with arsenic and then put them in the run to poison the mole. No demand now for skins to make waistcoats.

19 October – POTATO FEVER

Park Farm is in the grip of potato fever. All day long, empty trailers hurry up the road, to return full of spuds. Jim has nearly eighty acres of them this year, which means lifting over 1,000 tons, quite a lot of potatoes. It's a race against time with the first frosts due at any moment, and meanwhile too much rain.

And then, last week, labour trouble. Five women are employed on the machine. They stand together on a platform, muffled against the wind, and sort the potatoes from the stones and dirt, by hand.

Last week Jim encountered his female labour force walking back along Shoe Lane two hours before knocking-off time. A strike: not about pay, hours, conditions, demarcation, redundancy or even union recognition. In fact Jim had a job to find out what the strike *was* about.

It boiled down to a problem of human relations. Mrs A, one of the old potato hands, had fallen out with Mrs B, a newcomer, who's incidentally said to be Mrs Something-Else. They would no longer share the same platform. The others didn't want to get involved so everyone clambered off the platform and the potato-ing ground to a halt.

The management set up a one-man Arbitration and Conciliation Service on the spot and, after a spirited session, a compromise was reached. Mrs A and Mrs B agreed to return to work provided that the management came too. So Jim found himself sorting potatoes on the digger instead of driving the tractor to and fro. Worse, much worse, on Saturday morning he had to forego the first pheasant shoot of the season.

It's a case of spuds before sport, however, and no certainty that these troubled waters will yield to oil. 'Are Mrs A and Mrs B speaking to each other now?' I inquired. 'No, they glower.'

29 October – ON THE PLATFORM

A bright, blustery morning with a bitter north-east wind blowing. Jim was a woman short on the potato-digger so I had a morning on the platform. Gloves, two pairs of socks, two sweaters and a wind-cheater but it didn't cheat the wind. Up the moving belt came the potatoes, sometimes in driblets but more often in avalanches, together with many clods and stones which we picked out and thrust down a chute. You have to be quick-fingered. Now and again there's a yell of 'whoa-oa-oah' which, if loud enough, brings the tractor to a halt while we catch up with the avalanche.

With my whole attention fixed on sorting, my experienced companions' ability to make themselves heard over the clatter was impressive. Mrs A even managed to light a cigarette with one hand, despite the gale, while continuing to sort with the other.

'It gets you out into the open and brings in a bit of pocket-money.' Mrs A has been potato-lifting for seventeen years. But there's unease about the future. 'I like to be on good terms with them I work with. I don't quarrel with nobody.' Today everything ran smoothly because one of the quarrellers was absent, but this is only a respite.

This digger will lift up to thirty tons a day, but may already be out-moded. Michael has been to inspect the last word in potato-harvesters, worked by electronic eyes. Up come the potatoes with dirt and stones which electronic eyes can't penetrate, whereas potatoes offer no resistance. So potatoes fall in one direction, dirt and stones in another. No women are needed, no human beings at all. Expensive, of course, but if you work out the cost of wages, it may be cheaper in the end.

29 October – LENGTHMAN

Dotted along below the railway embankment you could see, in pre-war days, little wooden shelters for the gangs who looked after the permanent way. Platelayers, these men used to be called; nowadays they're known as lengthmen. Five men went to a gang, and each gang looked after two-and-a-half miles of line. They had to keep it clean and under observation, weed it, and do running repairs.

Fred, now round the eighty mark, worked as a lengthman for forty-three years and always on the same two-and-a-half miles, between Kemble station and the road-bridge on the Oaksey–Somerford Keynes road.

When the Cheltenham and Great Western Union line was being laid in 1841–2, the lord of the manor of Kemble was Robert Gordon, MP. He was a man of some influence and, at the crucial time, Secretary of the Treasury. Naturally he didn't want the trains to spoil his view from Kemble House, so the line was banished underground through a tunnel, 415 yards long, just before it reaches the station.

The same two-and-a-half miles for forty-three years, from six in the morning until half-past-five at night, might seem monotonous, but Fred didn't find it so. He liked his mates and liked the work; wages were always a little above the farm wage (sixteen shillings weekly, when he started, as against fifteen), so there was a certain prestige attached to being a railway-man. Discipline was strict. If a man was even a couple of minutes late the ganger would swear at him and say: 'I'll wash your eyes out if you're late again.' After a single lapse, Fred said, he never was. 'You had to have a good watch.'

The job carried its responsibilities. If a gang failed to do it properly, a crack London express train might come off the rails. And then there was fogging. Every lengthman was liable to be called out at any hour of the day or night to stand with a lantern, red or green, at intervals along the permanent way, to warn oncoming train-drivers. Fogs were much more common then than now, and much thicker. Once it took him two hours to grope his way to Oaksey Halt (since abolished), about half a mile away.

The only time Fred left his native village was in World War I. He returned unscathed, but one brother was killed and the youngest, Walter, met with a tragic end here at home. (He was named after Walter Long, Mrs Martin's brother; when he was born, Mrs Martin used to come from the Park to wash him, and help generally in the cottage; 'they were good people,' Fred said.) When young Walter left school at thirteen, he went to work for Robert Warner, and one day when he was harrowing in a field called The Lynch, using a ducksfoot drag drawn by three horses, a shot was fired nearby, and the horses bolted. Walter was caught under the tines and mauled so badly that he died.

Fred never aspired to rise above the rank of sub-ganger because promotion might have meant leaving Oaksey. Here he was born, here he's raised his family of four, here lives a married son (an agricultural engineer) with his family, and here Fred lives himself, a widower, at the respectable end of Bendybow. There are two Bendybows: the respectable end where most of the old Oaksey families have gathered, and the newer houses – all equally unpleasing to the eye – which accommodate the foreigners and hooligans.

Fred has seen a lot of changes. When he was a boy, the biggest day of the year in the village, after Oaksey Races, was the Camp, the annual gathering of Methodists from miles around in a field behind the chapel at Earl's Corner for buns, hymns and general jollification. A brass band paraded through the village; the children had an outing in farm carts cleaned and polished, drawn by horses groomed until they shone; it was a great occasion. The Methodists were stronger, then, in the village than the Church. After the second war, they dwindled; services ceased; the chapel was used for storing hay; finally it was turned into a comfortable modern house of just the right size, as it is today.

The greatest change he's seen, Fred considers, has been the rise of hooliganism among the young. 'Nothing like it in my day.' The hooligans are right here in Bendybow, keeping people awake at nights revving up motor-bikes, pinching cars and crashing them, even throwing stones at trains. Police cars, I'm told, are as common as wasps in August round strawberry jam. 'What, again?' the officer says wearily when summoned to yet another incident – luckily, at the other end of Bendybow. Fred's grandsons live at the respectable end and are all right. One is married, one studying to be an engineer like his father. Their parents' recreation is ballroom dancing, enjoyed every Monday evening in the Minety village hall. They've passed their test for the bronze, hope to get their silver next year and then their gold.

31 October – PANNAGE IN FLUSRYGGE

Flisteridge wood has become so overgrown with brambles and bracken, its former paths so churned by horses' hooves, that I don't enjoy my walks there as I used to; anyway, it's not the same without a dog. So instead of scrambling through the undergrowth, I explore the wood more comfortably, if less healthily, in the library. It's not a large wood (about ninety acres) but, as part of the former Braden Forest, not without its history.

To reach it, you cross the Swill Brook by a small bridge on Park Farm, near the buried Roman brick-kiln. This brook was the Forest boundary, and throughout the Middle Ages people who lived on one side of it were governed by a set of laws different from that governing people living on the other side. Forest law was even harsher than the ordinary law of the land. In the Forest, you might take dead wood for firing, but woe betide you if you lopped a tree or trespassed in the 'vert' (the undergrowth). On the mere suspicion of having killed or wounded a deer, a man could languish for years in a dungeon, or have a hand cut off, which might have been preferable. If he kept a dog, it had to be 'lawed' – three claws on one forefoot amputated, so as to lame it for life.

Should the carcase of a deer be found, there had to be an inquest attended by men of the three nearest villages, together with a phalanx of officials. Courts of Attachment were held every forty days, presided over by the King's foresters and verderers, without a jury. The Chief Justice of the Forest held his courts only once every three years, and the ordinary Justices of Assize not at all. Opportunities for a forest-dweller to get his own back on an enemy were almost limitless. Roger Tuck, for instance, must have had such an enemy. In 1209, the bones of a deer were discovered in his dwelling. His story that one of the King's huntsmen had kenneled his hounds there for fifteen days was of no avail; Roger 'lay for a long time in prison so that he was nearly dead' before the truth of his story was admitted. He was freed, but lost everything and was banished from the Forest for ever.

So, by and large, the citizens of Oaksey were extremely lucky to live on one side of the Swill Brook instead of on the other. They had no distance to go to fetch a load of firewood, and if a deer should happen to stray, no inquest need be held on its carcase; if, indeed, a carcase was ever found, which seems unlikely.

The privilege which the villagers valued most was their right of pannage in the wood of Flusrygge (to use contemporary spelling). Flusrygge had belonged to the Abbots of Malmesbury ever since it had been given to them in AD 681 by King Ceadwealla, as part of the manor of Crudwell. But King John 'enforested' it, i.e. put it into the Royal Forest, so depriving the Abbots of their rights. Naturally, it became a bone of contention; and eventually an arrangement was reached by which the Abbot 'had the same wood out of the regard and in severalty against all men's right from Michaelmas Day at noon until Martinmas Day at noon, for the preservation of the mast'.

But by long tradition, and under Forest Law, the citizens of Wockeseye, and of other villages just outside the Forest, had rights of pannage in Flusrygge. So in 1277, the third Earl of Hereford, 'being at his manor of Wockeseye'

there came his people and put the demesne hogs of the Earl and the hogs of his people of the town of Wockeseye into the afforesaid wood; then came the Abbot's people and impounded the Earl's hogs and the hogs of his men, at his manor of Cruddewell. Soon after came the demesne people of the Earl and the people of the town with great force, and broke down the gates and forcibly took out the hogs, and wounded the Abbot's people, even to the death so that the coroner was sent and all the country to look into this great affray. The hogs they forcibly drove back to the wood of Flusrygge and kept them there for fifteen days and upwards with great force of people, so that no one of those who were with the Abbot dared to come near the wood. They forcibly kept them there until all the mast was consumed.

From this extract from the Malmesbury Cartulary (translated by J. Y. Akerman and published in *Archaeologia* xxxvii) we know that the third

Earl of Hereford, who inherited in 1275 and died in 1322, was in residence
at our Court in 1277, which at least provides a firm date. It would have
been a new place then, perhaps not even finished, if the assumption is
correct that it was built by this third Earl's father sometime between his
inheritance in 1220 and his acquisition of a licence to hunt hare and fox
in Braden Forest in 1253.

This second Earl of Hereford, Humphrey de Bohun (the builder of our
Court) was a great grandee: hereditary Constable of England, Marshal
of the Household, former pilgrim to Santiago and Knight Crusader,
ambassador to Prince Llywellyn ap Gryffedd, a member of the Great
Council of 1248. The arrival of such a nobleman with his entourage of
knights and pages, heralds and squires, and a whole army of servitors with
troops of horses, must have created a great stir in our village on the ridge,
whose mud-and-wattle dwellings clustered round the only stone buildings,
the magnificent new church and the even greater Court or Castle almost
adjoining, with its towers and keep and battlements. Strange tales must
have been told of an evening, concerning distant lands and peoples, by
men who had accompanied their lord on the Crusade and fought the
Saracen.

The lord's arrival must also have placed a great strain on the resources
of the neighbourhood; it must have seemed as if a swarm of locusts had
gone through the village when the Earl and his entourage had departed.
One wonders whether the villages hid away their daughters, indeed their
wives, and whether the ancestry of a good many families runs back,
could the truth be told, to some lusty young Norman knight; or, more
probably, to some humbler character: perhaps the serf who tapped the ale.

November

5 November – A BAKER'S TALE

Herbert, my next-door neighbour but one, can turn his hand to anything, and whatever he does, he does it well. I envy him more than I can say and depend upon him, too much I'm afraid, to do things for me that I ought to do myself, but can't. After tea today, for instance, he put a new light into my cold frame.

Icing cakes, strangely enough, is one of his skills. He started as a baker's boy, he told me, at Minety, in 1922. It was a hard training. At three in the morning, on an empty stomach, he had to turn the handle of a machine that mixed the dough. Then he had to fire and rake out the bake-ovens and help the baker, an old man of seventy, slip the loaves in, two by two, with a wooden rake called a peer. And then take the loaves round in a pony and trap, later a motor van. A two-pound loaf sold for 4½d in old currency (less than two new pence.)

When the baker retired, Herbert filled his place, and got good money for those days: forty-four shillings a week. He was married by then, paying a rent of half-a-crown a week for a cottage. The work was still hard, starting at 3.30 am and ending at about 9 pm, six days a week, and on Sundays there was cleaning up to do. 'I was strong then,' Herbert said. 'I could carry a sack of wheat on my back up a ladder, two and a quarter hundredweight, and think nothing of it.' He is strong still.

The depression came, and Herbert's wage dropped to thirty-eight shillings; he made the money up by selling cakes after hours. The art of confectionery he learned by watching his sister, and he practised until he could ice a three-tier wedding cake with professional skill.

When he heard that Arthur Rich was looking for a chauffeur, he applied successfully for the job. How did he cope with that formidable character? 'I got on all right with him because I stood up to him.' There was a moment of truth between them. Arthur, in the back seat, lost his temper and began to cuss and swear in his usual fashion. Herbert put his foot down on the accelerator and drove along the winding, narrow lanes at seventy or eighty miles an hour, taking the corners on two wheels and ignoring Arthur's frenzied bellows. When the car squealed to a halt at Court Farm, Arthur said: 'Parker, don't you ever do that again!' 'I never had any cause to,' Herbert told me. 'Old Arthur quietened down after that.'

'There's never been a man like him for cattle,' Herbert recalled. Tens of thousands of beasts passed through his hands and he never forgot one. He remembered where each animal had come from, what he'd paid, its age and weight. When he went out hunting, he did so less for the sport than for the opportunity it gave him to ride over other people's land and appraise their cattle.

You couldn't cheat Arthur, but nor did he cheat others; he stuck to his bargain and expected you to do the same. When one of his neighbours sold him an animal, he'd leave the cheque behind a clock in the hall and tell the farmer to come and collect it. He was tight with his money – very tight. 'He told me to paint the kitchen once,' Herbert said. 'I said I'd need a brush. "You go out and borrow one", said Arthur.' He left over £130,000 in his will. 'I got on with him all right,' Herbert concluded.

21 November – A COWMAN'S STORY

November goes on, wet and grey, grey and wet; no colour, no movement of air. A kind of limbo. Walls fall down and lie strewn over the verges.

Tractors scatter mud over the roads, cattle stand in gateways hock-deep in slush looking downcast and shaggy. Birds are either black or look it – rooks, blackbirds, starlings.

In Minety Lane I met Tom Boulton hobbling slowly and painfully along with two sticks. He used to be so active and strong. How often have I encountered him and his wife Annie cycling along The Street in single file carrying buckets full of mash on the way to the allotments, and full of eggs on the way back. Sometimes Annie carried home four hundred eggs on her bike, she told me, and then she had to wash them. 'I never broke one.' She and Tom fattened pigs in a shed at the bottom of the garden and she boiled up potatoes for them every day in an old copper.

From school, Tom went to Park Farm to help milk Harry Westlake's cows for 3s 6d a week to start with, and stayed there for twenty-two years. When Harry Westlake left he moved to Dean Farm, still hand-milking; he said he milked seventeen cows twice a day by hand, until machines came in during World War II. He married a daughter of the carter, Albert Picter.

After twenty-five years as cowman at Dean Farm, arthritis forced Tom into retirement. He still manages to work a quarter of an acre of garden but it's painful to see him digging or hoeing away in all weathers, with a chair nearby to rest in now and then. If he gave up working altogether he'd probably give up living.

Tom told me that it wasn't arthritis, as I'd thought, that crippled his father, but *locomotor ataxy*: and all brought on by a tug-of-war. The rope broke not once but three times. Old Tom was 'anchor-man' at the end of the rope, and came down with a heap of men on top of him. 'And they were big men then,' Tom said. Joe Hanks marked on a farm door the weights of everyone who worked at Dean Farm; the lightest was eleven stone and the heaviest, Joe himself, seventeen.

Old Tom went on working for several years after that but gradually grew worse, suffering from cruel bouts of pain. 'Scilla would sit up with him all night sometimes, after her day's work. 'She was a wonderful woman,' her son said.

24 November – VILLAGE CARPENTER

The parish registers provide good quarrying on a wet November day with lights on at noon. The first name is that of William Dicks, buried on 2 October 1670 – the day before a new Rector, Robert Dalton, Master of Arts and Fellow of Queen's College, Oxon, was inducted by the Vicar of

Kemble. The last Dicks of the name, Edwin Orchard, was buried in Oaksey churchyard on 20 May 1938, aged eighty.

There's no proof, of course, that Edwin Orchard, born in 1858, and his father James, born in 1834, were direct descendants of the William buried in 1670, but it seems highly probable, since the name occurs at intervals without a break for three hundred years. Both Edwin Orchard and James were carpenters and Dicks' may have been carpenters long before that; it was only from 1837 that occupations were given in the registers.

Edwin, known as Ted, married twice but had no family, and now there are no Dicks's in the village. Older people remember him well. A sturdy man with strong features and mutton-chop whiskers, and a great teller of tales. Dolly recalls visits to Sodam where he came to do estate repairs. Over a cup of tea in the kitchen the children would crowd round to listen to his stories. At this distance of time, nearly seventy years, naturally she can't recall their content, but remembers one of his remarks. 'When she married, she was a tip-top lady, but now she's the dirtiest effut in Swindon.' Effut is a local word for newt.

Proceeding on an old-fashioned bicycle down The Street from the Wheatsheaf, he rode with his heels pressed down on the pedals and his knees wide apart, looking like a waddling duck. But when on foot he sometimes looked, in Sid's words, more like 'an old hen without feathers'. When he wore out the seat of his trousers he put them on back to front; his trouser-seat ballooned out in front and the fly-buttons strained across his behind.

But what he's most remembered for is his bizarre end. 'Ah, yes, Ted Dicks, he passed on in the lavatory.' What's more he was found there by Lady Florence Eden, an old lady of the old school. (When we first came here, she was the only person who left a calling-card.) Ted Dicks's wife was blind, and Lady Florence came to read to her. One day when Ted failed to return from a visit to the garden, she went to investigate and there he was, dead in the privy. The last of the Dicks'.

25 November – THE MARRIAGE PATTERN

As a change from tracing individual families in the parish registers, I've been trying to get a picture of the village as a whole and of the trends, if any, that have been at work in the last couple of hundred years.

The first thing that strikes one is the stability, the slow rate of change.

We don't, of course, know what the population was in 1670, but although it was almost certainly smaller, I doubt if it was much smaller than in 1811, when the number in the parish stood at 372. In 1972, it was 416.

The annual marriage rate has tended, slightly, to decline. In the last half of the eighteenth century, 1754 to 1803, 136 marriages took place in the Church of All Saints, an average of just over two-and-a-half a year. Exactly a century later, the number fell to 97, an average of less than two a year. This has since remained constant; in the half-century from 1913 to 1962, 98 couples were wed.

Inter-marriage between about a score of Oaksey families has occurred again and again. Until about a century ago, it would have been almost impossible to have been born in the parish and not to be related to the Bakers or the Boultons, the Hawkins or the Sparrows or the Kents, or to families now locally extinct such as Oatridge, Manby, Kight, Haviland, Cove, Dicks or Goddard. The genes of Oaksey must be as inter-tangled as a bramble thicket, but people seem none the worse for that. Physically they are good specimens, often handsome, and village idiots few and far between.

In the first half of the eighteenth century, eighty-eight of the marriages, just over sixty-four per cent, were between partners both 'of this parish'. Only forty-eight Oaksey girls, roughly thirty-five per cent, 'married-out', and most of those looked no further afield than the neighbouring parishes of Crudwell (14), Kemble (6) or Minety (4). Somerford Keynes, Ashton Keynes and Charlton each provided two mates, and the rest were singletons from seventeen different parishes, all of them in Gloucestershire or Wiltshire.

The first reference to a partner from outside these two counties doesn't appear until 1824, when Ellen Holtham married Underwood Price from St Saviour's parish in Southwark, then in the county of Surrey. Even after communications improved and people moved about more, when choosing mates the girls stuck to their home ground or near it. Besides Mr Price of Southwark, during the whole of the nineteenth century I could find only six real outsiders: two more from London, two from Wales, and one each from Somerset and Yorkshire. This is all the more remarkable in that the great majority of girls went straight from school into service and left home, many of them for London. It seems that nearly all resisted the lures of the non-natives and came home to settle down with local boys.

I don't know what this proves except, like most bits and pieces of sociology, something we knew already, i.e. that people in villages used to inter-marry a great deal, and did so less when they could get about more. A change that one could almost describe as dramatic came about after World

War I. The number of marriages between partners 'both of this parish' fell from just over sixty-four per cent of the total (1754–1803) to just under thirty per cent (1912–62); while the number of 'out' marriages rose from about thirty-five per cent to over seventy per cent, and the girls of Oaksey drew their mates from no less than sixty-nine far-flung parishes.

Diversification has been a twentieth-century trend not only among mates but among occupations. In the last century, about twelve out of every twenty infants baptized in Oaksey had plain 'labourers' for their fathers. Between 1913 and 1936, only about three out of every twenty fathers were so described. Two tendencies seem to be at work here. One is greater specialization and a wider range of available jobs; the other, a habit of calling the same job by a grander name. A man may still, in fact, be a labourer, but will describe himself as a stockman, tractor-driver, building operative, County Council employee (i.e. roadman), and so on. And hitherto unknown forms of employment appear, such as marine fitter, machinist, mental hospital assistant, panel beater, golf professional, insurance representative – there's even an ice-cream manufacturer on the books.

Throughout the nineteenth century, only three 'gents' appear on any of the registers. These were William Maskelyne who was at the Park (a tenant) when his son George was baptized in 1817, and in 1839 when his daughter Maria married a surgeon; William Henderson of Flintham House in 1821 and 1823 when his sons were baptized; and Maurice Maskelyne who registered the baptism of a son in 1834. Between 1813 and 1870, the fathers of twelve infants were described as paupers, and forty-two bastards were baptized.

Certain families led the field in the fecundity stakes throughout the centuries. The over-all average wasn't all that high; an average of 3·3 babies were baptized each year between 1837 and 1870. This, of course, leaves out of account those who died before they could be christened. Two brothers Jones, both masons, fathered between them sixteen baptized children. A shoemaker, William West, registered nine; and then there were the Coves. In 1864 Mary, wife of Thomas Cove the blacksmith, produced quadruplets; almost miraculously, in those unhygienic days, all appear to have survived. Blacksmiths' wives have been especially prolific. Ten years before the Coves' quads, triplets had been born to Ann Howse, wife of Thomas Cove's predecessor at the smithy. They survived, too.

Life may (or may not) have been nasty and brutish but it was by no means always short. In the century between 1813 and 1912, nine people lived to be over ninety (Hawkins, Dust, Browne, Mayo, Holtham, Wallace, Boulton twice over and one of the Bakers), and sixty-seven octogenarians

were recorded, many also with familiar names. (Hawkins again, also
Boulton, Sparrow, Manby, Dicks, Mayo, Kent, Oatridge, Hitchings,
Uzzell). The palm goes to Jane Talbot, who, according to *Wilts and Its
Worthies* by Joseph Stratford, died in Oaksey in 1765 at the age of 105;
but she couldn't have been buried here, as her name is not in the register.

Considering the size of the population, a pretty high percentage, for
those days, reached a ripe old age. Perhaps we must thank our 'verie
wholesome aire'.

26 November – A FIREMAN'S TALE

'Spare a thought,' said the rector, 'for the Great Western Railway,' an
institution dear to his heart; the Rectory is hung with drawings of early
locomotives, a brass number-plate in the hall commemorates an engine that
has passed on, old plates and books emerge from drawers, the name Brunel
is greatly revered. There's little the rector doesn't know about classes of
engines and their performances, or the course of vanished branch lines.

It's hard to realize that the Great Western has passed into history. We
still have Kemble station, almost a ghost station when one recalls former
days. No longer a junction; both its branch lines, to Cirencester and to
Tetbury, were Beeching-ed to death and now it's a single-track line from
Swindon run by a computer. No signal boxes, no squad of stalwart porters
and no courteous station-master in peaked cap and freshly pressed uniform,
greeting regular passengers respectfully by name.

The station just before the departure of the 9.05 am for Paddington on
Mondays was a sight in those days. Rolls-Royces disgorged pin-stripe-
trousered, bowler-hatted company directors to mingle with tweedy farmers
emerging from Land-rovers, bound perhaps for the Dairy Show, and ladies
en route to their hairdressers making dates to lunch at Fortnum's; and of
course lesser fry. The third-class day return on Wednesdays cost five
shillings. Now and again the station was a-twitter, as if invaded by a flock of
exotic birds, with girls in maroon-coloured cloaks, clasping lacrosse sticks –
Westonbirt School assembling or dispersing.

There were seasons also for gun-cases and fishing rods. In summer the
platform resembled a herbaceous border with ladies in print dresses,
matching coats and eye-arresting hats bound for Ascot or the Centre Court
at Wimbledon. There were some splendid Guards moustaches, a whiff now
and then of subtle perfumes, ripe Eton and Oxford accents, the words

White's and Boodle's could be heard. Sometimes a young man leading a goat was to be seen. He lived in the Sapperton woods among foxes and badgers, lectured at the Royal College of Veterinary Surgeons and sometimes took his goat with him, I don't know why.

And then there was the Cheltenham Flyer, which in all its pride and glory thundered under our road-bridge past Oaksey Halt. It wasn't merely the Great Western's crack train, it was the fastest train in the world. Railwaymen came from many countries to admire and emulate. In April, 1931, the Canadian Pacific captured the record with an average speed of 68·9 miles per hour. A short-lived triumph; three months later the Cheltenham Flyer clocked up an average of 69·2 miles per hour, and on a famous day in June, 1932, the Treganna Castle (4-6-0), Driver Ruddock and Fireman Thorp, set up a record never broken in the days of steam by covering the 77¼ miles from Swindon to Paddington in 56 minutes 47 seconds, an average speed of 81·6 miles per hour, with a maximum of 91·4 on several stretches between Didcot and Reading. (This, however wasn't a record for *maximum* speed; that was achieved by the City of Truro (4-4-0) drawing the Ocean Mails Special from Plymouth to Bristol, with a top speed of 102·3 miles per hour.)

The Cheltenham Flyer was the 2.30 pm from Cheltenham, 3.48 pm from Swindon, to Paddington, and I don't think I ever travelled on it. Our 9.05 am non-stop from Kemble, drawn also by a Castle engine (green and black), covered the 99 miles to Paddington in 80 minutes and must have travelled very nearly as fast, but it wasn't actually the Flyer. All those trains flew, however; bowler-hatted gentlemen with rolled umbrellas would pause beside the hissing engine on their way to the barrier at Paddington to congratulate the driver and fireman, whose grimed faces looked down with Olympian superiority upon the human stream debauching from their carriages; watches were actually set by it, and should it be even one minute late there were tut-tuts and head-shakings. To be more than five minutes late was unthinkable, and had such a thing occurred it would have been headline news. Time was a god in those days.

Until the rector told me, I had no idea that we have in the village a man who was once on the footplate of the Cheltenham Flyer. I've known Doug Jones for years (Charlie Butcher's brother-in-law) but was in ignorance of this past glory. Today, after tea, I rectified the matter. Doug is a first-rate raconteur and recalled the great moment of his life in vivid detail, hurling imaginary coals in great shovelfuls on to his electric heater with such vigour that one could almost hear the thunder of the wheels and the hiss of steam as the Flyer sped on its way.

Doug started as a learner engine-cleaner in Swindon and had risen to become a junior fireman, working on goods and slow passenger trains, when his moment came. He was sitting in the firemen's hut at Swindon station, awaiting his next assignment, when a breathless foreman arrived. 'This is the day of your life,' the foreman said. 'Get on your bike and ride like hell to number one platform. You're to fire the Cheltenham Flyer.' 'He'll never take me,' Doug exclaimed, conscious of his inexperience. 'He'll bloody well have to,' said the foreman. Doug stayed to hear no more.

He learned later that the Flyer's fireman had been taken ill soon after leaving Kemble station. The driver had scribbled a note, wrapped it round a lump of coal and thrown it out as they passed the signal box on the approach to Swindon station. The signalman telephoned the message through to the station-master – 'replacement urgent'. Doug was the only fireman on hand.

The Flyer with its Castle engine took off from Swindon dead on time and covered the 77 miles to Paddington in the scheduled 59 minutes. 'You did all right, son,' said the driver as they drew up in a cloud of steam. Not far off forty years ago but Doug remembers it as if it had been yesterday.

There was an art in firing steam locomotives, as in most things. The shovel had a short handle, with a face about two feet wide, and could lift half a hundredweight or more at a time. You must keep the fire steady, always at the glow. 'Never put coal on coal,' Doug said. 'Sounds funny, but you must never stifle the glow.' When all was going smoothly, you could pick a time to make tea. You boiled the billycan on the glowing coals, whirled it round your head two or three times with the milk and sugar, and there was your brew.

Or you might fancy bacon and eggs. 'A fireman kept his shovel polished till it shone like silver. A dirty shovel was a disgrace. So on the footplate all you had to do was to give it a wipe with a clean rag, and there was your frying pan – cleaner than most women keep theirs.' Eggs and bacon cooked on a shovel tasted better than any you'd get at home.

Of all Doug's former mates, he remembers Driver Topper Moss with most affection. A stocky man, shortish, who walked about with eyes half closed but missed nothing. 'When he opened them, they were the most beautiful blue you ever saw.' He was a comedian. When they approached a platform lined with passengers, he'd fix a bit of greasy waste to his face to resemble a big black moustache, and lean out waving his arms. Doug would look back to see the waiting passengers doubled up with laughter.

He disappeared once in Box tunnel. Doug looked up from his firing and the driver wasn't there. Gone. 'Rule fifty-five came into my mind.' This stipulated that should a driver suddenly be taken ill in a tunnel, the fireman was to stop the train immediately, get out and cut a wire which set the signals on both sides of the tunnel to Danger. Before he could do this, Topper Moss reappeared. There was a narrow footwalk round the nose of each locomotive, used for inspection purposes and sometimes on trial runs. But never on express runs in tunnels. Topper had felt like taking a stroll with an oil-can to see that everything was all right.

Topper was also a collector. If a train was halted for a while by signals he'd dismount and go in search of what he could find. Blackberries, possibly, or mushrooms. Once it was a sack: 'always come in handy'. He shook it, and a cloud of flour turned him and his fireman into white apparitions; people stared at them amazed when they steamed into the next station. Another time, he saw a roll of wire at the bottom of a flooded ditch. 'Just what the missus wants for a new washing line.' Trying to haul out the wire, he fell into the ditch. Back on the footplate, he took off his clothes to dry and steamed through the next station stark naked.

Rabbits were collected by a form of barter. As the train passed those little shelters beside the line for the use of lengthmen, Doug would throw out a shovelful of coal. On the return run there'd be a lengthman standing by the line holding up a rabbit on a stick, or sometimes several rabbits strung together on a stick bent into a loop, the ends tied to form a bow. Doug would slip his arm through the loop as they went by and scoop up the rabbits.

Water was taken in not only from tanks which stood at many stations, but also from a trough between the rails. As the train sped on at full speed, the fireman let down a kind of scoop; the train's impetus drove the water into it, and then the fireman raised the scoop to fill the locomotive's boiler. Exact timing was demanded for this.

The war came, Doug was in a reserved occupation, wanted his release and grew a bit rebellious. First he deliberately mistimed the scoop, sloshing water all over the cab and into the shoes of a driver (not Topper Moss) he didn't care for; then he tipped out tealeaves from his billycan into the faces of passengers looking out of their windows; he did other frowned-on things, was reprimanded, finally got his release and joined the Forces. After the War he didn't go back to the railway. 'Everything had changed, and so had I. I'd never want to drive a diesel. Might as well drive a tram.'

Meanwhile he'd married an Oaksey girl, so he settled in Bendybow, put up a small shed in the garden and filled it with precision tools to make small objects whose names and purposes I could never attempt to understand. Some are concerned with defence. Also he repairs and reconstructs old clocks. The other day he bought a ninety-year-old bicycle, did it up, and sometimes rides about the village on it, saving petrol. 'I love old things,' he says; and makes new ones. How enviable the craftsman's hand and eye.

29 November – FIREBACKS AND CORN DOLLIES

Since it seems no longer possible to close one's mind to thoughts of Christmas shopping, I headed for the Civic Centre (formerly the Town Hall) in Malmesbury where a craft show has opened. All sorts of crafts from all over the West of England: hand-woven rugs, leather bags, pottery jugs, bowls and ash-trays, engraved glass, saddles, iron firebacks, wax candles, corn dollies, hand-painted door-panels, terra-cotta figurines, tiles, dried-flower pictures, wooden salad bowls and cheeseboards, basket-work, soft toys . . . No end to what craftsmen are producing, beavering away in studio and kitchen.

I think my problem is simply age. As age advances, wants decline, and the space available for objects, whether hand-made or not, declines even faster. It's not only objects I'm unlikely to need like saddles, dog baskets, firebacks and modern refectory tables. Where can one put, in a three-bedroomed cottage, even an extra ash-tray, pottery jug, salad bowl or terra-cotta figurine? And what would I do with a painted door-handle, a cigarette box decorated with sea-shells, or a corn dolly?

One is, of course, in search of presents, but potential recipients of the same age group have the same limitations, although I suppose a hand-woven tie could be squeezed in, even a fat candle or a tile.

Business was brisk however; many craftsmen say they can't keep up with the demand. Such is our nostalgia for a vanished age peopled by honest craftsmen toiling industriously amid the smell of sawdust or leather, throwing pots in the tradition of the Romans, or weaving with homespun yarn, vegetable-dyed, from fleeces of a kind of sheep surviving only in a remote island in the Hebrides.

Back home with two soft toys, a cheeseboard and two framed prints, I encountered Gladys near the church. She'd been cleaning the brass, and complained that 'those boys' had left empty beer-cans in the porch and were knocking bits off the stonework. The telephone kiosk is full of broken glass, old cartons and litter.

'Those boys'. What a different world they live in from the dedicated makers of iron firebacks, painted door-handles and decorative corn dollies.

So does Jack, a pensioner, who came to help me plant three young trees – well, plant them really; he worked at one time for the Forestry Commission so understands trees. 'Always put the stake in first.' (Also, when sowing peas, put in some holly leaves; they keep off mice.)

He told me that when he was a small boy in Hankerton, his father was thrown from a trap and killed at the age of twenty-eight. He and his brother and sister were brought up on what his widowed mother could earn taking in washing and working on farms. The world slump came when he was twenty-one or so, he lost his job as a farm hand, there was no dole, and he was up against it.

He saw an advertisement in the local paper for a carter to look after thirteen horses on the other side of Reading. He walked to Reading, sixty-two miles, and got the job. For the next few years he had charge of four plough-teams (three horses to a team), to be fed and watered, groomed and dressed, their harness oiled and polished, and out by six o'clock in summer, first light in winter, all the year round. Hard work but he loved his horses and was happy there.

He ended up looking after boilers instead, at the airfield, with good pay and short hours, but it made him ill. Like Gladys, he hasn't much time for 'those boys'. His garden is his love now, together with a cat and a small black poodle.

December

3 December – SMALL PRINT

The files of our local newspaper, the *Wilts and Gloucestershire Standard*, start in 1852. Then, as now, disasters and horrible crimes, however far afield, stole such headlines as were considered seemly. Ghastly Murders in Kentucky, Massacres in Ethiopia, Family Burnt to Death in Huddersfield, Railway Disaster in Chile. People were constantly getting mangled in threshing machines, crushed to death in Swindon's workshops, hurled out of overturned carriages, dragged to death behind runaway horses, set on fire by lighted candles, found with throats cut from ear to ear.

Then, as now, the business of the Courts filled much of the newspaper. A sturdy character called Sergeant Bustard stationed in Malmesbury was indefatigable in tracking down crime. 'The Apprehension of a Gang of Fowl-Stealers' was one of his *coups*; four fat fowls valued at twelve shillings had been swiped from the yard behind the King's Arms and poultry thefts were rife all over town. The gang proved to consist of three boys, the eldest of whom was six years old. They were sent to a reformatory for three years.

Teenage vandalism is no invention of our times. In 1868, a gang of eighteen boys threw stones at the Abbey Church during divine service. Sergeant Bustard caught only three, who were fined 3s 6d each; the rest eluded him. Penalties were surprisingly light. Two poachers with several previous convictions, who were making a business of it, were fined £4 each or two months in gaol.

Traffic offences, if not as frequent as today, were of much the same nature – causing an obstruction on the highway and driving without due care and attention. Stephen Pettifer of Crudwell went to sleep while driving a trap, and his horse trespassed on to the footpath; unluckily for him, Sergeant Bustard, clearly one of those men who's everywhere at once, happened to be passing, so Mr Pettifer found himself before the Bench. He was fined one shilling. His son, a retired veterinary surgeon, lives in Crudwell today and frequently, no doubt, watches his own famous son Julian on television.

Oaksey didn't feature much in print; the only crime reported in the 1860s was the case of a young man had up for ravishing a girl from Eastcourt. The annual visit of the Malmesbury Band of Hope, an offshoot of the temperance movement, was well reported. There were high jinks in the school: a lavish tea for thirty children, a Christmas tree, the room 'very nicely decorated with suitable devices and mottoes,' and recitations and dialogues after tea, ending with the doxology.

In this same year (1866) Malmesbury was rocked to its foundation by a *cause célèbre*. The town's physician, Dr Salter, engaged a Mr Fuller as his assistant. Mr Fuller proved to be a most personable young man, aged twenty-seven, who within a month had proposed to four young Malmesbury ladies. One of them, Miss Alice Perring, aged seventeen and a beauty, eloped with him to Cheltenham where they were married. She had a *dot* of £1,500.

It wasn't long before a cheque for £15 cashed by Mr Fuller at a local bank turned out to be a forgery. Sergeant Bustard apprehended Mr Fuller and brought him back to Malmesbury in custody. So convinced were the townspeople of his innocence that some of them smashed the windows of the house of Widow Perring (Alice's mother) who had laid the information.

Mr Forrester, the solicitor, whose descendant practises in the area today, ferreted out the antecedents of young Mr Frederick Fuller. His name wasn't Fuller at all, he'd had several aliases and two previous, and living, wives. As a lad he had enlisted, gone with his regiment to India and married the daughter of a sergeant. After he'd deserted her and returned to England, he bigamously married a well-endowed young lady from Surrey. In turn deserting her, he carried off Alice Perring, the belle of Malmesbury.

In the dock at the Assizes, dressed in black from head to foot and 'looking every inch a gentleman', he had 'a careworn expression', and no wonder. The game was up and he was sentenced, by a rather sympathetic Judge, to five years' imprisonment.

The year 1868 saw a general election. In Malmesbury, the sitting member was a Liberal, Viscount Andover, son and heir of the seventeenth Earl of Suffolk. His Tory rival, Mr Walter Powell, said that he employed three thousand men. 'I consider,' he observed, 'that the man who is an employer of labour is a fit man to represent it.' However apoplectic such an opinion might render a modern trade union leader, it evidently commended itself to the electors, who unseated Lord Andover and returned Mr Powell by a majority of twenty-three (337 to 314).

Probably the Viscount wasn't unduly despondent because a month later the whole neighbourhood turned out to give him a magnificent reception at Charlton Park when he brought home his bride. The train, with a special coach, stopped for them at Minety station where they passed under an arch, adorned with the words 'God Bless the Bride', to their carriage. Along the seven miles to Charlton, mainly through the Suffolk estate, every farm house and cottage was illuminated and several other 'tasteful arches' marked the way. At least two thousand people roared out their welcome on the village green, where the horses were replaced by men who drew the carriage to the mansion. Here a massive silver candelabra, for which fifty-eight tenants had subscribed, was presented to the bridal couple. A memorable feast, with brimming punch-bowl, followed. The Liberal voters, though they failed to return their man, presented his bride with a gold bracelet set with diamonds and turquoises. So the loss of the election can't have seemed an overwhelming disaster to the future eighteenth Earl.

The name of Sergeant Bustard cropped up many times, always in a favourable light; I expected at any moment to come upon a report of his promotion. Far from it, alas. Disaster struck. In 1869 he was suspended from duty for slandering his Superintendent and being in 'a filthy dirty state and covered with vermin'. His wife, it seems, had suffered a long, expensive illness, he'd got deeper and deeper into debt and had finally despaired. A year or so later he petitioned Quarter Sessions for a pension. It was refused, and ex-Sergeant Bustard sank out of sight.

4 December – THE VESTRY

At intervals in the *Standard* files appears a small paragraph headed
'Malmesbury Union' and listing the number of inmates. In mid-1867, there
were 68 adults, of whom 50 were non-able-bodied, and 59 children. A new
relieving officer was appointed that year; there were fifteen applicants, the
salary £90 a year.

A group of about fifteen parishes, of which Oaksey was one, sent its old,
sick and infirm to the Union if their families couldn't support them at
home. Destitute children went to the Union school. At parish level, all this
was in the hands of the vestry. Each parish looked after its own aged and
infirm, as well as idiots and paupers, by means of a poor rate levied on
everyone who owned any property, from the lord of the manor to the
smallest cottage or garden. No subsidies, grants or fairy godmother ex-
chequers in those days. In fact the vestry was a Ministry of Social Security
all on its own, one for each of the ten thousand or so parishes in the country.

'To Jane Barnes, 27 weeks at 2/6 a week, £3.7.6' is the first entry in the
oldest surviving Oaksey vestry minute and account book for 1829. Accounts
were made up half-yearly and were in two parts: outdoor relief in the shape
of weekly payments to the sick, infirm and out-of-work living in their own
homes; and occasional payments. For the year 1829–30 the total was
£314 19s 1d, fairly equally divided between the two heads. Weekly payments varied between 1s 6d and 4s 0d, and were generally about half a
crown or a bit more.

Minuscule by modern standards but, by the standards of the day, a
sizeable sum to be voted in a parish of less than four hundred souls, including women and children and the lame ducks themselves, of whom, in
1829–30, thirty-two received outdoor relief. (The majority were women.)
Not only did the parish get no help from outside sources, it had to contri-
bute from its own meagre funds to the county exchequer.

In 1842, the only year for which the rate-roll survives, the parish had
fourteen farms, on which most of the tax fell. The annual rateable value of
the largest, Park Farm, of just under three hundred acres, was £327 0s 2d.
Next came Court, Church, Moor and Dean Farms, rated respectively at
£160 3s 1d, £157 5s 0d, £154 12s 9d, and £153 2s 0d. The parish was lucky
to have a railway line running through it whose rateable value was assessed
at £416 13s 4d. The total, after deduction of tithe, came to £3,037 1s 4½d,
and the rate was 1s 11d in the pound.

The vestry appointed annually two of its members to be Overseers,
responsible for fixing and distributing relief. They were respectable citizens,

of necessity literate and supposedly honest; in 1830 one was a farmer and butcher Abel Cole, the other a yeoman, John Miles. Both churchwardens, one appointed by the rector and the other elected by the vestry, were *ex officio* members, and the parson often, though not always, presided. No one was paid except the clerk, who got £2 2s od a year and had a great deal to see to, as the Occasional Payments show.

Most of these were for clothing and coals. In 1829, John Taylor got 9s od for a pair of breeches and William Short 2s 2d for shirts. Ann Short got 17s 4d for coals and Hannah Matthews' boy 8s 6d for shoes. Sarah Boulton's boy was paid 1s od once a fortnight: an apprentice perhaps? (To aid apprentices was one of the vestry's duties.) There was unemployment relief: Thomas Baker, no work; Simon Haviland, no work; John Brown, no work; each 10d a day.

There are some cryptic entries. 'To Mr Thomas for return of Idiots.' This item recurred once a year. 'To a man with a pass', 1s 6d. 'The Irishwoman', whoever she was, got a princely payment of £3. Twice a year the clerk took the books to Malmesbury to be audited; the return fare, by William Collett's horse and cart, was 2s 6d. Another regular item was £1 10s od every half-year to John Kent for catching moles.

The clerk had also to attend petty sessions, 'take Rachel Bayliss to Mr Mullings,' deliver sick people to the infirmary in Malmesbury and collect them if they recovered. Postage on letters was variable – you paid on receipt. From Chippenham, seventeen miles, the clerk paid out 1s 11d for a letter, but only 9½d for one from Fairford, fifteen miles. A letter from Newent in Gloucestershire, and another from London, cost 9½d each. In March, 1830, sickness was so rife that between April and September the Overseers disbursed more than fifty weekly payments to sick persons. There was a big bill, £20, to Mr Smith 'for smallpox' – presumably the doctor. The rate rose to 3s od. in the pound, and brought in £357 4s 4d.

One gets the impression, looking through these columns so gracefully written in a hand so much clearer than any today, that no one could go really hungry, fall sick, shiver with cold, go about in rags and tatters or fall into dire need without someone doing something about it: not much by modern standards but something; parsimony no doubt there was, but not indifference. The Overseers were people living in the parish, perhaps next door. They had to sort out the malingerers, and when they'd done so, no detail was too small. In 1830 John Taylor got 1s od for a pair of stockings and in the following year 4s 10d for a smock frock in December, followed by 2d for its buttons and thread in January. Twice a year, M. Burgess was paid 8s 4d for washing and shaving him; evidently John Taylor was infirm.

There was a night stool for William Herbert, 8s od, and a new pot for John Major, 5s od; bread for J. Essex 8½d, shoes for Daniel Beard 6s 9d. One hundredweight of coal for Thomas Wilton, 1s 4d. Coffin for Major's child, 7s od. Half a pint of brandy for P. Ellison, 2s od, and 2 lb of mutton for Thomas Reynolds, 1s 2d. Bedding for Hester Roseblade 12s od. Joseph Hubbard with a bad hand, 2s 6d. Howell Clark for lost time in the snow, 2s 4d. Charles Henden £1 5s od for straw to thatch his house. Twice, in 1833 and again in 1837, 'one shoe for Charles Henden'. A peg-leg, presumably: had he left the missing limb on the field of Waterloo? Bread and cheese and beer for Isaac Boulton's funeral, and 4s 6d for his shroud.

Eventually it all got too much for a small parish like Oaksey, which was by no means so small as many; Cholesbury in Buckinghamshire, in 1801, had a population of 122 of all ages, only two farms, and an annual rateable value of £121. A combination of poor crops and crushing rates drove out the two farmers, and their land lay derelict.

The poor laws had scarcely been altered since the days of Queen Elizabeth I, and in 1834 a great change was made. From 1836 on, our vestry book recorded no more payments for out-door relief of the able-bodied. Parliament set up a central Board of Guardians to even up the treatment of the poor throughout the country. No longer was each vestry required to shoulder the whole burden of its own sick and needy. Able-bodied men and women were sent off to the Union to work for their suppers, instead of having them placed, as it were, on their laps beside a hearth warmed by coals supplied by their neighbours. This was the beginning of the end of the vestry as a vital element in rural life.

From Michaelmas 1836 onwards, the Oaksey accounts noted only 'Disbursements ordered by the Board of Guardians not to be Entered in Account with the Union', which meant that they were confined to occasional payments. Able-bodied paupers, young and old, had gone off to the workhouse. The clerk still took the books to Malmesbury by William Collett's horse and cart, which still cost 2s 6d. John Taylor still had to be cared for; he got another pair of breeches and in the following year another pair of shoes. Soap for washing him cost 2s 11d. Sarah Boulton's boy went on getting his frequent payments of 1s od. In 1839 John Harding was paid £10 for Servicing the Poor with Coals and John Kent the mole-catcher continued to draw his £3 a year.

But the money at the vestry's disposal was cut back drastically, and after 1840 there were no more entries. They were resumed ten years later in the form of short notes of quarterly meetings, when two Overseers of the Poor and two Surveyors of the Highway were elected. From then on, no more was paid out for shrouds or shoes, coals or moles, or at least no records were kept if such payments were made.

As time went on, repair of the roads rather than of the villagers' apparel increasingly occupied the vestry's time. Shorn of its major powers, it continued to function until by degrees church and secular matters separated out, to be dealt with by two separate village councils, called parochial and parish respectively. The last entry in the old book is dated Easter, 1902. The Rector, the Rev. W. J. H. Faithfull, was chairman, and Arthur West (who kept the sub-post office) was clerk; the other members were Robert Warner, A. Morse (tenant of the Park) and Markwell Jennings (Dolly's father).

7 December – A FIFTH PERAMBULATION

Not the best time of the year for a perambulation, with gateways deep in mud and flooded brooks and ditches. The Braden area is wet. I started my perambulation by driving to Cricklade, hoping to follow, as closely as I could, in stages, the former boundaries of the Royal Forest.

The first question was, which boundaries? Through the centuries the Forest had swollen and shrunk like a courting bullfrog. Fifteen hundred years ago Braden was part of the forest of Sealwunddu stretching from the Thames Valley to the Blackmore Vale in Dorset, and Saxon kings hunted here; its first mention is in a charter of 796. By the time of Doomsday Book it had become much smaller; a rough estimate has been put at 15,000 acres. King John, an inveterate hunter, increased it, and by the time of the first recorded perambulation, in 1228, it had swollen again to enclose about 30,000 acres. A squirrel, according to Aubrey, might have jumped from tree to tree between Wootton Bassett and Brinkworth churchyard, about six miles – a red squirrel then, now, alas, all gone.

This first perambulation was a prelude to another bout of disafforestation, and perambulation number two, in 1278, showed a much reduced area. Then came a third perambulation in 1300, and another whose date is uncertain. The boundaries kept on being re-adjusted but after 1300 invariably contracted until the Stuarts snuffed out the Royal Forests for good and all.

My best plan, I thought, would be to take the 1228 boundaries as described in the *Victoria County History*, and try to trace them on the map and on the ground.

This definition starts at the Forest's most northerly point, Hailstone Hill on the Thames between Ashton Keynes and Cricklade. Then it runs along the Thames to Water Eaton→Spersholt→Lydiard Tregoze Pond→Midgehall→Webb's Wood→Brinkworth→Garsdon→Charlton→Braydon Brook →Pill Bridge at Eastcourt→Swill Brook→Stockenbridge→Steort Wood→ Py Hegge (Pike Corner)→along the Thames and back to Hailstone. So far as I can roughly estimate, this perimeter is between thirty and thirty-five miles.

I parked the car by the bridge over the infant Thames at Cricklade, and set off downstream along a footpath over the fields. The sky was dark with heavy cloud, all was sombre and soggy, even a cluster of geese on the bank looked mud-stained and disconsolate and honked in a despondent way.

After all but losing my gumboots in a gateway that had spread across half the field, I came to something worse, and all but indescribable. 'Works' seems the only word, but no one was working; piles of steel rails, planks, enormous concrete pipes, lay about on viscous churned-up clay intersected with ditches. Something was being done to the Thames, forced between huge palisades so far as I could see; and on the right, in the middle distance, enormous machines were pounding away in a field. The 'works' must be a bridge in an embryonic stage.

Squelching on, I found a stile, and then was back among the watermeadows with placid grazing cattle, a line of pollarded willows, grass still green as young apples, as yet untouched by frost. Peace at last, except for the distant rumble of bulldozers. The river, quite suddenly, widened out. It curled and jinked about for no apparent reason, since on either side the fields were absolutely flat.

Water Eaton came into sight: not a hamlet but a large farm. Just before you reach it, the little river Ray flows in on the right bank. The Forest boundary swung due south here to follow the Ray to Lydiard Tregoze, now on the outskirts of Swindon. Two furry young men were lying on the bank with fishing rods. They'd caught a chub, they said.

The early December dusk was falling as I turned back. How quickly can the scene change. All at once, the western sky lightened and colour returned; long banks of cloud stained rose and violet, apricot and dove-grey, swept across the western sky.

The river rippled quietly on, silvery-grey; the light faded; black cattle raised white faces from a pool in the middle of a field; a small vee of wild duck went over, very high. Nearer Cricklade, an alder rooted in the bank leant over the stream and, framed beneath it, against a rose-red sky, stood

out the marvellous four-pinnacled tower of St Sampson's church. An un-
forgettable moment of majesty.

I reckoned I had perambulated about two miles. Another thirty-two or
three to go.

12 December – THE SECOND POOR

Going up The Street to fetch our Christmas cake which Kitty's iced for me
– she's a superlative icer – I found Sid limbering up for an unaccustomed
walk to the church. It's the day for distribution of alms for the Second Poor,
as advertised on a notice in Rodney's shop window.

Who are the Second Poor and who left them alms? No one seems to
know, including the rector and George in his capacity of churchwarden,
on duty in the church to distribute the largesse. This used to be a tanner
each, Sid said, but now its been inflated to fifty pence. Anyone can apply,
but in practice the pay-out is confined to old age pensioners. Any pensioner – what about me? They shook their heads and said ah, well.

It was a dark, wet December afternoon and old Sid was the only
pensioner to collect his ten bob. The rest of the cash, it seems, is put into
envelopes and slipped through the letter-boxes of the other qualifying
individuals.

Since no one knew the history of this annual event, I wrote to ask the
Charity Commissioners, who in due course replied. According to the
Parliamentary Returns of 1786, Henry Pool left in his will the sum of £50
and John Archer the sum of £20, together bringing in £2 16s 0d a year,
for the Second Poor of Oaksey.

The Commissioners are as unclear as everyone else about what
happened to this money. An inquiry held in 1905 concluded that it wasn't
Henry Pool who left the £50 but Sir Robert Westley. Henry Pool must
surely have been the Henry Poole who was the last male Poole to be lord
of the manor and died in 1726; Sir Robert Westley was the former Lord
Mayor who bought the Park in 1732. Evidently the money got mislaid, for
the 'interest long remained unpaid'. When re-discovered, it was vested in
1805 in the names of Francis Webb and Joseph Pitt, and invested in four
per cents. (Today there's £100 worth of 2½% Consols.) Joseph Pitt, living
then at Eastcourt House, had 'frequently advanced money to the churchwardens to be given to the poor' at Christmas.

The question of whether it was Henry Pool(e) or Sir Robert Westley who
left the £50 has never been resolved. A declaration made in 1842 by three

rectors and Joseph Pitt, states without equivocation that Sir Robert Westley was the benefactor. The Assistant Commissioner concluded in 1905 that Henry Pool's £50 'must be regarded as lost or expended'.

As to the Second Poor, they consisted of people who received no parish relief and had no trade or business, but 'got their livelihood by day labour only'. The poorest of the poor, in fact. In 1904, 76 adults and 45 children received the charity – a matter of five loaves and seven little fishes surely, considering that the total sum officially available was five shillings. Joseph Pitt, perhaps, put his hand deep into his pocket. A different matter from 1974 when there were twelve qualifying pensioners of whom eleven didn't think it worth while even to apply, so got their mite slipped through their letter-boxes.

Christmas Day – AN OUTING FOR ANGELS

Well, it's over, the annual guzzle, peeling all those bright wrappings from presents, stringing up gay cards destined all too soon for the dustbin. So much care, skill and effort has gone into the production of those cards, and some are so attractive (Old Masters and birds and beasts particularly) that it goes to my heart to throw them away. Often I've kept a few favourite ones, to be used perhaps as book-markers, but in the end they clutter desk or drawer and must go. What a world of waste we inhabit.

The cottage reverberates with stentorian commands. 'NO, Jos, that frog is Alexander's,' 'Leave Hugh's rabbit ALONE.' Jos has taken to letting off steam almost literally, with a piercing high-pitched yell like a demonic engine. When the boiler and the cats join in and the radio's going, even the Red Arrows couldn't make themselves heard.

The painted wooden angels have come out of the loft for their annual outing. They see the light for about three days and then hibernate, and aestivate, for the rest of the year, like characters in some Greek myth about fertility. They must be forty years old, bought for a few dollars on Madison Avenue and gradually matured into a family tradition. All with trumpets, wings and halos. One has lost her halo over the years.

Rain all day, thinning to a drizzle and then surging back into a storm. An afternoon walk across sodden fields towards the Swill Brook, all deserted, no cattle in the fields, only rooks flying over, an occasional blackbird chattering in a bare hedge, a solitary heron flapping slowly. It might have been the heron who deposited in the middle of a field a grey bivalve, former home of a Swan mussel.

Back to tea and Christmas cake, a faithfully observed tradition but after Christmas Day the cake hangs around and never gets finished; none of us is a tea-eater. 'NO, Jos, do NOT throw your fire-engine at your brother.' 'Yes, thank you for telling me that Hugh's been sick on the floor.'

After quiet reigns upstairs, a goose for our own dinner. I singed it, as advised by its breeder, out of doors, over a pan of methylated spirit, an alarming procedure amid leaping flames fanned by a strong wind. Eyebrows got more effectively singed than the goose.

A wild night, storms continuous and a gale battering the trees and howling and beating at the windows. Snug inside. A typhoon has destroyed the town of Darwin in Northern Australia.

27 December – BRAYDON POND

In the triangle between Minety, Purton and Brinkworth there's a tangle of narrow lanes that twist about among scattered farms with names like Battlelake, Ravensroost, Moonsleaze and Gryphon Lodge, where to get lost isn't just easy, it's almost inevitable. In search of Braydon Pond on a dark night, invited for a drink by its owners, I turned off the road up a muddy track through woods that shook and soughed before a half-gale. No moon, no stars, no lights anywhere. I wasn't sure if I was on the right track and there was no one to ask. Bump bump bump through the puddles. Almost, one began to think of wolves.

Then a gleam shone through trees which thinned out to reveal a fine big house, lights streaming through uncurtained windows, a glimpse of elegantly clad figures within moving about a gracefully proportioned drawing-room. Could this be real? Or a fairy palace in the heart of Braydon?

An old tale came to mind, one of those perennial stories told in many versions and varying in detail, but in essence all the same. A pair of travellers, lost amid remote country lanes, drive up to a mansion brilliantly lit (like this one) and with a sound of music pouring from its open windows. Inside, they see a gay concourse of gentlemen and ladies in silks and satins, wigs and jewels. Clearly, a fancy-dress ball. The travellers summon courage to approach the portico, climb the steps and ask a liveried footman for directions. He obliges, they press a half-crown into his hand and drive away. They come to a village, and put up at the inn.

What, they ask the landlord, is the name of this mansion, who is giving such a splendid ball? The landlord shakes his head, looks puzzled and says he knows of no big house like that in these parts. So next morning, off they go to search. They find nothing. At last they come upon a track that seems familiar, but much more overgrown and rutted than the one they had followed the night before. It peters out among nettles and brambles amid which are fragments of old walls. A glint of something bright catches their eye. On top of a ruined flight of steps among the brambles lies a new half-crown.

Although tonight there was no ball or spectral footman, it was a surprise to find myself in such well-groomed company, listening to a retired ambassador discuss the qualities of different French wines, and a perfectly gowned American lady touch upon the relative merits of Whitstable and Baltimore oysters. Eventually the subject of Braydon pond was dealt with, and I came away with a most interesting survey.

For centuries this pond, the largest in Wiltshire (thirty-nine acres) had been a nesting-place of ducks, a haunt of coot, snipe and heron, and a resort of anglers who sat hopefully for hours beside its reedy fringes. Also a happy hunting ground for pike, which gobbled up the desirable kinds of fish like tench and carp.

About four years ago, the pond and its environs were bought from Lord Suffolk's Charlton estate by a fugitive from City life, Mr Roger Grafftey-Smith, whose ambition was to stock it with trout. To do this, the pike must be eliminated, and the only way to get rid of them was to drain the pond.

When draining operations were well under way, Mr Grafftey-Smith discovered that others had had the same idea before him, probably several centuries ago. To control the level of the pond they had plugged its outlet with a massive elm bung attached to a long oak beam, a crude but effective apparatus whose existence had been unsuspected. The beam and bung were so heavy that he had to get a JCB to move them, and so well fitted that, when removed, water gushed from the pond in a tremendous torrent.

When the pond had been drained almost dry, a chemical called Rotonone was sprayed over its bed and all the fish were knocked unconscious. They were then netted, hauled to the shore, given a fresh-water shower, and put into tanks of oxygenated water – all except the pike, which were left to die. The other fish, mostly tench, recovered, and the dead pike were gobbled up by herons and seagulls.

This flat, squelchy area with patches of scruffy plantation, once the heart of Braden Forest, is actually a watershed between Thames and Avon; so it's not surprising that men from the Avon River Board arrived to find out whether any of this potent chemical was getting into their river. There have been several fish disasters in the Avon in recent years. The chemical was, however, cleared of suspicion, and the now pike-free pond refilled, to offer once again the shelter of its banks to nesting waterfowl.

It remains to be seen whether, in the mysterious way fish have, pike will re-colonize it, as they must have done after it was drained, presumably by the Earl of Suffolk's agents, several centuries earlier; and possibly even before that, when it belonged to the monks of Malmesbury Abbey anxious to make sure of their Friday dinners.

28 December – THE DISAFFORESTATION OF BRADEN

The Pooles of Oaksey were closely concerned with the disafforestation of Braden. This didn't, incidentally, mean cutting down the trees; it meant freeing the area from the Forest law and, as a consequence, enclosing it; as a further consequence, most of the trees *were* cut down. In 1606, Sir Henry Poole (the first of Oaksey) and John Warnefield reported the Forest Lodges to be in such poor condition that one at least was fit only to be demolished.

Did the Sovereigns lodge at these lodges when they came to hunt? Almost certainly not; they would have stayed with one of the lords of nearby manors. When Henry VIII hunted here, he was lavishly entertained in Malmesbury by William Stumpe, 'an exceeding rich Clothier', who, on the surrender of the Abbey in 1539, bought from the King the whole complex of buildings, gave the main part of the church to Malmesburians to serve as their place of worship (as it still remains), and filled the rest of the 'vaste Houses of Office that belonged to thabbay fulle of lumbes to weve Cloothe'.*

'There are many great spoyles, wastes and distractions made and commyted in our Woodes within our Forest of Braden,' complained a Com-

---

* These included, besides part of the church, 'cloisters and chapelles adjoyning, the Dormitory, Chapter-house, Fraytre, Barbary, Infirmary with all lodgings then adjoyning, the Cellarers Chambre, the Squires Chambre, Seint Maryhouse, the Chaundry, the Convent Kitchyn, all the houses in the Sextrey ende, the Stewards Lodging, the Storehous, the Slatterhous, the Stable, and all the other houses in the Utter Courts'. All these were 'committed to the custodie of Wm. Stumpe, deputie to Sir Edward Baynton, Knt' [John Leland, antiquary to Henry VIII, d. 1552]. Wm. Stumpe's son Sir James, MP for Malmesbury 1555–6, was to marry Sir Edward Baynton's daughter; and their daughter and heiress Elizabeth in turn to espouse Sir Henry Knyvett of Charlton. Their eldest daughter Katherine married Thos. Howard, 1st Earl of Suffolk, in 1583.

mission appointed in 1611. James I decreed heavy fines, or failing that 'corporal punishment upon such of the poorer sorte of people as shall bee found offenders'. Pasturing cattle, lopping trees and taking firewood were the main offences. Not that it was only 'the poorer sorte' who offended by any means; Lord Danvers 'hath so lopped and topped the trees that the wood is almost destroyed'. Whether from motives of mercy, or because matters had gone too far to be controlled, on offenders 'faithfully promisinge never to offend againe', the Commissioners inflicted no punishment.

Two years later, yet another Commission reported that 'this Forest hath but a small game of Deere in it for that, by reason of the surcharge of cattell, there is no feed for the deere . . . This Forest yieldeth the King no profit at all more than this game of deere for the keeping whereof the King is at a yearly charge.' Royal forests, in fact, had had their day and the time had come to abolish them. The King, moreover, was desperately short of ready money. So in 1630 the Court of Exchequer decreed the final dis-afforestation of Braden, declaring its lands and woods to be 'the proper soyle of His Majesty and that he might inclose the same,' and ruling that all commoners' rights were to be extinguished. Charles I lost no time in leasing the area declared to be his 'proper soyle', about 3,700 acres, to his Court jeweller, Philip Jacobson of New Fish Street in the City of London, to whom he owed between £8,000 and £10,000. Jacobson set about clearing forest, selling timber and sub-letting parcels of land, and two other City gents, James Duart and Roger Nott (another tailor) joined him in the venture.

If the natives had resented the tyranny of the Forest's officials, they resented even more these alien City merchants who were extinguishing ancient rights of commonage for their own profit. Enclosures would be 'the utter undoeings of many thowsands of poore people,' a local resident deposed, 'that now have right of common within the said Forest, and do live thereby'. No more pannage for the hogs of Oaksey.

The King had undertaken to secure 'quiet possession' for his lessees. Possession proved anything but quiet. In 1631 there was rioting, destruction of landmarks and a threatened attack on Great Lodge where Jacobson's agent was installed. The Sheriff was called out, rioters arrested and gaoled and there was general turmoil; as a result, the commoners won a few minor concessions. But the rest of the land was soon enclosed and let off as farms with substantially the same boundaries as they have today.

The three principal landowners continued to be James Duart, with 1,281 acres; Roger Nott the tailor at Great Lodge with 790 acres; and Philip Jacobson the jeweller with 1,315 acres at Hatton Lodge. These three

City businessmen evidently settled down as country gentlemen. Nearly two centuries later, the Notts were still at Great Lodge and were renting Hatton Lodge as well from Jacobson's descendants; and in 1817, when the Crown finally sold the land, Mrs Catherine Nott still held the lease of Great Lodge and its farmlands.

29 December – SQUIRE MASKELYNE'S YELLOWHAMMERS

The subsequent history of the Forest is bedevilled by a confusion which arose between which parts had formerly been administered by the Duchy of Lancaster, and which by the Exchequer. As both belonged to the Crown, this could scarcely have mattered less; it was a question of two sets of civil servants fighting it out to the finish, and it kept innumerable lawyers gainfully, if not usefully, employed for years.

A single case, involving the status and whereabouts of less than twenty acres, became a thirty years' war, lasting from 1772 to 1804, which must have cost thousands of pounds, and ended in a draw. No one ever did find out exactly what had happened to the nineteen acres, three roods and two perches leased by Queen Catherine (consort of Charles II) to Hippersley Coxe and sub-let to William Maskelyne. In the finish, William had to give up the nineteen acres, three roods and two perches, but as he had made a fortune out of growing wheat in the Napoleonic wars, he probably didn't miss this parcel of land.

There had been Maskelynes in and around Purton and Lydiard Tregoze since Elizabethan times and before that: landowners, farmers and lawyers, the senior branch seated at a house called Basset Down which has lately, like so many other old and interesting mansions, disappeared. One of the family, son of the William of the controversial bit of land and also called William, was the tenant for some years of Oaksey Park; two of his children were baptized in our church between 1816 and 1819. Maurice, probably a brother, had Flintham House at Oaksey, and yet another Maskelyne was vicar of Crudwell. The most famous of the Maskelynes was Nevill (1732–1811) who for forty-six years held with distinction the office of Astronomer Royal.

In 1692 the current squire, Nevill Maskelyn, married the vicar's daughter Anne Bathe. She dressed her brood of eleven all alike, changing the colour of their apparel every year. 'There go Squire Maskelyne's yellowhammers,' and old woman was heard to remark as the children filed into their grandfather's church. The Bathes, formerly de Bathe, were another old landed family in these parts, and this vicar, the Reverend William, added a wing to his parsonage at Purton in order to entertain in proper style his friend the Earl of Clarendon.

I was interested in these Bathes because old Priscilla Boulton of Earl's Corner, was born a Bathe and, her children think, had relatives at Purton. In a family history of the Maskelynes, Mrs Mary Arnold-Forster recalls two old sisters, Anne and Esther Bathe, no taller than children, who in the 1920s walked across the fields, winter and summer, to work in her garden at Basset Down, clad in striped Welsh flannel skirts, homespun jackets and, in summer, ancient quilted sun-bonnets, in order to support two half-witted brothers. Some folk rise, some fall in the social scale of the world. Anne and Esther Bathe were akin to old 'Scilla, plucking fowls to bring up her family, at least in name and spirit, and possibly in blood also; and perhaps, somewhere in the complex maze of genealogy, Squire Maskelyne's yellowhammers occupy a place in her ancestry.

January 1975

1 January 1975 – THE RIVER KEY

Battle Lake. A romantic name, the scene suitably melancholy; a dull, over-cast day, a footpath leading through a small plantation to a field so wet I sank immediately to the top of my wellingtons. Laboriously skirting it, I lurched from side to side while balancing on one leg so as to extricate the other, and came to a bulrushy ditch with pools of stagnant water which, from the map, appeared to indicate the upper reaches of the river Key.

Hopping from tussock to tussock, I reached a point where it broadened out and here was Battle Lake, fringed with rotting logs and straggly little oak trees. Only a solitary coot to be seen.

The Key picks up its spirits a little in the lake and emerges the other side almost briskly, about a yard wide, to trickle through woods en route for the river Ray, which in turn joins the Thames near Cricklade. On a slope above stands a grey-faced, three-gabled house looking down over a meadow. This must be Red Lodge, but it isn't red.

Battle Lake, despite a name so evocative of Arthurian legend, was made by Mr Joseph Neeld of Grittleton, who in 1829 bought most of the Hatton Lodge estate formerly belonging to Philip Jacobson. Deer once came to drink the waters of the river Key; the baying of hounds and the summons of the horn rang through these coverts, and kings and courtiers rode here; no wonder the river, in this plebeian modern world, has grown dispirited.

A track leads past Red Lodge, which turns out to have red sides if not a red front, and skirts a farm where I met a man exercising a black retriever. He told me that the house isn't called Red Lodge any more but Hatton Lodge, its original name. (It's also been called Webb's Lodge on occasion.) This was where Philip Jacobson settled when he eventually enjoyed the 'quiet possession' of his land.

There've been a lot of changes, said the man with the retriever, even among nightingales. These woods used to resound with their song. Last summer not a nightingale was to be heard. Cuckoos, too, are greatly diminished – only one pair last spring. Nuthatches, redwings come no more. Why, he didn't know. 'I don't suppose you've come across another dog with a name like mine,' he added. 'Gravy. I bought him off a man called Browning.'

Down the track to Gospel Oak Farm, then by car past Buryhill which has prehistoric burial mounds, so to the bridge over the Swill Brook. Dusk was falling as I stopped the car and took a turn along the Brook as far as Pike Corner, once called Py Hegge, which marked the northern limit of the Forest of Braden.

A woman was exercising a beagle along the bank as the day's greyness thickened into the greyness of nightfall. She'd been following hounds all day, she said, by car; riders, horses, hounds, cars, all were plastered with mud. So people are still hunting in Braydon, after at least a thousand years.

Had the hounds killed any foxes? 'Oh, no, they didn't *kill* anything.' She seemed surprised at the question. 'Just hunted around.' Her dripping beagle at last tore itself away from the water, she trudged off into the gloaming towards a waiting mini and I drove home in the dark.

4 January – AN OLD SOLDIER

You can't mistake an old soldier: upright as a ramrod, freshly shaved, alert of eye, trim and neatly dressed. A sergeant-major, surely, with that air of authority, but a gentle voice and a twinkle in the eye. A silent daughter keeps the cottage, he keeps the garden but can't work in it when the wind is blowing from the direction of evil-smelling broiler houses only a hundred yards away.

Eighty-four years ago George was born in Oaksey (called Woxey then, he said), where his father kept a butcher's shop; but at nineteen he grew tired of delivering meat, enlisted in the Royal Horse Artillery, went to India and was away for twenty-one years. One of his earliest recollections is the proclamation of King Edward VII's accession in the market place at Cirencester; only the children got the national anthem right, the rest sang God Save the Queen because they'd never sung anything else.

Then there was the swarm of wood-hornets which attacked the children nutting in Oaksey Wood. Robert Warner drove the children to Malmesbury Hospital in his four-wheeler, and that evening the oak tree that had housed the hornets' nest was felled, although it wasn't Warner's tree but Captain Burnaby's. Robert Warner was a JP which, seemingly, gave him authority to execute someone else's tree if it had done wrong.

George told me a lot about trees. In his youth, a man would cut and lay a hedge, and do out the ditch as well, for 3s 6d a chain (22 yards), and for every sapling spared he got an extra sixpence. So no young trees were destroyed. Once a year, the landlord's woodward came round to decide which trees would make good timber, and these remained the landlord's property; inferior trees he pollarded and these became the tenant's, to be used for repairing fences. No fence was patched with barbed wire in those days; gaps were replanted or made good with posts and rails. So there were no bits of barbed wire (the devil's invention) to tear the flesh of cows and horses, or injure sawyers by causing chips to fly in all directions.

'Have you noticed,' George asked, 'how many different kinds of oak there are on the Charlton estate? There's scarcely two the same.' This is because the present Earl of Suffolk's great-great-grandfather made a collection of acorns from all over the world. When he walked round parts of his enormous estate he'd drop an acorn in the hedge wherever he thought one would grow. Evidently he had good judgment, for a great many thrived and are there today. But as they die out, no one replaces them.

As a boy, George used to skate on the Oaksey pond called Bendybow; there was ice every winter then. Bendybow ice was peculiar, it bent in the middle without cracking – like a bow. This gave the pond its name, which, in due course the housing estate inherited.

7 January – AT THE MEET

The grey façade of Eastcourt House looked down benignly through the trees. Hefty ladies in rubber boots strode about with dogs on leads, gruffly exchanging news of litters, lamed ponies, the logistics of childrens' holidays. More elegant and mounted ladies in tailored coats of midnight blue reined in their well-groomed horses while they greeted friends. Children of all ages on ponies of all shapes and sizes adjusted girths, scrambled on, dug heels into tubby flanks to stir their mounts into activity. A man in a white polo-necked sweater came round with a tray of stirrup-cups. Along the narrow lane, a line of Land-rovers towing horse-boxes, and ordinary cars bumper to bumper, stretched out of sight.

The scene was set, and at a signal the jostling hounds surged off into a field, followed by a horde of horsemen funnelled through a gate. A young woman charged by on a snorting horse shouting 'I'm sorry, I've absolutely no control', as was apparent. In the field was a dead tree with two men standing beside it. One of those hoarse hunting screeches sounded forth as down the tree-trunk slid a fox, to lope across into the Eastcourt House garden. Commotion; in due course the hounds surged back, and eventually the pack and its followers disappeared into the middle distance, leaving car-borne hunters with the question of whether to proceed towards Flisteridge, or head back towards Hankerton.

Before this could be resolved, a stout bearded man on a stout horse appeared at full gallop crying: 'Land-rover! Land-rover!' in an important voice. A woman had been injured and was lying unconscious. 'Who?' 'I don't know. Riding a grey.' One of the many Land-rovers got under way, a woman clutching a first-aid kit climbed in, and the stout bearded rider set off again to show the way at full gallop. It wasn't long before back came the Land-rover, no casualty inside. 'No one there, she'd gone,' and so had the grey.

The next thing to appear was the fox in person. He loped towards us, clearly intending to cross the road and head for Flisteridge Wood; once there, he'd have little to worry about. His way was blocked by a line of cars and people holloa-ing and waving. Turning aside, he went back into the purlieus of Eastcourt House doubtless intending to make for Flisteridge by a different route, but still Flisteridge and safety.

He was an unlucky fox, because in recent weeks Braydon Brook has been mechanically scoured above Pill Bridge and now runs between steep, perpendicular banks which no fox could scale. He had no choice but to turn back towards Hankerton across open fields. Up came his pursuers, the riders clop-clop-clopping along the road. What a lot of road-clopping modern hunters have to do. Everyone disappeared; I walked a little way along the Brook running swiftly amid level meadows. Silence reigned; a light drizzle; I picked up several more Swan mussel shells. Then towards home.

Near Hankerton I met the hunt again in force, clop-clop-clopping along the narrow lane. I squeezed my car into the hedge and the riders squeezed by in single file, thanking me politely, touching their caps, sometimes thanking me *very much*. It was kind of them, but I don't know what else I could have done except charge them all head-on, a sort of Light Brigade action in reverse; and upwards of a hundred and fifty large horses with riders wielding whips, versus one small undefended 1100, could have ended only one way. Thus are the once-proud horsemen humbled: in every car may lurk an agent for the League Against Cruel Sports armed with cameras, spray-guns and sheaves of protests to Members of Parliament.

Some acknowledgement of all this gratitude was clearly called for, yet I could hardly say 'don't mention it' or 'you're welcome' to every rider as he filed past. Nor could I just sit and glower; I must at least smile in a friendly manner. I was then faced with a choice between sitting with a fixed grin on my face or switching it on and off rapidly, like an advertising sign. I tried a little wave, and felt as if caught up in a nightmare in which I was a trapped Royalty called on to review the Household Cavalry clad (as indeed I was) in a pair of muddy gardening trousers, a ragged Husky jacket and rubber boots. It was a relief when the last hunter filed by.

Plucking up courage, I asked a scarlet-coated gentleman on a glossy steed whether they had killed the fox. 'Yes, we did,' he replied. An unlucky animal.

8 January – WILTSHIRE ABORIGINES

To Cricklade to inspect the museum, a modest little place that was formerly a weighhouse, so modest it opens only for one hour on a Saturday afternoon. Here Dr T. R. Thomson, formerly the town's medico and now its scholarly historian, kindly showed me some of its possessions, such as coins minted here by King Æthelred, and relics of a wall built by King Alfred to keep out the Mercians just across the river. It enclosed about seventy acres, and to man it fully would have needed about 1,700 men, but it's most unlikely that it was ever manned on such a scale. Keep out the Mercians it did, but not Cnut's Danes who took Cricklade in the rear and burnt it down in 1016.

Coming to more modern times, there's a pedigree of Joseph Pitt of Eastcourt House, the land speculator, property developer and benefactor of the poor of Oaksey, and doubtless of other places as well. Land grabber that he was, he was 'of the strictest honour in his private life', according to a Lord Chancellor, which suggests that, in his semi-public deals, he wasn't as strict as all that. In 1815 he bought the manor of Cricklade, and represented the Borough in Parliament from 1812 to 1831.

So home by the turnpike past The Leigh and Minety, which he also owned. How different are these villages and market towns like Cricklade from those across the river, even a mile or two away. Here cottages are smaller, poorer, meaner, low-roofed; villages more straggly, less planned. These dwellings seem to acknowledge their descent from wood-cutters' cottages and charcoal-burners' shacks. Across the river you're in the Cotswolds with that mellow stone, that impeccable sense of design, all those rich wool merchants' houses; fanlights and porticos; magnificent churches. For centuries Braden was kept for the sport of kings, while across the river farmers and merchants rose to riches on the sheep's back.

Besides, over on this side, instead of oolite there's clay. Some of the clay gets up through the boots of moonrakers into their souls – as Aubrey noted.* How rude he was.† In North Wilts,

the Indigenae, or Aborigines, speake drawling, they are phlegmatique, skins pale and livid, slow and dull, heavy of spirit . . . they only milk the cowes and make cheese. They feed chiefly on milke meates, which cools their braines too much, and hurts their inventions. These circumstances make them melancholy, contemplative, and malicious; by consequence whereof come more law suites out of N. Wilts, at least double to the southern parts. And by the same reason they are generally apt to be fanatiques; their persons are generally plump and feggy: gallipot eyes, and some black: but they are generally handsome enough. It is a woodsere countrie, abounding much with soure and austere plants, as sorrel etc: which makes their humours soure, and fixes their spirits. In Malmesbury Hundred (ye wett clayey parts) there have even been reputed witches.‡

So that's what we looked like to a fellow Wiltshireman just three hundred years ago. We must take what comfort we can from those gallipot eyes.

* *Memoires of Naturall Remarques in the County of Wilts.* John Aubrey, 1685. Edited by John Britton.

† But not as rude as William Cobbett, who wrote 'I passed through that villainous hole Cricklade about two hours ago, and certainly a more rascally looking place I never set my eyes on . . . This Wiltshire is a horrible county.'

‡ Aubrey records elsewhere that in the 1670s a cabal of witches was detected at Malmesbury. 'I think there were 7 or 8 old women hanged. There were odd things sworne against them, as the strange manner of the dyeing of H. Denny's horse, and of flying in the aire on a staff.'

10 January – HATTON LODGE

Above the doorway of what's now Red Lodge, a hundred yards or so from what *was* Red Lodge but is now Hatton's, a stone set into the brick above the door, and carved with the date 1809, looks oddly at variance with the rest of the old red-brick farmhouse, obviously built at least a century earlier.

'Yes, the date's bogus,' agreed the owner, Miss Elizabeth Ward. When she moved here a few years ago from the bigger house, Hatton Lodge (now turned into flats), the inscription had read 1509. 'I knew *that* was wrong, and it annoyed me, so I changed it.' But why to 1809? 'It would have cost too much to have the whole stone taken out and replaced, but it was easy to change the 5 into an 8.' So 1809 the date became. The hunted beasts of Braden seem to have passed on the art of confusing a scent to their human successors.

The interior of this rambling, attractive old place, one part dating from the seventeenth century, is full of uneven steps, beams endangering unwary heads, oak panelling, terriers and hunting boots. From a chest in the hall Miss Ward extracted a cardboard box containing old parchment deeds in crabbed, illegible writing; rolls of maps; and documents of various kinds chewed by mice. All these she most kindly allowed me to take away. From them I learned that her grandfather had bought this property at a sale in 1901 from Sir Audley Neeld, and that it was the residue of that part of Braden Forest parcelled out in the reign of Charles I between Philip Jacobson, Roger Nott and James Duart. Over the years bits of it changed hands until this portion, centred on Hatton Lodge, passed in 1826 into the possession of the Earl of Clarendon, who in turn sold it to Joseph Neeld of Grittleton.

This Joseph Neeld was an interesting, if unattractive, character, who inherited when young an enormous fortune from a great-uncle who was a miser in the traditional style, starving himself amid a hoard of golden sovereigns. His heir made up for it and spent the money, but shrewdly, on property, not on riotous living. He made a grand marriage to Lady Caroline Ashley-Cooper, a daughter of Lord Shaftesbury, but either chose unwisely or had himself some odd shortcomings. After the honeymoon she went immediately to an hotel instead of to the mansion in Grosvenor Square he had prepared for her reception, and shortly afterwards brought a suit against him for the restitution of conjugal rights.

'Counsel advised me,' he wrote, 'that however unworthy your conduct might have been, you had not legally forfeited the claims of a wife.'

Whatever she had done, or not done, he had to take her back, but not to
the house in Grosvenor Square which he dismantled; they went to an hotel.
'My dinner hour is seven o'clock,' he added.

Dinner can't have been a cosy meal. Accusation and counter-accusation
flew between them; he said she was extravagant and spread 'base and
slanderous aspersions'; she said that he was cruel, locked her up, humil-
iated her before waiters and based his charge of extravagance on her use of
wax candles. One thing she couldn't accuse him of was impotence, since
an illegitimate daughter by, it was said, a beautiful Frenchwoman, was
one of the first ornaments to catch her eye when she arrived at his seat at
Grittleton. The final outcome was a legal separation. His heir was a
brother who was made a baronet and had six sons. The last survivor of the
six, not one of whom had surviving issue, was Sir Audley Neeld, who sold
the Braden property to Edward Ward, Elizabeth's grandfather.*

So that more or less rounds off the story of the disafforestation of
Braden, from Charles I and Philip Jacobson to Miss Elizabeth Ward. But
where, among all these Lodges, is Great Lodge of the original grant?
Vanished: but it's said that a bit of moat, or foundation, or wall, can still
be seen on Ravenshurst Farm. The shortest way to get there, Miss Ward
advised, was to follow a line of hunt jumps across the fields.

Reasoning that where a horse could go, there also could a human, I
scrambled over several hunt jumps and squelched across several fields
until Ravenshurst Lodge came into view; a four-square, red-brick, unpretentious house, surrounded by a gaggle of buildings and a remarkable
miscellany of objects such as bits of abandoned machinery and an unex-
pected row of old gas cookers by the back door.

The owner's son was vague about the moat, but believed there was something on or near 'the island', and led me to a patch of swampy ground
almost encircled by a flooded brook. No one could have built a Lodge here,
or anything else except a hut on stilts like ancient lake dwellings, but possibly the hedge between 'the island' and the farm buildings conceals
ruined walls; difficult to say amid the brambles, rushes and mud. A
drizzle set in, so I made for home.

A drizzle, yet not quite a drizzle; one of those days when rain isn't
actually falling, yet somehow wetness seems to arrive. No wonder foreigners don't understand our weather. Plodding back across the fields I
thought of an American friend who, on his first visit, found our weather
forecasts irresistibly comic. 'Showers, followed by rain,' or sometimes

* I am indebted for these details to Countess Badeni's *Wiltshire Forefathers*, a mine of
local information.

'rain followed by showers', vastly amused him. A legend printed on a box of what were then called gramophone needles also took his fancy. 'Approximately 200', it said. I couldn't see the joke but he thought it odd of us to be unable to make up our minds when rain was rain, and how many gramophone needles we had put into a box.

I don't know what he would have thought about these Braydon brooks. According to my map, the one that forms 'the island' at Ravenshurst Farm is called, unequivocally, Derry Brook. But older maps call it Sambourn, or occasionally Greenburne, and there are alternatives such as Ravensditch, Sandbourne, Three Gutters and Sparrow Brook. As for the River Key, it has a number of aliases; Spittlebrook, Dance Brook, Stokkenlade, Braden Brook, Lortingesbourne, Stoke Brook. The number of names attached to a stream seems directly proportional, inversely, to its' size. Only one Nile or Amazon so far as I know, but half a dozen Derry Brooks and River Keys.

Rain had been followed by showers, and showers by rain, before I reached the car and drove home, on the way just missing a fine cock pheasant, resplendent in his bronze and gold and purple plumage – such an alien, gaudy bird in our sombre black winter woods. I braked hard, and regretted doing so a moment later. Before long he'll be hanging in someone's larder in any case, so why didn't I accelerate?

For the weekend I decided to go a bust and have a pheasant anyway, the price being at its lowest, so rang up Mr Day in Malmesbury who still delivers on a Thursday. No longer in his van, he said, since the last rise in the price of petrol; a boy comes out on a bicycle. Surprised that any boy, these days, should be prepared to ride seven miles there and seven back on a bicycle, I inquired about him from Marjorie, a fellow customer of Mr Day's. 'Boy?' she exclaimed. 'He's an elderly man who does errands.' When delivering, he generally comes into her kitchen for a chat. Once, on a cold winter's day, he arrived about mid-day when she was making onion soup, so she gave him a bowl which he found delicious. Ever since, when he delivers on a Thursday, he's come at the same time, hopefully sniffing for onion soup.

13 January – COMMONERS OF THE KING'S HEATH

Malmesbury by lamplight, streets deserted, occasional footsteps clop-clopping, black shadows: a place of magic. You can feel age oozing out of ancient stones and flights of worn steps. Little houses huddle together as if on guard over treacherously narrow streets. Above it all, a broken symbol, stands the ruined Abbey. The High Street curls down to the river with St John's Almshouses, built in the thirteenth century, at the foot, the quiet Avon in its green valley almost encircling the town.

Few people were about and the footfalls of occasional passers-by echoed on the pavement. Shop-fronts at the top of the High Street were lit up but windows at the bottom and in the side-streets were dark, save where curtains had been left undrawn. Inside, there's the family sitting round the remnants of their tea with all eyes focused on a flickering screen in a corner. In every house I glanced into as I passed there was the same programme – 'Me and My Chimp'.

These Malmesburians are citizens of the oldest borough in England. This is a big claim but Stan Hudson assured me it's true. In the year 880 King Alfred granted a prescriptive charter to the town and in 939 his grandson Æthelstan, Malmesbury's own king who reigned and was buried here,* confirmed it.

I Athelstan King of the English do give for me and my Successors to my Burgesses and all their Successors in the Borough of Malmesbury that they shall always have and hold all their Functions and Free Customs as they held them in the time of King Edward my Father freely and honourably and I command to all under my Dominion that they do no injury to them and that they may be free from all Calumny and of Burghboote Brugboote Wardwhite Horngeld and Scot and I give and grant to them the royal Bruery of five hides of land near to my town of Norton for their assistance in my Conflict against the Danes.

These were the words, an extract from King Æthelstan's charter, recited to me from memory by the current High Steward of the Malmesbury Commoners, who was born in this town, schooled here, worked here all his life and lives here now in his retirement, in a plain and dignified late Georgian house in the High Street, with a garden running down to the old wall above the Avon. A spare, upright, slender man nearing eighty, with all the courtesy and kindliness of his generation.

Over one thousand years ago an ancestor of his fought for Æthelstan against the Danes, and in return for services rendered by this ancestor, Stan Hudson today receives the rent on ten and five-eighths of an acre of farm land on the King's Heath, part of the five hides 'near to my town of Norton'.

---

* The exact whereabouts of his tomb remains unknown. It has been suggested that it lies in the garden (and formerly under an asparagus bed) of Abbey House, which was built on the site of part of the Abbey after its destruction.

The King's grant amounted to 570 acres. There were, in Æthelstan's day, 280 Commoners each entitled to one acre. In course of time, by seniority, twenty-four of these Commoners became, and become, Assistant Burgesses, and receive an extra acre or so from a pool called the Hundred. From among these Assistant Burgesses twelve are chosen to be Capital Burgesses, which entitles them to a further allocation of land. There is also an Alderman, in effect the Mayor in former times, and, at the top of the hierarchy, the High Steward, the only one who doesn't have to be an hereditary Commoner. For about nine hundred years these fourteen men governed the Borough.

Today there are 240 Commoners, only forty less than in the tenth century. It's astonishing to think that there are 240 men living today in the Borough whose ancestors were living in the same place a thousand years ago. Women can't be Commoners, but men (who must be married) can inherit the right through their mothers; and the husbands of Commoners' daughters are eligible. Mr Hudson has three daughters and their husbands can be Commoners, but only if they live in Malmesbury. (As well as being High Steward, he's an hereditary Commoner.)

In former times each man got his own plot of land which he could, and did, cultivate; now it's all let off as farms, and the Capital Burgesses manage it as a small estate, paying each Commoner his share of the rent. The ancient ceremony of initiation is still held, though no longer on the King's Heath. The newcomer used to dig a hole in his plot and throw in a silver coin while one of the Burgesses, the Clerk to the Common, touched him with a twig, reciting:

> This turf and twig I give to thee,
> As free as Æthelstan gave to me,
> And I hope a loving brother thou wilt be.

Nowadays, a square of the appropriate turf is taken to the hall where the Burgesses meet, and Young Commoners are sworn in there. Four Courts a year are held in an oak-panelled court room in St John's Almshouses by Goose Bridge at the bottom of the High Street, built in 1263 by the Knights of St John. It used to be a schoolroom, for one of a Commoner's privileges was free schooling for his children.

There were other privileges not, we may safely assume, foreseen by the King. Formerly the twelve Capital Burgesses, plus the High Steward and the Alderman, not only ran the borough, but chose two Members of Parliament to be returned to Westminster.

In practice, control by fourteen men generally boiled down to control by one, the High Steward. This rich honeypot naturally attracted influential flies, prepared to pay as much as £9,000 to persuade the Burgesses to elect them. The Duke of Argyll was one – the man Giles Earle deserted; Giles Earle held the office in 1741; others included an Earl of Suffolk, and Henry Fox who represented Malmesbury from 1774 to 1780. He joined with Suffolk to pay the Burgesses £30 each, plus two feasts, annually for seven years, remarking that 'it is hoped by this to prevent the Burgesses from being necessitous'.

The literacy rate among Burgesses appears to have been low. Fox's successor Edmund Wilkins is said to have placed a card in front of each Burgess bearing in large letters the name of the man he was to vote for. 'Memorise the look of it' he advised. Joseph Pitt, one need hardly say, served a term as High Steward and was evidently more generous; the Burgesses were known as Pitt's Pensioners during his stewardship.

The Reform Act of 1832 put an end to this cosy system, but the Burgesses continued to function as the *de facto* rulers of the Borough until their powers were shorn away by the reform of local government in 1886. After that the Old Corporation, as the Commoners' Court came to be called, was replaced by an elected one with a proper mayor. All that's left today is the King's Heath and some other property, a good deal of ceremony and tradition, some valuable records, and four seventeenth-century maces. A hollow shell: yet not entirely. Malmesburians continue to take up their Commoners' rights; and to be elected a Capital Burgess, even more a High Steward, still carries local prestige.

But now Malmesbury's claim to be the oldest borough in England has gone by the board, because boroughs themselves have been swept away by the local government reforms of 1974. Malmesbury has degenerated into an unimportant part of the North Wilts District Council. Its Burgesses feel the insult deeply, and have tried hard to rescue their borough from the sea of bureaucratic anonymity; but despite a direct appeal to the Queen as King Æthelstan's successor, their attempt has failed.

One question that has never been settled is the place and nature of the services rendered to Æthelstan, for which the first Commoners received their reward. Was it for loyalty in general during his campaigns, or for valour at some particular battle? Brunanburgh, fought in AD 937 somewhere in the north and by the sea against the kings of Dublin and of Scotland, was Æthelstan's most famous victory over the Norsemen, but there were other battles closer at hand. Stan Hudson has a theory, based partly on an observation of Aubrey's, that the Danes were vanquished just outside Malmesbury itself, at a place called Winnies Hill.

21 January – SALISBURY CLOSE

A perfect winter's day to visit Salisbury Close. After so much lashing rain and sodden cloud, the sun illuminated as with a searchlight that marvellous silvery cathedral spire rising from its throne of pinnacles, and cast long, sharp shadows on the grass. All the kindly houses in the Close, each so pleasing and each so different, seemed to smile at passers-by, promising comfort within and, without, the peace of walled gardens.

What sheltered lives these houses enjoy. Here also Mrs Frances Salisbury, lady of the manor of Oaksey from 1814 to 1862, and her two unmarried daughters, enjoyed, it's to be supposed, sheltered lives for over forty years. This was Trollope country, Trollope time; did Bishop and Mrs Proudie attend her Thursday afternoons in a brocade-upholstered drawing-room? Did Sophia and Maria hopefully work designs in wool on curates' slippers – alas, in vain?

Mrs Frances Salisbury had three daughters. The youngest, Anne Caroline, espoused Captain Edwyn Burnaby of Baggrave Hall in Leicestershire in 1829. Sophia Frances and Maria never married. After their mother's death in 1862 they enjoyed a life tenancy of the Park but never lived here, or visited it so far as we know.

Their sister Anne Caroline Burnaby became a progenitor of our present Queen. One of our former rectors compiled a family tree showing that her daughter, Louisa Caroline, married the Rev. William Cavendish-Bentinck; their daughter Nina married Claude Bowes-Lyon, 14th Earl of Strathmore; their daughter Elizabeth married King George VI; and then came Queen Elizabeth II.

Number 16 The Close, today renumbered 14 and 14A, is a handsome, late-eighteenth-century brick house (now regrettably painted café-au-lait colour) up against St Ann's Gate. Opposite is the former town house of the Harris family, Earls of Malmesbury, from whom Mrs Salisbury's father, Francis Webb, bought our manor.

In 1818, the Procurator and Commonalty of the Vicars of the Cathedral Church of St Mary, known as the Vicars Choral, granted a forty-year lease of Number 16 to Mrs Salisbury for an annual rent of ten shillings, to be paid in quarterly instalments on the feasts of St Michael the Archangel, the Birth of Our Lord, the Annunciation of the Blessed Virgin Mary and the feast of St John the Baptist. Half a crown a quarter, with an extra one and sixpence to be paid at Michaelmas: why did Mrs Salisbury get her fine house virtually for nothing? These deeds provide no clue.

Eight years before her death, Mrs Salisbury made over the remainder of her lease to Sophia and Maria. Then in 1863 the Misses Salisbury assigned the rest of it to a Mr E. P. P. Kelsey, and left The Close forever.

Mrs Frances Salisbury of Salisbury and her two daughters remain mere names on paper, and these old leases can do nothing to give them life. Other documents, however, preserved among the diocesan records in Salisbury do provide some glimpses into parochial history. The brevity of the earliest scrap of parchment, a churchwardens' report submitted to the Bishop in 1607 on the occasion of a Visitation, suggests that everything was going smoothly; but in 1662 Minety had got into a dreadful state.

The church had no chalice, no flagon, no carpet for the Communion table, no patten for the bread, no 'decent crimson cloth'; the Bible had no binding, some windows no glass.

Two coppices sold by the parishioners in the troublesome times and the . . . trees cut down to make the churchyard and . . . without the comfort of the Vicar. Heaps of rubbish in the churchyard . . . notwithstanding frequent warning.

Wm Webb and Wm Taylor churchwardens for that year 1661 . . . encrocahed on by Nicholas Pleydell, his owne . . . enlarged without any authority . . . besides much indecency and disorder by boys . . . The Minister wears not his surplice, because there is none.

This was by no means the whole story. One of the parishioners 'much offends by gambling openly and tipling in alehouses'. Two of William Hawkins' children had not been properly baptized. Easter dues were unpaid, children would not come to catechism, Nicholas Pleydell's will had been tampered with by his son, John Morse excommunicated.

Minety affords only one example of the state of disorder and neglect many parishes and churches had fallen into during the Civil War and after. Three and a half centuries earlier, affairs had been temporarily just as chaotic. Minety church had been put under an interdict by the deans of Malmesbury and Cricklade, who instructed the parishioners to worship at Oaksey. This was because a forester called Little John, with several companions, had forcibly occupied the church in the name of Peter of Savoy, Dean of Sarum, a relation by marriage of Henry III. The office of dean carried fat pickings and no duties, and the appointment of absentee foreign nobles was bitterly resented by the native clergy. Little John had presumably come to collect the dues for his master Peter, and staged a sit-in at the church.

By the time the churchwardens made their report in 1682, Minety church was back on its feet again. In Oaksey, in 1692, Thomas Sparrow and John Keight were able to depose that 'we the churchwardens do present omnia bono'. In a Visitation of 1783 the rector reported that Oaksey had normally about ten communicants and no Papists, Presbyterians, Independents, Anabaptists or Quakers; also no charity school or almshouse. Crudwell, on the other hand, had a school for seven children, endowed by a field let for £3 a year with a house and garden, and founded by the Duke of Kent, son of Baroness Lucas who was the lady of the manor.

22 January – TRANSPLANTED COCKNEYS

In the early days of World War II, a wave of London's East-Enders swept into the villages of England, our own amongst them. When it receded, the only Cockneys who'd taken root were Billy Williams, who went from school to work at Park Farm and is there today, and the Jolly family.

'Mrs Jolly would go back tomorrow,' Albert said. 'But not me.' They're both around the eighty mark, settled in Bendybow (the quiet end), with two married children living in the neighbourhood. They were showing me photographs of their golden wedding, with a concourse of grandchildren gathered in their kitchen round a table-load of iced cakes. It all brought back the days when evacuees were dumped here by bus, confused, bedraggled, apprehensive, uprooted, feeling as if they had got to the end of the world.

The children came first, a whole school from East Ham complete with its teachers, and that was very well organized; billets had been settled in advance and everyone was ready to take the children to their hearts. Among these children were two young Jollys from Plaistow, to be followed about a year later, when the bombing began, by their mother Edie with the other four; and, before the end of 1940, by their father. Albert was an air raid warden and saw a man decapitated before his eyes. 'People say everyone was brave in the blitz. You don't want to tell me that. People's nerves gave way.' He joined his family, and somehow they all squeezed into a tiny, cold, bare hovel at one end of The Rucketts, empty because it had been condemned. But the Jollys hadn't been used to luxury and it was luxury enough to be free from bombing. Within a fortnight, Albert had found a job as roadman for the County Council and, except for an occasional visit, they've never been back to Plaistow since.

Albert was one of ten, he told me; his father was often out of work and the family hungry. On leaving school he answered an advertisement for emigrants to Australia, concealed his age and, with eleven other boys, reached Melbourne on his fifteenth birthday.

Australia was hard. He started on a farm where, on his first evening, he nearly severed a finger while trying to clean a cracked lamp-glass. Next morning he had his first lesson in milking a cow; he can remember to this day how the milk stung his finger. After a year he left with his savings of £2 10s and lost it all on his first evening in a pub. Pinching an old bike, he proceeded on his way with nothing but a billycan, chopping wood to earn his supper, sleeping rough, and fetching up in Sydney, where he saw a home-bound Orient liner lying in the harbour and shipped in her as a trimmer.

Then, World War I. Albert joined the Navy and on 8 August 1915 HMS *India* was torpedoed in the North Sea and sank in seven minutes. Albert was one of the lucky ones; he scrambled into a lifeboat, it capsized, the sailors clung to its upturned hull and sang 'Nearer My God to Thee' (except for one who tried 'Tipperary' – 'but he was only a boy') until a Norwegian fishing smack rescued them. They got to Narvik and spent the rest of the war in an internment camp, where at times the temperature sank to 33 degrees below zero. Albert learned to ski. He also married; internees were sent home for one month's leave a year and during 1917 he espoused his Edie in Plaistow, where they set up home after the war and reared six children.

Albert's days of travel weren't over. He signed on as a stoker and for the next four or five years roamed the world's oceans and sea-ports until he came back to Plaistow. Then it was a question of work sometimes, sometimes not, the dole, factory jobs, whatever came along. They ended up, so unexpectedly, in Oaksey, finally in this council house where, drawing their pension, they will live out their time.

'I reckon we're better off now than ever we were in all our lives before,' Albert said. He showed me a photograph of his mother: an intelligent, alert, high-cheekboned face. 'She knew more poverty than ever we did,' he said. 'D'you know what she used for tea?' I guessed some kind of herb. 'Bits of burnt toast.'

26 January – AN OLD WAGON

Sunday. Colin Ettles walks down the Park road with his dog and a golf club to practise driving, though he never plays.

For how many generations have the men of his family followed the trade of carpenter? His father Joe is a wonderful cabinet-maker. Joe's father Walter was a carpenter and wheelwright at Eastcourt, and so was his father, John.

About a century ago, John Ettles built a wagon for Thomas Hislop, then of Oatridge Farm. A good solid wagon that took the corn to Garsdon Mill. Later, it stood about neglected and would have rotted away like so many others if it hadn't been bought and restored by a wheelwright at Coates, Dennis Tugwell, who sold it to the owner of the Cotswold Farm Park, where breeds of farm animals in danger of extinction are preserved and bred. The ledges along its sides are finely chamfered, and it's said that the famous Ernest Gimson of Sapperton drew inspiration for designs from this traditional chamfering on West Country wagons.

Joe Ettles said that in his youth a wagon like this, complete with ladders fore and aft, all brightly painted, cost about £30, and would last several lifetimes. His father gave up making them because of bad debts.

Now Jim Hislop, grandson of the man who bought the wagon, lives within a mile of Joe Ettles, grandson of the man who made it. Thomas Hislop, the purchaser, came from Perth in Scotland as gardener to Captain Arthur Randolph of Eastcourt House. His Scots pertinacity, intelligence and drive won him the position of bailiff to the Randolph estate, and at Oatridge Farm, then a part of it, the Hislops reared four boys and four girls. Each of the boys got a tenancy of one of the farms on the estate; the daughters married respectively a farmer, a miller, a butcher and a baker; so all held to the land and its fruits. There is still a Hislop, another grandson of Thomas from Perth, at Oatridge Farm.

30 January – JOSEPH PITT OF EASTCOURT

It was a coincidence to come across, among the county records at Trowbridge, and within a few days of talking to his grandson, an account book kept in 1877–1885 by Thomas Hislop, bailiff to the Eastcourt estate. In it is a 'flint account' relating to the flints dug in Flisteridge Wood and sold to the Crudwell parish council for roadmaking at 1s 10d a yard. Some of the older Eastcourt people can remember passing, on their way to school, heaps of flints by the roadside, and men breaking them with a hammer, a kind of iron vizor protecting their eyes.

Captain Arthur Randolph was then the owner of this beautiful estate of about 1,500 acres which included nine farms, each with its substantial buildings, big old barns and rich pastures and cornfields. (Hill Farm, now John Oaksey's, was among them.) Before him at Eastcourt House was Joseph Randolph Mullings and, before him, Joseph Pitt.

The name of Joseph Pitt crops up everywhere, buying properties great and small, acquiring advowsons, taking out mortgages, and launching the fashionable development in Cheltenham, Pittsville, with its graceful Pump Room intended to rival that of Bath, which commemorates his name. Yet with all these interests, living in affluence at Eastcourt House, keeping Malmesbury's burgesses at his beck and call, lord of so many manors, everything collapsed in ruins about him and only death, and the willingness of Joseph Randolph Mullings to bide his time, saved him from penury and disgrace.

A document in the Trowbridge Record Office tells the story. It's a deed drawn in 1841 between Joseph Pitt and Joseph Randolph Mullings, a prominent Cirencester solicitor (his descendant practises in the town today), by which Mullings advanced Pitt the sum of £9,000. Relentlessly, like a hammer striking nail after nail into a coffin, this deed recites Pitt's indebtedness to his solicitor: loan after loan, mortgage after mortgage, amounting to £42,625 before the final £9,000 was paid. Mullings didn't foreclose. Pitt was over eighty, the pike was in the net, the net was closing and in the following year it closed. After Pitt's death on 26 February, 1842 the High Court of Chancery ordered the sale of his property to go towards his debts and funeral expenses; and in came Joseph Randolph Mullings.

Pitt's will, in the light of this, is rather pathetic. He was survived by five sons and two daughters, and was at great pains to convince his family, and no doubt himself, of how much he had already done for them in his lifetime. Cornelius had the advowson of Rendcomb; 'therefore I do not give or devise to him anything else'. Charles had the advowson of Ashton Keynes and enough in cash to enable him to buy a house in Malmesbury, so he got no more either. Nor did William, who already had property 'of considerable value'. 'I have also at great expense provided for my son George and I therefore give him no more.' There must have been some glum faces in Mullings' office at the reading of the will.

The Misses Pitt, Ann and Henrietta, did a little better, but not much. They already had property to the value of 'nearly what they would have been entitled to under their grandmother's will,' which included 'musical instruments and appendages and musical books in my dwelling house at Eastcourt,' also the furniture of the rooms 'usually called their own'. Each could select £400 worth of plate, linen, china and pictures, but no other provision for these spinster ladies was made. Everything else went to Pitt's son Joseph – everything meaning nothing. In effect, Mullings got the property for £51,625, plus expenses. He lived there until his death in 1859 and left it to his son Arthur Randolph Mullings.

Rather less than twenty years later (in 1877), the signature on documents relating to the estate ceased to be that of Arthur Randolph Mullings and became Arthur Randolph. This was confusing. But two of Thomas Hislop's grandchildren, Albert and Dorothy, explained the matter. Captain Arthur Randolph changed his name. He dropped the Mullings. The reason was a scandal connected with a divorce.

The current Mr Mullings, head of the family firm in Cirencester, confirmed this but knew little more about the scandal, save that it was of such a shocking nature that every document connected with it had been committed to the flames by his predecessors. All he had gathered, handed down to him in a hushed voice by the senior partner when he joined the firm, was that the scandal was on the lines of 'what the butler saw'. The captain had divorced his wife, dropped the sullied name of Mullings, left the neighbourhood and let the house to a succession of tenants. In due course his son, who became a judge, inherited.

The only tenant who impressed himself on local memory was Walter Powell, MP for Malmesbury, who disappeared in his balloon. Sid Cook told me the story. The Prince of Wales, he said, had accepted an invitation to lunch with Mr Powell at Eastcourt House. It was to be a great occasion. The local gentry were invited to a sumptuous meal in a marquee on the lawn, and free beer was laid on for the villagers. The *pièce de resistance* was to be an ascent by Mr Powell in his balloon.

All was prepared, the guests assembled in their best, the hour came – but no Prince. The company waited and waited. At last they could wait no more. Mr Powell opened the marquee and told the villagers to help themselves to the goodies within. Then, slighted and despondent, he stepped into the cage of his balloon, cast off the moorings and rose above the trees. Soon he was out of sight for ever; neither he nor his balloon was seen again.

Sid likes to tell this story, with embellishments, in broad Wiltshire. He had it many years ago from Albert Picter. 'Vivty-vor-er years ago it was,' Albert said, ''ee disabeard. I knows 'cos I were there.' Sid thought a little. 'You was there, Albert?' 'Ah, that I were. You never seen such vict'lls in all your life as there was in that girt te-e-ent. You could have fatted all the pigs in Wiltshire just on what was left on 'm pla-a-ates. You could of villed the la-a-uk twice over with t' beer.' Sid thought some more. 'Ow old bee'st thou, Albert?' 'I be vivty-vor-er today.' 'Well then, Albert, if thee be vivty-vo-er today, 'ow can thee remember that was in that girt old te-e-ent vivty-vo-er year ago?' 'Our mother was there and she were carrying I, so it sta-a-ands to reason I were there too.'

February

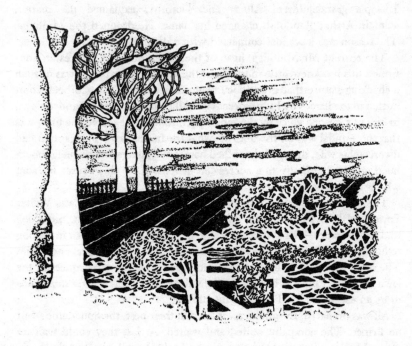

7 February – THE JUDGE AND HIS LADY

Despite having lived so close for so long, until a week ago I'd never set eyes on Manor Farm, Hankerton, where Albert Hislop lives in retirement with his sister Dorothy. It lies way off the road, an old Cotswold stone farmhouse with immensely thick, ivy-clad walls. It's been a farm now for about three hundred years but before that it was a small manor house lived in by the Earles until, enriched by trade in Bristol, they built the grand new mansion nearby at Eastcourt.

Traces of its manorial status remain in a moulded ceiling with a Tudor rose at each corner, and parts of it were built in medieval times. A notable oak stairway winds steeply up inside what was once a turret, with narrow slits in the stone walls, and ends abruptly on a small landing; evidently, when the need for defence was over, the top of the turret was demolished and the place modernized, sometime in the sixteenth century. Across the yard are two enormous barns, with doorways high and wide enough to admit a fully loaded wagon, such as you find in all such ancient barns. The girt oak beams (as Sid would say) must be hundreds of years old and the roof's stone tiles, tens of thousands of them, were quarried by hand in a field between here and Crudwell.

Above the doorway of each barn are the initials G E and two dates, one 1707, the other 1708. G E stands for Giles Earle, grandson of the Giles who built Eastcourt House and the place-hunting crony of Walpole's. He died in 1758 and there's a tablet to his memory in Hankerton church executed by the sculptor Nollekens.

After the Earles at Eastcourt House came Pitt and Mullings, and finally Judge Joseph Randolph, Captain Arthur's son. A fine, upstanding gentleman, Albert said, but not communicative. He'd stride over the fields with his stick, say 'good morning' or 'nice day', but only once, in all Albert's experience, did he pause for a chat, and then not for long. What did they talk about? 'The plantations, I expect. He loved trees. Almost every day, he'd walk to Flisteridge Wood.'

His wife was every inch a lady, as he was every inch a gentleman. She wrote books and entertained literary people; the Poet Laureate, John Masefield, was among her guests. Wherever she went, to church for instance, her maid went with her, and both dressed alike. 'A tall, good-looking woman,' Miss Hislop recalled. 'Neat as her mistress and dressed the same yet not quite the same, if you understand.' The Randolphs had no children. When the Judge died in 1936 the property passed to a nephew who was killed soon afterwards in a flying accident, and then the whole estate was sold.

Donning an ancient mounted infantry hat with a chin-strap (Boer War design), Albert took a bowl of crusts out to three hens who share the girt barns with a rusty mowing machine of about the same vintage as the hat. 'I've mown a lot of grass with that,' he said reflectively, and added: 'I had good horses. I never used a whip. Everything was done with the voice.' Then, in the war, came tractors, and one had to move with the times. He kept the last horse for several years rather than let it go to strangers, or to the knacker's, and then had it shot. I don't think that for Albert, after horses went, farming was ever quite the same.

He saved one crust for a tame blackbird that hops about near the back door.

Margaret Thatcher Day – THE BALLOON WENT UP

Walter Powell, MP, didn't start on his last and fatal balloon ascent from
the lawn at Eastcourt House, as Sid had thought, but from the gas works
at Bath. The balloon, named *Saladin*, bearing Mr Powell and two companions, was last seen passing over the Hope Rocks at Eype near Bridport.
Two men jumped out and the balloon 'rushed out over these cliffs at a
terrific rate and at a great height, directly the two gentlemen fell from it'.
The gentlemen were Captain Templer and Edward Agg-Gardiner, who
broke a leg.

I gleaned this information from Stan Hudson, whose chronicle of local
history, the product of long research, has been gestating for years. Clearly
such an event as this balloon disaster wouldn't go unrecorded in the local
press, so I made my way to the offices of the *Wilts and Gloucestershire
Standard* to continue burrowing in its files. And there was the full story.

The three men went up from Bath on 3 December 1881; Captain
Templer was making meteorological observations for the War Office.
Saladin passed low over the cliffs near Bridport when Templer and Agg-
Gardiner jumped out and Walter Powell was seen, as the balloon shot
upwards, to wave his hand.

A tremendous search followed on both sides of the Channel. Nothing
was seen. A week or so later, part of a thermometer was washed up at
Portland and identified by Captain Templer as having come from *Saladin*.
No other trace was ever found.

Walter Powell was thirty-nine, a bachelor, and had represented Malmesbury in the Tory interest since 1868 when he had defeated Viscount
Andover. He came from Newport, Monmouthshire, and was a director of
the Penarth Railway Company. Not long before the balloon incident, one
of his brothers, accompanied by wife and son, had gone to Abyssinia on a
shooting safari and all three had been massacred by a savage tribe.

Walter seems to have been a generous and genial man. Each Christmas
he gave fifty tons of coal to be distributed among the Malmesbury poor,
and he built and presented a reading-room to the town. His magic-lantern
displays were immensely popular, sometimes causing 'roars of laughter and
cheers'. He hunted with the VWH and entertained house-parties for the
Hunt's Bachelors' Ball. His name 'was well-known in connection with many
kind and thoughtful actions' – even to the end, when he saw his two friends
clear of the balloon and vanished with a wave of the hand. The captain who
went up with his ship.

12 February – GOD BLESS THE PRINCE OF WALES

But how had Mr Powell's demise got mixed up with the luncheon party at Eastcourt House to which the Prince of Wales didn't come? There must have been some connection. Continuing my researches in the *Wilts and Gloucestershire Standard* files, I took down the 1877 volume more or less at random and there I found it.

In February of that year, the Prince visited Cirencester for a few days' hunting, throwing the townsfolk and the *Standard*'s reporters into paroxysms of loyalty. Cheering crowds, red carpets on the station platform, brass bands, decorated carriages, arches with the words God Bless the Prince of Wales: the town seems to have become almost hysterical with enthusiasm for this stout Germanic prince. He was the guest of the Master of the VWH Hunt, the Earl of Shannon of Castle Martyr, County Cork, and his lady, as bold a rider to hounds as her lord.

Next day there was a meet at Coln St Aldwyn and, the day after that, with the Cotswold Hunt at Five Mile House. This so excited the reporter that he burst into verse.

> The carriages were various too
> For some had an outrider,
> While others drove a pair horse fly
> And one, I think, a spider.
>
> Don't talk about dead Caesars,
> See how their glory pales,
> No men there were who could compare
> With our own Prince of Wales!
>
> Then prosper old Corinium!
> And the lord that hunts the vales,
> Lift up your voice and raise the shout
> God bless the Prince of Wales!

On the third and final day the meet was to be held at Eastcourt House at 11.30 am and Walter Powell to be host. Long before the appointed time a dense crowd assembled and 'in front of Eastcourt House were erected tents in which was spread a bountiful luncheon'. The night before had seen a hard frost and there were doubts about prospects for the hunt.

The hour came and went, then noon, everyone waited. 'One o'clock passed, and yet no sign of the Prince.' In fact, it had been decided to postpone the meet for two hours, but in the absence of a telephone, nobody at Eastcourt was aware of this. At last, at 1.30 pm, up cantered the Earl of

Shannon waving his hunting crop to clear the road. Then came the Prince 'attired in VWH pink', and his entourage. It was too late to sit down to the bountiful luncheon; off went hounds and riders across the fields, and the carriages tried to turn and follow. A terrible traffic jam developed and carriages could scarcely budge. 'O what tedious work it is!' lamented the reporter. 'Hundreds of vehicles crushed into the gateway and the exodus obliged to be made in single file.'

How familiar it all sounds: even to the finding of a fox up a tree, just as on the day I attended a meet at Eastcourt.

Suddenly a check occurs, the whole line of carriages comes to a stand . . . See! the varmint addicted to airy lodgings near Crudwell church has of a truth been found, and the hounds are racing him along parallel with the road in beautiful style. Glorious sight! . . . HRH well up and he has numerous followers.

The fox, bundled out of his tree, made for Flisteridge, just as the fox I'd seen a few weeks ago had done, but on this occasion with success. The hounds changed foxes in the wood, number two ran past Minety to Ravens-roost where the hounds lost him. From Braydon Pond number three led them, sure enough, back to Flisteridge, where number four took over and led the cavalcade back to Charlton and a withy-bed 'where night came and the curtain fell'. Back at Cecily Hill in Cirencester, hungry no doubt after missing his luncheon, the Prince was entertained by singers on the lawn whose 'sweet melodies' proved so pleasing that the performers were invited in.

No word was said about the Eastcourt orgy. When the hunt belatedly took off, Mr Powell had doubtless opened the tent to the multitude and everyone had surged in. 'People were running about with legs of mutton,' said Albert Hislop, who'd heard the story from his grandfather. Mrs Picter, carrying Albert, must have got home just in time before her pains started. It's good to know that Walter Powell didn't go to his death with a heart broken by royal discourtesy.

17 February – SEVENTEENTH-CENTURY JUSTICE

Some, no doubt, were hunting foxes in the mud, under a grey sky drip-drip-dripping as if someone was wringing out an enormous dirty dishcloth overhead; I was hunting Pooles in the library, snug and warm, amid a faint smell of books and wet plastic macs.

The quarry is elusive, but occasional glimpses can be had among the records of Quarter Sessions; most of the senior Pooles sat on the Bench, generally at Devizes. The earliest case I came on, heard before Sir Henry Poole of Wockseye in April, 1615, concerned a bone-setter called Edward Shaile. Suzan Hedges, servant of Anthony ffrie of Brinkworth, deposed that in order to treat 'a greiffe in her necke,' Shaile 'with bothe his hands did turne her necke upright and in doing thereof hee harde some of the veins and sinewes of her necke goe cracke,' which left her with impaired speech and a neck permanently awry.

Edward Shaile denied the charge of professional incompetence; he had treated many patients who were 'never speechless or impaired in their witts thereby'.

The original cause of the injury had been a blow or blows by Suzan's master, but there was a conflict of evidence; one fellow-servant said that, after his assault, her neck had been red and swollen with kernells in it; another that the blow, only one, had done no harm, and Suzan had gone to bed without 'any showe of greiffe'. Sir Henry Poole committed Suzan 'to a house of correccon there to remaine till she be retayned into some honest man's service'; a judgment which at first glance seems harsh, but was probably designed to get the girl away from her harsh master Anthony ffrie. Possibly Sir Henry passed the word round that a useful servant-girl was to be picked up at the house of correction, even if she held her head to one side.

Then Edward Langdon came before him, also at Devizes, indicted for sorcery; he had sold to a cousin of Nicholas Reade of Myntie a charm 'of such a strong operation that yf yt were hanged about a cocke's necke then noe man should have the power to kill the said cocke'. The verdict is not recorded, nor that on John Browne of Potterne who came before the Bench for 'suffering of Rookes too Build and Breade about his House there to the great annoyance of Corne thereabout'.

One gets the impression, slenderly based perhaps, that Sir Henry Poole, the first of Oaksey, was a kindly man ready to do a good turn, when he could, to a neighbour. The year before his death at sixty-nine he wrote from Oaksey Park to intercede for a young clergyman at Kemble, Thomas Earle junior, son of the incumbent, who'd been bound over for paying improper attentions to a parishioner's wife; and there is something endearing about the instruction given in his will to his son and heir, to be loving and kind to his brother and sister and 'good unto my tenants, suffering them quietly to enjoy their several estates'.

Most of the cases heard at Quarter Sessions were humdrum affairs, but one stands out for its nastiness; the Justices aren't named, and I don't believe Sir Henry can have been among them. In 1632 Katherine Peters, a young widow nursing an infant son, was accused of stealing a tablecloth and a sheet from a hedge where they'd been put out to dry. For some obscure reason, she refused to plead; and it was for this, not for stealing two cloths valued at ten shillings each, that she was condemned to a punishment so appalling that even to read about it, in the comfortable security of Malmesbury's library more than three centuries later, chilled the blood.

She was to be 'brought to a close room and there to be layed upon her back naked from the middle upward, her legges and arms stretched out and fastened forewards towards the four corners of the room, and upon her body to have so much weight and somewhat over that she is able to bear'. On the first day, she was to have 'three morsells of coarse bread and noe drink, the second day drinke of the puddle of water, not running, next to the place where she lyeth and noe bread, so every day in like manner till she be dead'.

It seems incredible that such a dreadful torture should have been imposed merely for refusing to say whether or no she had stolen a tablecloth and sheet. Had she pleaded guilty, all her goods and chattels would have been forfeited; if she died without pleading, she could pass them on to her heirs. Had such a woman anything to pass on? Could she have been motivated by a resolve to leave what little she had to her infant son? That, too, seems incredible. There is something odd about this case. Harsh as judgments were, torture was normally reserved for much more serious offences such as treachery. Habitual felons were branded on the left hand with the letter F, for lesser offences a normal punishment was to be whipped till 'the boddye be bluddye'. In Katherine Peters' case the sentence 'de paine fort et dure' was carried out and she was slowly crushed and starved to death. Eighteen years later, the parishioners of Standen petitioned to be released from the obligation to support her son.

In the eighteenth century sentences became much less barbarous, though some of the crimes did not. In 1764 Henry Timbrell, a farmer from Malmesbury, was committed to gaol for castrating two lads he had undertaken to 'breed up for a small sum'. He hoped to take advantage of the good market then prevailing for *castrati*, mainly an export market to Rome. For this he got only four years and a fine of 26s 8d. This sentence was considered to be so light that 'it was with the utmost difficulty that he was preserved from the rage of the populace'.

Crime and punishment was only one of the concerns of country magistrates; they had also to carry out the rudimentary functions of a welfare state. They heard many petitions for pensions from old or disabled soldiers; matters of public health, poverty, wages and housing came before them. In 1636 forty-seven 'aged impotent decayed persons young children and infants which have no livelyhood but are ready to starve', dwelling in three score houses within the precincts of Malmesbury Abbey, appealed to Sir Nevill Poole and other magistrates for the 'consideration of their distressed care and examination'. Even worse off were 'two ancient people' of Broken-borough who, in default of any better dwelling, lived for a month in a hollow tree.

Minimum wages were fixed at Quarter Sessions and employers could be summonsed for failure to pay them. In 1655 the annual rates, which included meat and drink, were as follows:

Chief shepherd with 5,000 sheep and over, £5
Shepherd with 600 sheep, £3 6s 8d
Chief carter, £4
Common servant of husbandry, £3
Chief woman servant, £2 10s 0d
Every other woman servant, £1 10s 0d

There were also daily rates, as follows:

Mowing with meat and drink, 8d
Haymaking, 6d
Mowers of corn with meat and drink, 8d
Hedgers, ditchers, threshers and others, 3d

Or work could be paid for by the acre: 3d for reaping and binding corn, 7d for barley mowing, oats a penny less, pease 4d, grass 12d, ditching 6d a perch, and sawing 1s 10d a thousand feet.

'Ah,' as Sid sometimes remarks, 'money wuz worth zummat in them days.'

26 February – A BABY IN A BOX

Let sleeping scandals lie: that would be the polite course, but today, yielding to curiosity and with the aid of my old friend the *Wilts and Gloucestershire Standard*, I got to the bottom of the matter which caused Captain Arthur Randolph Mullings of Eastcourt House to change his name.

Mullings versus Mullings was heard before the Divorce Court on 25 July 1874. Ten years earlier, the Captain had espoused Bellamira Emma Primrose, aged eighteen, and one of the distinguished Scottish family headed by the Earl of Rosebery. Far from settling down in North Wilts among all those milk-dulled wits and gallipot eyes, the young couple took houses in various parts of England and on the Continent. In 1871–2, they had a house in Dresden.

Here the marriage went awry. The Captain 'frequently had cause to complain of his wife's levity of conduct and her indiscreet familiarity with gentlemen, and their disputes on this subject led to their occupying separate bedrooms'. That was her undoing. In November, 1872, she went to England with her maid and two children (leaving her husband in Dresden) to stay in Torquay, where a sister married to a parson was living. Unknown to her husband, Bellamira was pregnant, and had made arrangements with a doctor in London to have the baby there the following January.

Nature, however, intervened; the baby arrived prematurely in Torquay in such secrecy that even the servants in the house where she was staying, presumably her sister's, didn't know, or so Bellamira believed – optimistically, as it proved; to prevent a household staff from knowing that a confinement was taking place upstairs would have been a remarkable feat.

Even more remarkable was Bellamira's. No sooner was the baby delivered than she packed it in her trunk and caught the next train to London. The doctor, alerted by telegram, met her at Paddington and took her to Bayswater, where lodgings and a nurse awaited her. The baby was unpacked 'not much the worse for its journey'. Bellamira must have done a superb job of packing, especially when this was a task her maid would normally have performed.*

Torquay to Paddington is a long journey – the question of just how long was immediately answered, unlikely as this may seem, by our rector who, whipping an ABC from a shelf, ascertained that in 1873 Bellamira would, almost certainly, have caught the 11.30 am from Torquay (single first-class fare 25s od), changed at Exeter and reached Paddington at 6.10 pm. Then she would have to get to Bayswater, so the journey must have occupied at least seven hours in all, probably nearer eight.

What a nightmarish journey, with a charge of murder, not to mention social ruin, as its outcome if the baby didn't emerge alive from its trunk.

* My mother, who was born in 1885, tells me that in her youth a kind of trunk made of wicker-work, with a domed lid, was in vogue among fashionable ladies. If Bellamira had a trunk like this, it would explain how the baby survived without suffocating.

But emerge alive it did, and when the case was heard eighteen months later it was thriving.

Two months after the confinement, in February, 1873, the still unsuspecting Captain joined his wife in Torquay. Here 'what the butler saw' – or perhaps an under-housemaid – was communicated to him, and the divorce ensued. The suit was undefended.and the co-respondent not named, but Bellamira told the nurse who had attended her that he was 'a military officer in Dresden'. Soon after the decree *nisi* was made absolute, Bellamira married Geoffrey Darley Beswick, so presumably her lover was a British, not a German, military officer: possibly a brother-officer of Captain Mullings' in the 15th Hussars.

A man who divorces his wife, himself the 'innocent party', doesn't usually change his name as a result. Two reasons suggest themselves. The baby in the box would bear his name; perhaps he didn't want to share it with another man's child. And, within about two years of dropping the Mullings, the Captain married an American heiress. In the idiom of the day, his name had been 'dragged in the mud'; perhaps he wanted to offer a cleaner one to a new bride.

Bellamira, a woman of thirty when all this happened, lived only for another six years after her re-marriage. Captain Randolph had a son and daughter by his second wife; the son was killed in action in 1915, and *his* son, who became Judge Randolph's heir, was killed in a flying accident. So the Randolphs of Eastcourt House came to an end.

Going through the old files, a notion that there was something familiar about this bizarre story niggled at my mind. A baby in a box in a railway carriage: of course – Miss Prism and the infant Ernest deposited in the cloakroom at Victoria Station. There are discrepancies; Miss Prism's baby (or rather her employer's) never actually travelled, the stations were different, but the basic idea the same.

Oscar Wilde would have been an undergraduate at Oxford when the case was reported in the newspapers, and no doubt much talked about. Here surely is the seed which was to lie dormant for some twenty years and then germinate and blossom into *The Importance of Being Earnest*.

27 February – FOUR WILLIAMS

Fog every morning, reluctantly dissolving as the day goes on and an anaemic sun emerges, little brighter than the full moon which shares the heavens with it in the late afternoon. Catkins hang limply on bare hazel twigs. Oaksey Wood is a morass with yellowish water lying deep in slithery tractor ruts.

Gum-boots, or wellingtons: one of those unsung inventions which, unlike so many, have brought unalloyed benefit to country dwellers. Bill Sherwood and I agreed on this when we met in the wood. 'I had the first wellingtons in Oaksey,' he said. Geoffrey Lawrence brought a pair from London and got another pair for Bill, he thought in 1930. Before the days of wellingtons, no farm worker went dryshod in winter and despite thick socks, heavy boots and gaiters, their feet must have been permanently chilled.

Bill retired two years ago after working at Hill Farm for forty-eight years, in fact he still works there, part-time. His family occupied the last thatched cottage in the village. One day, when they were sitting at tea, the roof collapsed on top of them, burying everyone in straw, rotten timbers, old birds' nests and dismayed sparrows. They all climbed upstairs, and were eventually rescued by means of ladders.

Soon after came World War I and Bill's father, also a William, went off to enlist, although he was the father of five. His wife tried to stop him by letting the air out of his bicycle tyres but he borrowed another machine and cycled to Devizes. His family didn't see him again for three and a half years. No one, it was said, could thatch a rick or lay a hedge better than Bill the first. He came back safely and lived to be seventy-five.

Bill the second went when he was seventeen to Hill Farm and has been there ever since. His boss, Geoffrey Lawrence, then a busy barrister of the Inner Temple, started in the early twenties to breed pedigree Guernseys, and Bill became herdsman, eventually foreman. Soon there was a nursery at Hill Farm and each of the four little Lawrences learnt, in turn, to ride on a Shetland × Welsh pony called Mince Pie. It was Mince Pie on whom John, at the age of two, first practised the art of horsemanship in which he was to earn such distinction.

Bill married the nanny, so Lawrence and Sherwood lives became closely intertwined. In due course the Sherwoods produced another William, and the intention was to summon Mince Pie from his retirement in Wales to teach William the third how to ride. Before the intention could be executed, Mince Pie died, aged thirty-five. William the third became a policeman, so perhaps motor-bikes were more in his line. Now a fourth William has been added to the list.

28 February – SPRING POISON

At last, an early spring morning, soft and hazy, sunlight with a bit of warmth in it and moist earth smelling of growth; blackbirds whistling, promise in the air. This clay soil is still too wet to dig or hoe but there's much crying out for action.

The lawn, for instance. A small lawn but plenty big enough, and not at all lawnlike. Already a crop of grass thick enough for silage has come off it; the electric mower got even more exhausted than I did and had to be recharged twice. Then I've raked it twice, hard; broadcast lawn-sand; and today I sprayed it with one of those nameless chemicals, designated only by a number, that smells horrid and is guaranteed to kill everything except grass.

I didn't enjoy it. There were the daisies, some in flower, tucked so tightly into the ground as to dodge the mower and, when all's said and done, brightening up a gloomy winter scene. Neat little flowers with their yellow centres, perfectly harmless. Why should they be killed? Or indeed the clover, looking so green and healthy. Moss I don't mind about. The only plant that really is unsightly is the coarse couch-grass, and the spray won't kill that.

Why, on this fine sunny day with buds swelling, growth beginning, multi-coloured crocuses brilliant in the orchard, do I distribute poison, with its acrid smell that pollutes the air? Why do I want the lawn free from weeds?

This is hard to answer. I'm afraid it's a case of conformity, pressure of advertising, keeping up with the Joneses. Not that I'm ambitious about the lawn but gardening papers keep telling us that we must spray, rake, aerate, fertilize, spread peat and all the rest of it. Charles, at weekends, frowns at the plantains and removes them with a knife. One feels a sense of guilt about a neglected lawn. Visitors, if any, will lift an eyebrow. Do I care? Not really, yet the pressure's there, and on this sunny afternoon I distribute poison and murder daisies.

March

11 March – TRUE BLUE

Some of the village elders talk about a Captain Burnaby who was lord of the manor seventy or eighty years ago, but, like all our later lords, never lived here: a famous figure who died a hero's death in the Sudan. They recalled a portrait of him making a last stand with a broken sword amid a horde of howling savages all but, though not quite, engulfing the Union Jack. But George White, the old soldier, told me that it wasn't this Burnaby, but a cousin, who had owned the manor, and came occasionally 'to collect the rents'.

By a coincidence, there's a Burnaby-Atkins, a member of this military family – himself a Colonel – living, or at least weekending, in the village today: a son-in-law of Marjorie and Geoffrey Oaksey's Freddie lent me a book about his once famous, now forgotten cousin, who's depicted on the jacket reclining elegantly on a white settee with a cigarette between his fingers, wearing a spiked moustache and a languid expression, with a plumed helmet at his side: a perfect Ouida figure. (This from a painting by James Tissot in the National Portrait Gallery.) The book, *A True Blue*, by Richard Alexander, says that he was the tallest and strongest officer in the British Army and that he once twisted a poker round the neck of the Prince of Wales. Like Walter Powell, he was an enthusiastic balloonist and made a successful flight over the Channel. Clad in a blazer and a pillbox hat, he ate a beef sandwich, drank a bottle of Apollinaris and smoked a cigar before landing in Normandy.

He met his end on the battlefield of Abu Klea, where a British force advancing towards Khartoum in the hope of relieving General Gordon was attacked by the fuzzie-wuzzies, who broke the British square. In the picture, a bearded sheikh plants his flag in the centre, declaiming from the Quaran before he falls. Colonel Frederick Gustavus Burnaby of the Blues has been speared in the throat.

'Oh, sir, here is the bravest man in England dying,' cried a young trooper who was the first to reach the stricken Colonel. Tears were streaming down his face. 'In my own detachment,' wrote a brother-officer, 'many of the men sat down and cried.' By then, every fuzzie-wuzzie who had broken the square lay dead. It was during this battle that General Stewart gave to Corporal Payne of the 60th Rifles the famous order 'Don't fire, men, until you see the whites of their eyes.'

Tradition has it that this dashing officer was seen sometimes in the village, visiting his cousin; but as Algernon Edwyn Burnaby (the cousin) never lived here, this seems unlikely. Algernon Edwyn inherited the manor from his grandmother, Mrs Frances Salisbury's youngest daughter Anne Caroline, but lived in Leicestershire and became Master of the Quorn; and famous, Freddie said, like all good MFH's, for his blustery language on the hunting field.

13 March – THE INSTITUTE

I took my projector and a box of transparencies to the Village Hall this afternoon for the Womens' Institute meeting. The transparencies and I have grown old together, they more restfully in the loft; it must be thirty years since most of them were made. Age doesn't seem to have dimmed them but it has crept up on the screen; a bit of the frame broke off as I erected it and only with the utmost difficulty was it persuaded to stand upright at a drunken angle, swaying dangerously.

Last night, when I ran through the slides, I was rather pleased with them; colours clear, outlines crisp, panoramic views. So this afternoon I switched on with confidence and the screen went black; no image, no anything. Witchcraft in the night? There seemed nothing for it but to proceed. 'Here, I think, if we could see it, is a herd of elephants. Browsing on acacia trees.' I tried a dissertation on the family life of elephants. 'I think the next is a view over the Rift Valley; magnificent if we could only see it.' Very gradually, like a winter dawn breaking, the screen grew a little lighter. My audience of fifteen middle-aged and elderly ladies was extremely sympathetic. 'I'm sure it will improve when it warms up,' said Mrs Gealer. 'I think it's clearing a little,' Mrs Bennett added. 'It just needs time,' Ruth agreed.

They were right; objects began to show up on the screen. Soon we had real pictures and everyone felt a lot better. My commentary now became all too explicit. 'This is a lion.' Its tawny torso filled the screen, it could hardly have been anything else. To finish up with, I had put in a few slides of our former rose-garden. First a bed of Iceberg, then Sid among the Superstars and then, suddenly, a group of melancholy camels beside a desert well. Hastily removed, it gave way to a street scene in Mogadischu. I must have left the audience under the impression that we'd had a camel farm down at Woodfolds, in a very odd climate.

I judged a competition for the Most Unusual Teapot – the winner was decorated with little animal faces – and had a cup of tea. Such a kind, polite, long-suffering audience; it's sad that so few now join the WI and that nearly all who do so are elderly. 'None of the Bendybow people come,' one member said with regret.

15 March – TAILORS

Mary Luce said that when she first came to Malmesbury early in the 1940s, 'the house with the mirror' on the sharp bend in Gloucester Street, where she lived and lives, was occupied by twenty-eight tailors who sat cross-legged on the bare boards of a room comprising the whole of the first floor, stitching away to fill orders for a London firm which charged enormous prices and paid the tailors very little. Tailors had occupied the house for generations, working from dawn to dark with all the windows closed.

Four quartets of maiden ladies, she added, then lived in the town. Four Misses Luce and four Misses de Bertodano at The Knoll and Cowbridge

House respectively, four Misses Pitt and four Misses Hanks in the town. Luce, Pitt and Hanks are all familiar local names, but de Bertodano? The four sisters' father was a Spanish nobleman, Baldo Hyacinth, Marquis da Mara, who cherished an ambition to become an English country gentleman. He bought a big house with a park outside the town, and settled in with all the appurtenances of rank; carriages, cockaded grooms, liveried footmen, Scots gardeners, horses, dogs, guns, tweed suits, the lot.

He, it seems, was happy in his rôle, but his daughters were lonely and never really took to gardening in thick brogues, let alone the hunting field. Staunch Roman Catholics, they were nevertheless obliged to worship at the Abbey, where services at that time were particularly 'low'. None of them married, and when their father died they lived on at Cowbridge, leading empty lives amid the pomp and circumstance until the last one died.

There's a local tradition that the Misses Hank, also the last of their line, shared a common ancestor with Abraham Lincoln. Abraham's grand-mother, Lucy Hanks, was born in Virginia, and it was to Virginia that Thomas Hanks of Malmesbury went as an indentured servant sometime during, or soon after, the English Civil War. In 1653 he secured the free grant of a hundred acres to which he was entitled on completing his indentures, so evidently he settled in Virginia; but whether Abraham Lincoln's grandmother, born about a century after Thomas Hanks emi-grated, was his descendant, it's impossible to say. The Hanks ancestry, an American historian has observed, is 'the despair of genealogists'; and if Americans can't reconstruct the President's family tree, then nobody can.

18 March – FOSSE GATE

On this crisp spring day, with an east wind blowing, a warmthless sun, blue skies and scudding clouds, I set out in pursuit of a long-standing ambition: to trace the Swill Brook to its source.

Starting at Pill Bridge where the Brook, as you go upstream, becomes Braydon Brook – or rather one of the Braydon Brooks, there are three – I followed the eastern branch which trickles past Eastcourt House. Earle, Pitt, Mullings/Randolph, Cooper, Pitman – five family ownerships, one lasting only a few years, in three centuries. A pair of mallards takes off from the stream, a twitteration of tits moves among the bare branches of hawthorn and alder. How neglected the trees look, festooned with ivy. Pylons straddle the Brook.

At Crudwell, it disappears beneath the A429. Emerging the other side somewhat disorganized (we are going upstream), it coheres again into a cross between a brook and a ditch running beside a very narrow lane; but instead of petering out, it takes again to the level meadows.

Such muddy, flooded, windswept meadows. I squelch along thinking that at any minute I'll reach a place that could be called the Brook's source. I should have known better. Streams here don't rise, that is merely a poetical expression; they seep out of ditches that are sometimes dry and sometimes not, and start from no fixed address. Celandines speckle the banks. The east wind bites.

I come to another narrow lane. I think I recognize it; it leads to a withdrawn, reserved hamlet called Ashley with a fine old manor house standing up against the parish church, formerly its chapel. Here once lived Sir Theobald Gorges, who married a sister of Frances, wife of our Sir Nevill Poole of Oaksey. Nowadays the manor house, like so many others which have survived, is a farmhouse, and its owner, a widow, does beautiful embroidery of birds and flowers.

We have come to Fosse Way. This sounds impressive and appears so on the map, a straight line cutting across-country from Lincoln to Exeter; but on the ground this section, between Kemble and Newnton, is nothing but a muddy track, puddled by the hooves of horses, running between brambly hedges, with gipsies camping at one end and badgers burrowing at the other. Fosse Gate is the name on the map.

It was hereabouts that King Æthelstan, riding along the Way, came upon a woman sitting on a stool, with a cow tied to the stool's leg. She explained that 'they had no common belonging to the Towne' (I suppose meaning Ashley or Newnton) so she was baiting her cow. The King immediately granted to the local people 'so much ground in common as the woman would ride round on a bare-ridged horse'. A knight was sent with her, the land set aside, and monks built a house for the hayward to live in 'to look after the beasts that fed upon this common'. Every Trinity Sunday (all this according to Aubrey) the commoners prayed and dined together. But the house was burnt down in the Civil War, and in 1678 the custom of the annual commoners' feast ended.

Braydon Brook goes under Fosse Gate through a little culvert and across a field on the other side. By now it's become so small, all but invisible, that surely it can be called a ditch. In a brambly thicket by the Fosse Way, I feel I can leave it with a clear conscience; this is as near to a source as I'm likely to get. It was snowing when I reached home.

21 March – LANDLORD AND TENANT

John Ody was cleaning out his fowl-house: an old-fashioned wooden fowl-house sheltering old-fashioned hens; he had a rusty wheelbarrow and an ancient prong. The barns look tottery, ivy grips the stone tiles of outhouses, pig-sties are falling in. There's a hand-pump just inside the back door, an outside privy, and electricity is the only new-fangled device that's been installed.

I asked him if his hens paid. 'Lord bless you no, if I got twice the price for my eggs it still wouldn't cover the cost of their feed.' Then why keep them? 'Well, the Colonel likes the eggs, he'd be disappointed.' The Colonel is the landlord, the man who, according to the book, should have had water laid on, yards concreted, buildings modernized and so on. Far from complaining, the tenant is well satisfied with his *quid pro quo*.

'He's been fair to me. He's not gone putting up the rent every year or two like most.' In fact, I believe he hasn't put up the rent at all, which must be a unique situation. So everyone's happy, more or less pretending that the twentieth century hasn't happened.

Things haven't always run so smoothly between landlord and tenant. When John Ody first came, he and the Colonel fell out over some timber and didn't speak for five years. Then a day came when, passing each other in the lane, the Colonel nodded. A year or so later he said 'good-morning'; matters progressed, and now they're on excellent terms.

24 March – THE POOLES OF POOLE

Church Farm at Poole Keynes, as the name implies, lies cheek by jowl with the church, turning its back on the road. Seen from behind, it looks much like any other old, substantial Cotswold farmhouse, except for an unusual chimney, quite round, and rising from a curved base. I thought I'd never seen another like it, and no wonder, for today Robert Hiscock, the farm's owner, told me that there are only three others of the same design in the country, or so he's been informed; and that it's medieval, dating, possibly, from the thirteenth century.

Once inside, there is the old baronial hall and no mistake. A wide oak arch, filled in now by a modern wall, rises to a ceiling fourteen or fifteen feet high. An oak beam runs the whole length of the house; it must have been cut from one of the mightiest trees in Braden. Underfoot, the old uneven flagstones remain. The walls are four or five feet thick.

It's magnificent, romantic even, but scarcely convenient and surely cold. Were I Mrs Hiscock, my thoughts would often turn towards a modern bungalow.

Indeed such thoughts, if not quite on the bungalow level, may well have occurred to Griselda, wife of Sir Henry Poole, and prompted him to build a residence at Oaksey in the modern style. Baronial halls with great archways and open hearths where whole sheep were roasted on spits, stone floors perhaps strewn with rushes, and hosts of servitors: such things had gone out of favour by the end of the sixteenth century. Oaksey Park was altogether cosier, warmer, more compact and even elegant, and Griseld was doubtless delighted when the new mansion was ready and the family moved, leaving the manor house at Poole for sons and brothers. Edward Poole, Sir Henry's grandson, was living here in 1644, when he had a tablet affixed to the wall of the chancel to commemorate his daughter Frances, who died at Poole at the age of three.

Edward and his wife Dorothea, or Dorothy, would not have been living at Poole in medieval grandeur, draughtiness and (to some extent) squalor; the house was modernized and extensively altered sometime, architectural evidence suggests, early in the seventeenth century. Probably the arch was then filled in, new windows made, and a large part of the old manor house pulled down.

There's a local tradition that it was badly damaged by fire in the Civil War when Cromwellian troops attacked its Royalist occupants. This can't be right, because its occupant was Edward Poole, a Parliamentarian. (He and his father, Sir Nevill, were among those charged with the collection of Wiltshire's assessment of £725 a week towards the support of the Parliamentary forces commanded by the Earl of Essex.) If the manor house suffered at all during the Civil War, it was much more likely to have done so at the hands of the Royalists, whose forces under Prince Rupert took Cirencester in February, 1643, and held the countryside around it for some time afterwards – even though Sir William Waller for the Parliament recaptured Malmesbury in the following March. It was all very confused. There seems to be no evidence one way or the other about a fire.

After his father (Sir Nevill) died in 1651, Edward must have lived mainly at Oaksey, because he entertained Aubrey there around 1670. Whether the manor house at Poole continued to be occupied by Pooles we don't know. Edward's son Nevill may have lived there, as he married several years before he succeeded his father. There were always sons and brothers to be accommodated. Edward's younger brother Gyles had the manor of South Cerney, but Sir Nevill (senior) left instructions in his will that the manor was to be sold to pay Gyles' debts, so he was evidently if not a black sheep, then a spotted one. The family also had at its disposal the manor house at Kemble, now Kemble House, since for eight generations they held as one these three adjacent manors – Kemble, Poole and Oaksey – plus others that came and went. The first Sir Henry's younger brother, Walton, had the manor of Ewen.

If we don't know when the Pooles left their manor house at Poole and allowed a farm tenant to occupy it, we can hazard a fairly close guess as to who built it. In 1241 Margery, widow of Roger Fitzpayne, was presented by Henry III with two bucks and six does from Braden Forest to stock her park at 'Pole'. A park implies a dwelling house, perhaps a new one since it needed to be stocked with deer. Roger Fitzpayne, living in the first half of the thirteenth century, seems a likely candidate as builder of this manor house now dwelt in by the Hiscocks, and that fits in with the probable date of the round chimney.

After the Fitzpaynes, the lease of the manor from the Duchy of Lancaster must have passed to a family called Pagan, for in 1315 an inquisition on the will of Robert, son of Pagan, itemized the manor's resources. There was a capital messuage with garden (the manor house), eighty-five acres of arable, seven acres of meadow, some pasture, and 'a certain grove of ten acres' bringing in five shillings a year. Dwellings on this manor of 776 acres were two free tenants, eleven 'natives' holding one virgate each, and five 'natives' each holding half a virgate.

Soon afterwards, Robert, son of Pagan evidently gave way as lessee of the manor to Sir John Maltravers, whose daughter and co-heiress married Sir John Keynes in 1327, and the village acquired the second half of its name. Then there's a gap in the records of nearly two centuries until, in 1517, the lease was granted by Henry VIII to Richard Poole. The manor house was occupied by his grandson Henry, who married Jane Nevill; part of his tomb and coat of arms can be seen on the wall of the little church today.

25 March – A HISCOCK DIARY

There have been Hiscocks living at Church Farm at Poole for well over a century, and relatives and forebears of Hiscocks for some time before that. Three families, the Hiscocks and the Reynolds and the Manners, inter-married and inter-twined in the usual complicated fashion. Robert Hiscock kindly lent me a diary kept by his grandfather Henry William, who was born here in 1858, and in due course inherited the tenancy of Church Farm.

Like almost all countrymen, he was fascinated by pedigrees, and starts his diary with the arresting claim: 'There is good reason for believing that at the time of the deluge our ancestors occupied a place in the ark.' (Their descendants must have felt at home this winter, with water, water everywhere.) Neatly written in a clear hand in small notebooks, it gives a vivid picture of the lives of yeoman farmers, which changed little over the centuries until after World War II: frugal, hard-working, God-fearing, sober, earthbound lives, the menfolk tending their livestock and working their land in all weather seven days a week, the women bearing babies almost every year.

Children were raised on plain fare. Fresh meat was bought only on very special occasions; for the rest, almost everything was home-grown. For breakfast, skim milk and wholemeal bread, home-baked; for dinner, bacon, potatoes, green vegetables when in season, and now and again a 'long apple-pudding'; more bread with skim milk or whey butter for tea, with a cup of weak tea but no sugar; and finally for supper a bite of bread and cheese. There's no mention of eggs, though fowls must certainly have been kept; probably Henry's mother sent them all to market to make every penny she could; egg-money traditionally belonged to the wife.

It was a struggle to survive, and the aim of every farmer to save enough cash to stock a farm for his sons when they married and secured a tenancy. If a father could provide £100 for every son, he had cause for satisfaction; a sum of £50 or even £10 each was as much as many could manage. A single bad season could tip the balance between solvency and disaster for these tenant farmers.

Tough as the struggle was, work as they did from dawn to dark and after, these yeoman farmers had their pride and status. The diarist's mother Fanny Reynolds was sent at the age of ten to one of the small, unsupervised boarding schools that seem then to have abounded, where for a fee of £20 a year she was treated as a maid-of-all-work and half-starved, rather than to the national school in the village where her brothers went. Her aunts, the Misses Reynolds, 'kept their proper station and could be very smart on occasion'. Henry remembers a large wooden box in which they kept their bonnets; these were made of cardboard, shaped like a coal-scuttle and covered with silk, with a lace border in front. Fanny's father kept for best 'a pigeon-tail coat with breeches of best cord, gaiters or top boots'.

The Reynolds were Primitive Methodists and Henry (Fanny's father) often walked across the fields from Church Farm to preach at Oaksey's chapel. On such occasions those children who were left behind could play in the garden, a frivolity forbidden on a Sunday under their father's eye. Henry Reynolds' cousin Joseph Hiscock had the tenancy of Park Farm at Oaksey; when he died in 1859 he left his wife eight shillings a week. She kept on the tenancy and one of her sons helped her until he cut off a hand with a steam chaff-cutting machine, and died as a result.

All these farms, in those days, were held on yearly tenancies from land-lords: in the case of Oaksey, Mrs Frances Salisbury; of Poole and Kemble, Robert Gordon, the man who had the Cheltenham line put through a tunnel. On his death in 1863 these two manors passed to his only surviving child Anna. She never married, and left not only Poole and Kemble but a whole bunch of other manors (Rodmarton, Tarlton, Hullesey, Culkerton and Hayley; she had already sold Nether Lypiatt and two in Scotland) to Michael Biddulph, the son of an old friend of her father's who had helped her to run her estates.

Michael Biddulph was raised to the peerage in 1903 and remained lord of all these manors, but after his death his son sold off most of the farms to their tenants for modest sums. Bob Hiscock's father bought Church Farm, medieval manor house and all. Two of his three sons work it with him; they'll be the fifth Hiscock generation to milk and plough on this fertile level land beside Flagham Brook, within three miles of the source of the Thames. And probably the last, since taxation is now ending the tradition of father-to-son that has for so many centuries governed the disposal of farm land.

26 March – COURT LEET AND COURT BARON

Bob Hiscock brought round for me to see not only his grandfather's diary, but the minute books of Poole Keynes' Court Leet and Court Baron with View of Frankpledge for the years 1845–1871, when the last such court was held.

Originally these manorial courts were held every year, but in later times became more irregular. The freeholders of the manor came to do homage to their lord, to pay their rents, and to elect a constable, a hayward and tithingmen. (A tithing was a company of ten householders, each of whom was responsible for the good conduct of, and answerable for any damage done by, every other member.) A jury of twelve was sworn; deaths were reported and tenancies surrendered, entered into or renewed; rights of way were confirmed, rules of husbandry laid down, and any point of general local interest discussed.

These feudal institutions ceased to have any relevance to social conditions when Acts of Parliament replaced fealty to the lord as the basis of land tenure; to go on holding them in the nineteenth century was a piece of flummery which Robert Gordon, lord of the manors of Poole and Kemble from 1809 until 1865, evidently enjoyed. Perhaps his tenants did too; it gave them an opportunity to air their grievances in public, and to settle matters such as a dispute between Poole and Oaksey over their boundary. Poole accused Oaksey of moving the boundary into their parish; the jury examined John Strange, aged seventy-three, and Thomas Uzzell, aged eighty-two, and found a brook called Highells to be the proper boundary. (It was probably Thomas Uzzell's son Cornelius who performed a remarkable feat, commemorated by a sampler hanging in the bar of the Wild Duck Inn at Ewen; he consumed six pounds of bacon, half raw and half par-boiled, at a single sitting.)

Now and again, the Court rapped someone on the knuckles. 'We present William Reynolds and James Pinnegar for ploughing up the footpath from Poole to Somerford.' People who deposited rubbish by the highway were reprimanded, and the hayward authorized to impound stray sheep and fine their owners one shilling.

When Anna, only child of Robert Gordon and his wife Elizabeth Anne (born Coxe, and great grand-daughter of Sir Robert Westley) became lady of the manor in 1865, she evidently decided that tradition, like time, must have a stop; only two courts were held, in 1867 and 1871, after the death of her father. Perhaps she felt that Frankpledge ('a court held periodically for the production of members of a tithing, later of a hundred or manor': OED) was, several years after the passing of the second Reform Act, a little out of date.

27 March – THE POOR DEAR GREAT WESTERN

Kemble House is another of those old manorial mansions that's become a farmhouse, in this case so thoroughly reconstructed in the nineteenth century by Robert Gordon that it's lost most of its medieval look, while gaining greatly in comfort. It lay empty for some time until, in 1946, the second Lord Biddulph sold it to Samuel John Phillips, a Cornishman who migrated to Gloucestershire with a few pounds in his pocket and built up a farming empire, which continues to be run as a company with his son at its head. Today his widow occupies the ground floor while the rest of the mansion, turned into flats, provides accommodation for members of the company's staff.

With the lordship of the manor and the land, the records of the Court Leet and Court Baron with View of Frankpledge came to Mr Phillips, and now are carefully preserved at Kemble House by Mrs Phillips. She'd laid them out for me to see on a polished table in a spacious drawing-room, through whose big bay windows I looked over smooth lawns flanked by splendid old trees towards fields, a small wood and the invisible railway line, concealed in its tunnel.

The earliest record, a scrap of parchment written in Latin, goes back to 1583, but the Court books as a series date from 1668, when Sir Edward Poole was lord of the manor. Whether he actually lived at Kemble or at Oaksey it is hard to say; one daughter was buried here at Kemble in 1672 and another later married in the church; perhaps he maintained an establishment in both places. Then came Sir Henry, followed by his son, plain Henry, who seems also to have had a foot in both camps. Two of his infant children were buried here at Kemble in 1700 and 1701 and a son, Nevill, baptized here in 1702, and he himself, the last of the male Pooles, was buried in the churchyard. On the other hand another daughter, Phenella, was baptized at Oaksey in 1697 and yet another, Stuart, buried there in 1714. Their mother Stuart, daughter of Henry Wallis of Groombridge, presented two large patens to Kemble church in 1708, but there is no record of her burial either here or at Oaksey.

It was her daughter Finetta (of the twenty-two children) who sold all three manors to Sir Robert Westley, and Westley's son John who split the property that had stayed as one since Tudor times. His sister Elizabeth, to whom he left Kemble and Poole, married Charles Coxe, and their grand-daughter espoused Robert Gordon, MP (1787–1864), which is how he came to receive the homage of the Court Leet and Court Baron of Kemble. He and his wife Elizabeth had an only child, Anna, the last of the line.

Anna inherited from her parents 8,000 acres of good Gloucestershire land, with a bit of Dorset and Scotland thrown in; it's surprising that she never married. Perhaps she felt that she'd be wooed for her acres rather than her charms. After her father's death in 1864, she devoted herself to carrying out her father's wishes. He was a strong supporter of the temperance movement, and to the day of her death in 1884, and beyond it, the

-'coffee tavern' at Kemble station was allowed no licence to sell beer or spirits.

Indeed, she fought a rearguard action against the station itself. Her father had wrung from the Cheltenham and Great Western Union Railway an undertaking that access to the station should be confined to a footpath from which the public should be barred; only the Company's staff might use it, and the Gordons themselves, who had the right to board a train by giving notice to the station-master at Cirencester. Everyone else had to go to Coates, then known as Tetbury Road, which was just over the boundary of the Gordon lands.

As time went on, public pressure for a proper station at Kemble, a junction for Tetbury and Cirencester, built up, to be countered by a 'polite refusal' from Miss Gordon. She evidently entertained herself no animus against the railway, referring to it as 'the poor dear Great Western', but her father's wishes were sacrosanct.

The crunch came when one of the directors of the railway, invited to a hunt ball at Cirencester by Lord Bathurst, on changing trains at Kemble found himself huddled with a score of other passengers into a tiny wooden shed, the temperature well below freezing point, obliged to wait a long time for the connection. Action was swift. A Parliamentary Bill concerning Great Western matters was in the pipeline, and into it was inserted a clause giving the Company powers to acquire land on the Gordon estate.

So the station came into being, but not the pub; after Anna's death the Biddulphs maintained her father's veto on strong drink, and it was not until they sold the property to S. J. Phillips that the Coffee Tavern became the Station Inn.

Maundy Thursday – THE TITLE DEEDS

A year ago, Jim promised to show me his title deeds as soon as he got them back on Lady Day and Park Farm became the unencumbered property of himself, his wife Renée and their two sons. Today, he's been as good as his word.

Forty documents, or thereabouts, were displayed on a table in the old granary. One of these, closely written on both sides of the parchment in a copperplate hand, covers over thirty pages and can be read only by spreading it out on the floor. In an entanglement of legal phrases it is possible to discover an arrangement, made in 1854 on behalf of Mrs Frances Salisbury and her trustees, to divide the inheritance of Oaksey Park, though not the estate itself in a physical sense, into three equal shares, one to go to each of her daughters and their heirs. Most of the facts I know already, but his deed ties up a few loose ends.

Thomas Salisbury and Frances Webb must have been a well-off couple. The Salisburys were a Yorkshire family. Thomas's father set up as a solicitor in Lancaster and made a modest fortune on the side by trading with the West Indies. Thomas followed his father in the law, moved to Dorchester (Dorset) and built up a substantial practice. The couple lived at Fordington nearby, never at Oaksey, which Frances brought to their joint settlement. After they'd had three daughters Thomas died, at the age of forty-nine, in 1810, and his widow went with her children to live with her father Francis Webb in Salisbury Close.*

The youngest of the three daughters, Anne Caroline, who married Edwyn Burnaby of Baggrave, had one son, Edwyn Sherard. He joined the Grenadier Guards, rose to become a Major-General, and was the heir to Oaksey Park and a progenitor of Queen Elizabeth II.

In the salubrious air of Brighton – No 1, Palmeira Square – Sophia Frances and Maria Salisbury lived well into their eighties, dying in 1882 and 1886 respectively. By this time both Anne Caroline and her son the Major-General had expired, leaving as the heir Edwyn Sherard's son Algernon Edwyn Burnaby who, under trust, found himself, in 1886, lord of the manor of Oaksey at the age of eighteen.

It was a hollow inheritance. Over the years, mortgage had been piled on mortgage, in part no doubt for the support of the two old ladies of Palmeira Square. In 1906, Algernon Edwyn and his trustees sold the property, shrunk by then to 532 acres, to Lawrence James Baker of Ennismore Gardens, London. When five mortgages totalling £15,879 had been paid off, Algernon Edwyn was left with exactly £200.

Jim's title deeds have cleared up one puzzling point. From time to time, the Earl of Ilchester's name has cropped up in various documents; an annual rent of £50 16s 10d was paid to him by the estate although he didn't own any property in Oaksey. King Charles II, it seems, was responsible. In 1671 that impecunious monarch set up a system of selling for substantial sums, and in perpetuity, the rents of farms that didn't belong to him. The Lord Ilchester of the day bought Wilts Nos 55 and 56; the first brought in an annual rent of £46 11s 11¼d from the manor of Wokesey, alias Woxey, Park. The Earl's successors continued to enjoy annual subventions from the

---

* For these particulars about the Salisbury family I am indebted to Mr T. G. Lister Salisbury of Wellington, New Zealand, a descendant of Thomas's brother Edward.

tenants of Park Farm until 1947, when these 'fee farm rents' were redeemed on payment of £611 2s 6d.

After the sale of the manor, or half-manor as it had by then become to Lawrence Baker in 1906, the property passed jointly on his death in 1921 to four of his children (Hugh Baker was one). Then came the end. In 1938 the Bakers sold the remains of the estate for £8,276 to Arthur Howard Smith of Ipswich, who offered it immediately for sale in separate lots at the King's Head in Cirencester.

The rest we know. Less than half the lots found buyers, even at minimal prices. Park Farm and 'the mansion' went to the Bruderhof, or Society of Brothers; the three remaining farms, Woodfolds, Manby's and Johnson's, went for their reserve prices, but most of the cottages remained unsold. After the auction, a number were sold for give-away sums to their tenants: two in The Street to Albert Picter for £95; one to Mrs Norris for £70; a strip of land along The Green, that would today be called a building site, went for £3.

Within two years the Bruderhof had sold Park Farm and 'the mansion' to the Cirencester Benefit Society for £12,000. Jim came in as tenant of the farm; 'the mansion' became RAF billets and then an unsuccessful hotel. In 1956 Jim demolished it, after it had stood for about 340 years.

So the manor house of Oaksey, alias Woxey, alias Wockeseye, alias many other names, has followed the castle that once belonged to kings into oblivion. The elms have gone, and the fritillaries, and deeper things: the coherence of a small community whose members faced together the pains and dangers of the world.

Well: there's a new James down at the Park, born on the first day of the New Year. April, the cruellest month, is upon us; April I distrust, yet before it's out there'll be daffodils, and swallows, and lambs. If four centuries saw out the castle, and another four the mansion, forty years may be enough for Bendybow. But something will be standing on our ridge, I shouldn't wonder, looking down across the Swill Brook towards Flisteridge, in forty, four hundred, forty thousand years.

GENEALOGICAL TABLES

LORDS OF THE MANOR OF OAKSEY

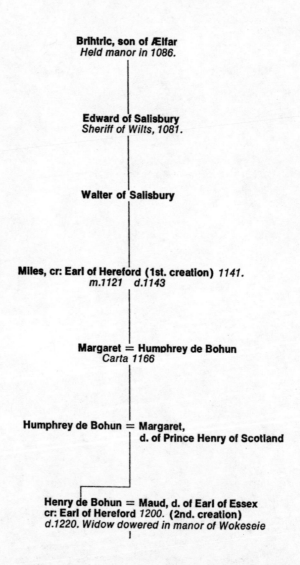

Brihtric, son of Ælfar
Held manor in 1086.

Edward of Salisbury
Sheriff of Wilts, 1081.

Walter of Salisbury

Miles, cr: Earl of Hereford (1st. creation) *1141.*
m.1121   d.1143

Margaret = Humphrey de Bohun
Carta 1166

Humphrey de Bohun = Margaret,
d. of Prince Henry of Scotland

Henry de Bohun = Maud, d. of Earl of Essex
cr: Earl of Hereford *1200.* **(2nd. creation)**
d.1220. Widow dowered in manor of Wokeseie

1

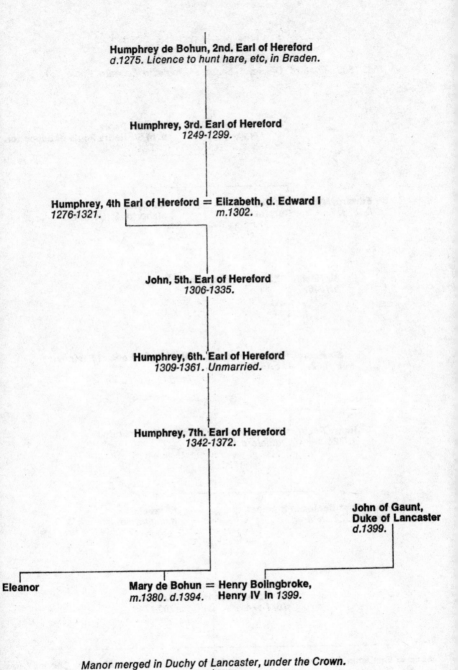

Humphrey de Bohun, 2nd. Earl of Hereford
d.1275. Licence to hunt hare, etc, in Braden.

Humphrey, 3rd. Earl of Hereford
1249-1299.

Humphrey, 4th Earl of Hereford = **Elizabeth, d. Edward I**
1276-1321.   *m.1302.*

John, 5th. Earl of Hereford
1306-1335.

Humphrey, 6th. Earl of Hereford
1309-1361. Unmarried.

Humphrey, 7th. Earl of Hereford
1342-1372.

**John of Gaunt,
Duke of Lancaster**
d.1399.

Eleanor   **Mary de Bohun** = **Henry Bolingbroke,**
            m.1380. d.1394.   **Henry IV in** *1399.*

Manor merged in Duchy of Lancaster, under the Crown.

**Henry V — Henry VI — Edward IV — Edward V —
Richard III — Henry VII — Henry VIII — Elizabeth I — James I**

Lease 1614 to
Sir Henry Poole, M.P. = Griselda
1563-1632. First of Oaksey. (Lease of Poole to Leonard Poole 1515.)

Sir Nevill, M.P. = Frances Poole,
1592-1651. **d. of Sir Henry Poole of Sapperton**

Sir Edward, M.P. = Dorothy or
1618-1673. **Dorothea**

Sir Gyles
Manor of S. Cerney.

Sir Nevill = Elizabeth, d. Maximilian Bard
b.1646.

Sir Henry = Elizabeth Earle, d. Sir Thomas Earle of Eastcourt
b.1672. | *b.1673. m.1694.*

Henry Poole = Stuart, d. Henry Wallis of Groombridge
d.1726 | *d.before 1714.*

Finetta = Benjamin Bathurst
m.1713. 22 children.

Elizabeth
d.unmarried.

Manor sold in 1732 to
Sir Robert Westley = Elizabeth
1671-1745. | *1700-1746*

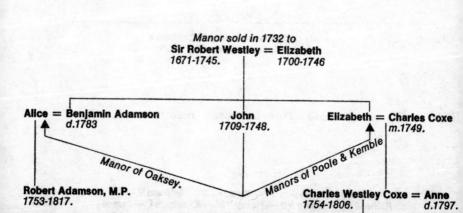

Alice = Benjamin Adamson
d.1783

John
1709-1748.

Elizabeth = Charles Coxe
| *m.1749.*

Manor of Oaksey.

Manors of Poole & Kemble

Robert Adamson, M.P.
1753-1817.

Charles Westley Coxe = Anne
1754-1806. | *d.1797.*

or of Oaksey sold at auction in London,
1787, mainly to
Iames Harris, 1st. Earl of Malmesbury
†6-1820. (Peerage 1788: Earldom 1800.)

Elizabeth Anne = **Robert Gordon, M.P.**
_m.1809._   _1787-1864._

Anna Gordon
_1809-1884._
Left manors of Kemble & Poole
to Michael Biddulph,
cr: 1st Lord Biddulph in 1903.

Manor sold in 1801 to
Francis Webb
_d.1814._

nces = **Thomas Salisbury of Fordington, Dorset**
_795._ | _d.1810_
_962._

ria   **Sophia Frances**   **Anne Caroline** = **Edwyn Burnaby**
_882._   _d.1886._   _1799-1867._

Major-General Edwyn Sherrard Burnaby   **5 daughters**
_1830-1883._

Algernon Edwyn Burnaby
_1868-1938._
Manor sold in 1906 to
Lawrence James Baker

Lawrence Ingham, Hugh, Charles and Alice Baker

Sale and dispersal of manor 1938.
Park and Park Farm sold to
Cotswold Bruderhof

Cirencester Benefit Society
_in 1941._

James Woodhouse _in 1954._
_1911-_

THE POOLES OF OAKSEY AND POLE OR POOLE

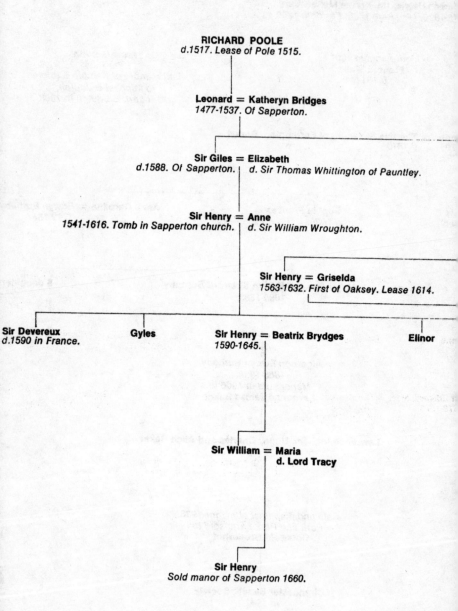

RICHARD POOLE
d.1517. Lease of Pole 1515.

Leonard = **Katheryn Bridges**
1477-1537. Of Sapperton.

Sir Giles = **Elizabeth**
d.1588. Of Sapperton. | *d. Sir Thomas Whittington of Pauntley.*

Sir Henry = **Anne**
1541-1616. Tomb in Sapperton church. | *d. Sir William Wroughton.*

Sir Henry = **Griselda**
1563-1632. First of Oaksey. Lease 1614.

Sir Devereux   **Gyles**   **Sir Henry** = **Beatrix Brydges**   **Elinor**
d.1590 in France.   *1590-1645.*

Sir William = **Maria**
                  d. Lord Tracy

Sir Henry
Sold manor of Sapperton 1660.

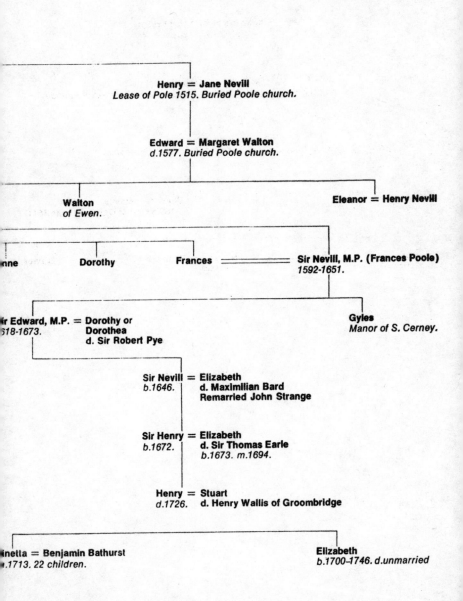

Henry = Jane Nevill
Lease of Pole 1515. Buried Poole church.

Edward = Margaret Walton
d.1577. Buried Poole church.

Walton
of Ewen.

Eleanor = Henry Nevill

nne   **Dorothy**   **Frances** ══════ **Sir Nevill, M.P. (Frances Poole)**
1592-1651.

ir Edward, M.P. = **Dorothy or**
518-1673.   **Dorothea**
        d. Sir Robert Pye

Gyles
Manor of S. Cerney.

Sir Nevill = **Elizabeth**
b.1646.   **d. Maximilian Bard**
       Remarried John Strange

Sir Henry = **Elizabeth**
b.1672.   **d. Sir Thomas Earle**
       b.1673. m.1694.

Henry = **Stuart**
d.1726.   **d. Henry Wallis of Groombridge**

inetta = **Benjamin Bathurst**
.1713. 22 children.

Elizabeth
b.1700–1746. d.unmarried

INDEX